BEYOND THE WALL

David R.Y.W. Chapman

Copyright © 2021 David R.Y.W. Chapman

All rights reserved.

ISBN: 9798779852449

For anyone who has been dealt a bad hand in life and those who have not been blessed with the same opportunities afforded to me.

CONTENTS

Prologue — vii

1. The Big Smoke – London, The United Kingdom — 1
2. The Forbidden City – Beijing, The People's Republic of China — 25
3. Heaven's Ladder – Huangyaguan, The People's Republic of China — 37
4. The Ledge of Death – Jinshanling, The People's Republic of China — 53
5. A Reluctant Striptease – Beijing, The People's Republic of China — 65
6. Drug Dealers, a Mermaid and a Dead Duck – Copenhagen, Denmark — 73
7. A Model City – Basel and Lucerne, Switzerland — 91
8. The City of a Hundred Spires and Constant Rain – Prague, The Czech Republic — 105
9. Twerk or Treat? – Tallinn, Estonia — 121
10. A Sting in the Tale – Helsinki, Finland — 137
11. Sun, Sea and Bloodshed – Benalmádena, Torremolinos and Seville, Spain — 147
12. Continent Hopping – Tangier, Morocco — 167
13. A Change of Course – Barcelona, Spain — 181
14. All Aboard! – Marseille and Avignon, France — 199
15. Jeans, Volcanoes and the Mafia – Genoa, Pompeii, Sorrento and Messina, Italy — 217
16. Lessons Learned – Sidi Bou Said and Carthage, Tunisia — 231

Epilogue — 239

PROLOGUE

As I surveyed the scene in front of me, it truly felt like a life-changing moment; or at least the culmination of a week that I would treasure for the rest of my existence. The Great Wall of China followed the course of the hills on which it was built on, dramatically rising and falling, and snaking from side to side whenever nature dictated. I had been exposed to countless images of this remarkable structure during my previous twenty-eight years, but it was something else altogether to see the wall, which almost appeared to be part of the landscape itself, extend as far into the distance as my eyes could see.

The past week had been exhilarating. I had travelled extensively before, but until this point I had not been on an adventure like this. Although I had witnessed scenes of immeasurable beauty on previous trips, I had never been presented with the opportunity to spend so long admiring what was before me. Picture-postcard vistas of the rolling hills had become the norm; how would I cope without being treated to such magnificence on a daily basis? I had become accustomed to the sensation of taking step after step along the wall; how could my body and mind adjust from trekking for mile upon mile to spending a sedentary eight hours in my employer's office five days a week?

The trips I had previously undertaken were usually carefully planned so that everything was under my control and that I did not have to rely upon anyone else. This had been totally different; I had been required to put my faith in our guides and trust that their expertise would be sufficient to safely lead the group to each checkpoint along our route. The fact that I had trekked along the Great Wall with forty strangers took me further out of my comfort zone. An introvert at heart, I had been forced to participate in a level of social interaction that I was not used to. Forming friendships with strangers had been more pleasant, and less difficult, than I had anticipated.

Still, I savoured these moments of solitude when I had time to take in my surroundings whilst gathering my thoughts.

    With such a momentous week behind me, I was wary of how this was likely to play out. My desire to embark on epic journeys of this nature was exciting my soul, but I was acutely aware of how the circumstances and constraints of everyday life so often mean that such ambitions are shelved for long periods of time, often indefinitely. I had a nine-to-five job and a girlfriend whom I loved dearly. She enjoyed travelling almost as much as I did, but the prospect of putting our lives on hold, including deferring payments on the mortgage she had taken out prior to meeting me, seemed fanciful at best. Perhaps I could find a compromise and squeeze a similar trek into each year's schedule? It would be difficult to take so many days off work to travel, in addition to our other plans, and the costs involved were another obstacle. Would this trip be as far as I went in terms of escaping the ordinary, or could a life of truly exploring the planet go beyond the wall?

1. *THE BIG SMOKE*
**LONDON, THE UNITED KINGDOM
FEBRUARY 2013**

It was less than a month until I was scheduled to trek along the Great Wall of China. I had hastily signed up for the challenge in December 2011 after hearing that Anthony, who was a friend of a friend, had done so a couple of weeks earlier. Shortly after registering for the trek, which had been organised by the Help A Capital Child charity in conjunction with Discover Adventure, reality set in. Participants were required to fundraise a total of £3,200 in order to secure their place on the plane to China. After a lifetime of shying away from social interaction, I would finally be required to come out of my shell, as I needed to engage with enough people to ensure that I raised the required amount.

Upon digging deeper into the financial details, I had discovered that around half of this amount would go towards the cost of the trip, with the rest being allocated to Teenage Cancer Trust units across the United Kingdom. With that in mind, I paid more than £2,000 out of my own pocket. I was now free from any guilt caused by the possibility of my friends and family paying for me to go on the adventure of a lifetime. This also meant that my fundraising target was a more realistic figure of £1,200. I treated this like an assignment from my school days: I buried my head in the sand and told myself that I could complete the task closer to the deadline.

By the summer of 2012, I had still not started fundraising. I was unsure of how Anthony was getting on with this undertaking, but at least he had organised a five-a-side football tournament at our local Soccer

Dome. The day was a success, with a few hundred pounds raised towards Anthony's target. More importantly, my team won the tournament and I took home the prestigious Help A Capital Child trophy! It still stands proudly on top of a bookcase in my mum's house. I thought that this would spur me on, but it took another couple of months for me to get into gear with my fundraising. Against all my introverted instincts, I reached out to my small number of friends, family and colleagues. They pledged enough to take me close to my target. Carol, who was my girlfriend but has since become my wife, held a charity event that raised the remaining amount. I can assure you, however, that my decision to eventually wed her was not solely based on her securing my place on the trip!

With all financial hurdles successfully cleared, including the purchase of expensive hiking gear, the trek suddenly seemed real. It would not be long until I was flying to the other side of the world with a large group of strangers and walking long distances each day, deprived of any home comforts. Before all that, though, Carol and I had booked a long weekend in London, which provided me with one last taste of a conventional holiday before the trek.

* * *

After spending the first night of our trip in Stevenage – at the home of Carol's sister, Michelle – we took the train to the 'Big Smoke.' Apparently, London's nickname dates back to the nineteenth century. The Industrial Revolution had resulted in the large-scale burning of coal, which caused a thick smoke to envelop the capital city. This was a startling sight for visitors from rural areas; hence, the nickname. The air pollution in big cities around the world today may be worrying, but it was even worse in nineteenth-century London. Climate change has rightfully become a pressing concern in recent times, but at least the quality of air in the United Kingdom's capital is not as bad as it was back then. It would not be long until I was visiting a city that is currently more deserving of the 'Big Smoke' moniker. After all, Beijing is renowned for its air pollution and lack of visibility due to the smog that often engulfs the city.

It was clear that China was already on my mind, as I could not help but make comparisons between the city we were travelling towards and the one that I would touch down in prior to my trek. The train that we had boarded at Stevenage was much better than what I was used to in the north of England, but it was still overcrowded and basic when compared to its overseas counterparts. The quality of the railways, and the trains themselves, were likely to be far superior in Beijing. Although I was probably not going to be using this form of transport during my time in China, the standard of rail services on offer had become vastly superior to the British equivalent.

China has invested a considerable sum in improving and developing its rail infrastructure over the past few decades, whilst the pioneering British railways that were once exported around the globe have been left to fall into a rather sad decline. High-speed rail highlights the contrasting levels of progress made in the two countries in recent years. At the time of our trip to London, the HS2 project had barely got going since it was first proposed in 2009. Not much has changed in the following seven-plus years. Although there are obvious environmental concerns regarding HS2, and there are many people who make a persuasive argument against the completion of the project, it is notable that China has created the world's longest high-speed rail network. Remarkably, they have already built over 36,000 kilometres of high-speed rail track. To put this into context, the circumference of Earth is only a slightly higher figure, at 40,075 kilometres. China is on course to reach the 70,000-kilometre mark by 2035!

Upon arriving in London, I felt uneasy about the prospect of taking another form of public transport. The London Underground is one of the world's most iconic rail networks. Its history can be traced back to 1863 with the opening of the Metropolitan Railway, on which steam locomotives transported passengers along the world's first underground rail network. I find it extraordinary that many of the tracks and stations that were used in the mid-nineteenth century are still in operation today. The service offered to modern-day Londoners is efficient and extensive; however, my childhood memories of the Tube were mostly unpleasant. Mum used to take me and my brother, John, to my Uncle Wai Lun's house 'down south' during half-term holidays. As a child, the Underground felt like a scary place consisting of confined spaces and large crowds of people bumping into each other. All whilst we were what felt like hundreds of miles beneath the city. The fact that I had absolutely no idea where we were supposed to be heading to hardly helped ease my anxiety. I am unsure of how Mum kept her composure to guide two disinterested and surly young boys to our destination.

Having extensively prepared for the Tube prior to our trip, I felt somewhat confident about being able to guide us from our current location at King's Cross to the various destinations we required. Descending the escalators beneath the bowels of London did not seem so scary anymore. It did not take long, however, to notice that this was a place of abject misery. Smiling seemed to be strictly forbidden and eye contact was a rarity. Being an introvert, this did not bother me on a personal level, but it gave the impression that an unpleasant series of journeys lay ahead.

"Londoners aren't as friendly as us 'up north,' especially Wiganers," Carol remarked.

"To be fair, they have just been on the Tube. Maybe we will look like that in half an hour!"

Thirty minutes later, we emerged from Victoria Underground Station with our smiles intact. "That was not so terrible," I said to Carol. "A little cramped, but not as bad as I expected."

"I can see why Londoners look so miserable though. I would not fancy using the Tube every day."

"London is a hectic city. The combination of such a fast-paced, business-orientated lifestyle probably makes people seem less welcoming."

"I still say that us Northerners are more friendly!" Carol concluded.

The first port of call was at the residence of London's most famous part-time resident. Well, we stood outside the grounds and took some photographs of the building through the wrought iron bars of the gates. This would be regarded as strange and obsessive behaviour if I were referring to the home of David Beckham or Elton John, but it is deemed acceptable to do this at Buckingham Palace. I guess that Queen Elizabeth II and the Royal Family do not mind too much, as they are fully aware that the income generated by tourists is often used to justify the lavish cost of such buildings and various royal activities. The history of the site that the palace is built on goes back to the Middle Ages, but it did not become the official London residence of the British monarch until 1837, starting with Queen Victoria.

Intriguingly, it was home to one of the world's most famous refugees until his recent passing. Prince Philip, born Philippos Andreou of Schleswig-Holstein-Sonderberg-Glücksburg, Prince of Greece and Denmark, was exiled from Corfu when he was just eighteen months old. He was taken off the island in a cot made from a fruit box, first spending some time in Italy and France before settling in the United Kingdom. I guess that I am being unrealistically optimistic in hoping that all refugees escaping danger in their home nation are embraced so warmly by their adopted countries.

Hordes of tourists, like ourselves, had gathered in front of the palace grounds. As Carol posed for a photograph in front of the gates, there was no chance of waiting for the crowds to diminish enough to capture the perfect image. We had to make do with a photo that resembled something from the pages of the *Where's Wally?* book series. Except anyone looking at it was tasked with finding a woman from Wigan who had made the questionable decision to wear double denim.

Itching to move away from the crowd, I suggested that we move on to the next point of interest.

"Do you not want your photograph taken?" Carol asked.

"Not particularly."

"Go on, have a photo."

"OK, but I am not jumping the gates to meet the Queen!"

The presence of armed guards, and the probability of her being in her weekend home of Windsor Castle, meant that even if I were a royal fanatic desperate to meet Her Majesty, I would not have succeeded in such a mission. Just to clarify – I am not a royal fanatic. I have not even seen a single episode of *The Crown*. Shocking, I know! In fact, my lack of interest in the Royal Family is best demonstrated by my reaction to an anecdote that was recently aired on an episode of *I'm a Celebrity...Get Me Out of Here!* One of the contestants mentioned that she had been involved in a romantic relationship with Prince Edward, before going on to describe her unusual encounters with the Royal Family. Whilst most viewers were probably discussing the juicy details of her revelations, I simply asked Carol: "Who is Prince Edward?"

Photographs taken, we set off towards our next destination. At this point, I must confess that my recollection of the order of events has become a little hazy. The nature of the London Underground network only adds to my confusion, as it is extremely easy to make illogical and unnecessary Tube journeys if one is unfamiliar with the city and its public transport. When examining a map of the Underground, if the only knowledge you possess is the name of the station closest to the relevant point of interest, it is likely that you will board a vehicle before changing to a different line, possibly several times, only to end up a few hundred yards from your departure point. The map, of course, does not remotely reflect the geography of the city.

The original version, published in 1908, attempted to do so, but it was rather messy. As the network was expanded, it looked even more absurd. With a cluster of stations in the city centre and just a smattering of them on the outskirts, it became undecipherable, almost to the point that it was indecipherable. It took the personal endeavour of a discarded engineer for the Tube operator to clean up the map. Rather than becoming bitter about losing his job due to funding cuts, Harry Beck spent his free time creating a version that prioritised the ease of which it could be read rather than its geographical accuracy. To add insult to injury, the company initially rejected his suggestion. Undeterred, he tried again and was successful. His design was tweaked as the network continued to expand, but we can thank Beck for the iconic map, which is much easier on the eye. The downside to this, unfortunately, is that tourists are often unaware of the distances between each station, or the direction one must travel in to get from one to the other.

    This means that it is possible that Carol and I walked back to Victoria in order to take a ridiculous Tube journey that involved heading to Green Park before changing to the Piccadilly Line and travelling to Hyde Park Corner. This long-winded route would have been a farcical waste of time, as Hyde Park Corner is a mere 0.6 miles from Buckingham Palace. Considering my lack of geographical knowledge of London in 2013, I suspect that we may have taken such a needless journey! I can assure you all that this foolish behaviour has been consigned to history – albeit a history that nobody cares about – as Carol and I have recently got to grips with the layout of the city. On our last trip to the capital, we travelled entirely on foot, aside from excursions to Camden and Notting Hill.

    Incidentally, we managed to locate a few famous sites featured in the film *Notting Hill* whilst we visited the West London district of the same name. Unfortunately, at the precise moment we were taking a photograph of the book shop that Hugh Grant's character owned, an intoxicated man decided to defecate on the doorstop of the shop next door. Nothing takes the fun out of a situation quite like another human being taking a big dump just yards away from you! He was in such a state that he did not seem the slightest bit bothered that he was performing this bodily function next to a busy street in broad daylight. On the bright side, no such incidents occurred whilst we took photographs of the famous blue door that featured in the film and the colourful houses that have become synonymous with the area. In order to save whatever shred of street credibility I still have – and it has probably taken another hit as a result of my refusal to shorten the phrase to 'street cred' – I will point out that Carol has long been a fan of the film; I just watch it every so often in order to perform my role as a dutiful husband. Obviously, it is not because I also enjoy watching it!

    Hyde Park is huge, both in terms of its size and its standing within the world of city parks. It is almost three times the size of Vatican City, which is of course a sovereign state. It may have been surpassed in size by the likes of New York's Central Park, but few other green spaces have so much history and interesting features. Many notable events have taken place here since Henry VIII took the land from the church in 1536. It has hosted May Day parades and rock concerts performed by the likes of The Rolling Stones and Queen, whilst it has also been the site of public demonstrations, including those in the name of the Chartist and Suffragette movements. Various anti-war protests have also been held in the park throughout its history.

"I am a big fan of green spaces within cities," I declared.

"It's just a shame they tend to be so busy."

"Bloody tourists, hey?!"

It did seem to be exceptionally busy, even by London standards. There was barely a patch of land that was not currently occupied. I am not keen on large crowds, but it seems that there are others who have even stronger feelings about the matter. As one group tried to manoeuvre past another, a woman appeared to use her pram to clear the path in front. A woman from the other group gestured to kick the pram, which resulted in a heated argument. I guess my dislike of crowded places was put into perspective at that moment! After all, I am yet to resort to kicking prams!

Multiple trips to Hong Kong, and a recent visit to Macao, had helped in this regard. Both are even more crowded than London, with the latter recognised as the most densely populated region on the planet. The population density of London is more or less 15,000 per square mile, which pales in comparison to Macao's respective figure of about 55,000! Still, London is far more densely populated than other cities in the United Kingdom. With a higher cost of living and a greater concentration of international businesses, London is almost regarded as a separate country by those who live 'up north.' This can create a strange feeling amongst northern tourists, as if one is visiting a foreign land where the average price of a pint of beer is twice as much as it costs in some British towns. The improbability of someone striking up a conversation or even smiling at you whilst you are on the Tube only adds to this impression.

As we strolled alongside the Serpentine, which is the name of one of the park's lakes rather than anything more sinister, Carol steered our thoughts towards my upcoming trek: "Do you think you will see many parks in China?"

"I would imagine so, but it will depend on the itinerary, I guess."

"I picture huge cities full of skyscrapers when I think of China, although I've also seen documentaries about the amazing wildlife."

"I think Beijing will be full of tall buildings and smog. I am looking forward to seeing vast areas of uninhabited land whilst trekking along the Great Wall though."

Our assumptions about China had more than an element of truth to them. The rapid economic growth of the country had resulted in a boom in construction that had contributed to worryingly high levels of energy consumption and carbon emissions. China has not just been building within its metropolitan areas, but it has been constructing large cities almost from scratch. Rural areas along the high-speed rail routes have been transformed into large cities, some of which have been faced with the problem of enticing enough people to relocate there. Something similar happened in Britain, with railway towns such as Crewe developed in a bygone era. There has been, however, a recent effort to create more green spaces within the cities and to commit to greener energy. I was not aware of this at the time, but Beijing has numerous parks, many of which have a longer history than Hyde Park.

After ambling along for a few minutes, we reached the Diana, Princess of Wales Memorial Fountain. The shape was not what I expected; the 4,000-square-metre oval-formed feature sees water flow in two directions, before converging in a pool at its lowest point.

"What do you think of it?" I asked Carol.

"It's different. I think I would have preferred a standard fountain design though."

"I am unsure whether the design reminds me of a street gutter, albeit a pretty one made from granite, or the world's most gentle waterslide. I'm not saying it's unattractive, but as you said, it is different. That's probably fitting, as she seemed quite different to a typical member of the Royal Family."

"I liked Diana. I think she was lovely."

"I'm largely indifferent to the Royal Family, but she seemed a relatively kind person and more willing to engage with those from outside the upper echelons of society."

We crossed over into the home of Peter Pan. I am obviously not talking about Neverland, although that would have made this paragraph far more interesting! I am referring to Kensington Gardens, of course, where one can find a statue of J.M. Barrie's most famous creation. We decided that we did not have time to locate this, instead electing to wander past the Albert Memorial, which is an ornate pavilion-shaped monument that commemorates Prince Albert, on our way to the Royal Albert Hall. This is the most recognisable and revered concert hall within the United Kingdom, which has seen artists from across the globe grace its famous stage since its opening in 1871.

We took some photographs of the Grade I listed building, capturing both the impressive dome and the terracotta mosaic frieze in all their glory, but we did not have time to enter. Little did Carol know, but she would return the following year to attend a concert by one of her favourite singers, Julio Iglesias. The Spanish crooner has reportedly slept with over three thousand women, so perhaps I should have been worried that Carol went to see his show without me! She said that the concert was fantastic and that, thankfully, the only performance he put on was on stage.

We left Kensington Gardens and Hyde Park without paying a visit to one of the latter's most celebrated areas. Speakers' Corner is a renowned place for public debate, with the likes of Karl Marx and George Orwell amongst the most well-known figures to have given speeches in the area situated on the north-east edge of the park. You do not have to be famous or qualified to speak to the masses; it is commonplace for people to turn up unannounced and address any given topic, as long as it is not deemed unlawful. This section of the park has been set aside for public speaking since Parliament approved the Parks Regulation Act of 1872.

"I don't think it would have been worth adding to our already tight schedule by visiting Speakers' Corner. I can't imagine that there is much going on at the moment anyway," I stated.

"Did you not fancy addressing the people of London?" Carol asked, knowing that this would be my worst nightmare.

"If I didn't have such an aversion to public speaking, I guess I could start a debate about the merits of having pineapple on pizza. Mind you, that could lead to the unnecessary deployment of riot police."

"I would love to see you addressing a large crowd! You would need a powerful megaphone as you are so softly spoken and shy."

"On a more serious note, we should be grateful that we at least have the option of openly debating issues in public. Free speech may be seen as a basic human right over here, but the Chinese authorities clamp down on this. Television broadcasts and newspapers are broadly controlled by the state, with censorship blocking much of what could be used to criticise the ruling Communist Party. Facebook and Twitter are blocked within China."

"But you have relatives in Hong Kong who are on Facebook."

"Hong Kong is a Special Administrative Region of China, where partial freedoms are in place. At least until 2047," I began, unaware that the erosion of such freedoms would be accelerated in the following years. "Within mainland China, however, the internet is censored. Some people refer to this as the 'Great Firewall of China.' If someone within China searches the internet for the Tiananmen Square Massacre of 1989, the results will not include any mention of the deaths that resulted from the government sending in armed troops to crush the protests. It is like China has erased this event from history."

Hundreds, possibly thousands, of peaceful protesters were killed in June 1989. Many of them were students. There is a concerted attempt to suppress such information in the build up to the anniversary each year, and on the rare instances when the government has addressed the issue, they have simply referred to the 'June 4th Incident.'

A brisk walk through the swanky streets of Knightsbridge took us to Harrods. Having visited the Diana Memorial Fountain, it seemed fitting that we were now stood outside a store that had such strong links to her lover's family. Tragically, Diana and Dodi Fayed both died in a car crash in 1997. Dodi's father, Mohamed Al-Fayed, had owned the famous department store from the mid-1980s until he sold it to the sovereign wealth fund of Qatar in 2010.

Carol had frequently mentioned buying a teddy bear from Harrods during a previous visit. As she had seemed so pleased with her purchase, which she said was just about the only thing she could afford, I suggested that we venture inside to hunt down another 'bargain.' Harrods has over one million square feet of retail space, making it one of the largest department stores in Europe. Still, we were unable to find many reasonably priced items. Even some of the teddies now cost more than thirty pounds. This makes the store motto, *Omnia Omnibus Ubique*, which is Latin for "all things for all people, everywhere," seem rather detached from reality. Somehow resisting the urge to spend thirty pounds on a bar of chocolate, we admired the aesthetically pleasing displays of products we could not afford before exiting the store to pose for photographs in front of the building.

We either headed back to Buckingham Palace and then walked the length of The Mall to Admiralty Arch, or more likely we took the tube to Piccadilly Circus before changing to the Bakerloo line and disembarking at Charing Cross. Admiralty Arch is an impressive sight to behold. Commissioned by King Edward VII in memory of Queen Victoria, it serves as the ceremonial entrance to Trafalgar Square. After taking some photographs of it from The Mall side, we decided to walk through the arch.

"Do you feel like a king making your entrance onto Trafalgar Square from The Mall?" Carol asked.

"I constantly feel like a king," I replied, lying through my teeth.

I have always found Trafalgar Square pleasing on the eye. Grand buildings such as the National Gallery and St. Martin-in the-Fields Church frame the square, and a couple of fountains enhance the aesthetics whilst also serving as places for people to gather. As with all good squares, there is a large open area that serves as a public space. As with many places in London, however, it can become difficult to appreciate its splendour when there are throngs of tourists bumping into you every few seconds. It is not just humans that you must look out for though. Pigeons have been known to wreak havoc around Trafalgar Square since its opening in the early nineteenth century. At one point in time, the square was thought to be home to around 35,000 pigeons! Thankfully, measures to reduce this number, including a ban on feeding the birds within the surrounding area, were introduced in the early-2000s.

Whilst this has come as a relief to a pessimist like me, who constantly fears being used as a toilet by those that fly above our heads, it was a blow to vendors who sold bird feed to tourists at extortionate prices.

The central feature of Trafalgar Square is, of course, Nelson's Column. Reaching a height of just under 170 feet, the figure of Admiral Horatio Nelson looms large over the square. Nelson died at the Battle of Trafalgar in 1805, having secured one of Britain's greatest naval victories; thus, leading to the immediate desire to commemorate him in this manner. The monument, which was constructed in the 1840s, is what one would expect: a statue of the admiral on top of a tall column that rests on a pedestal. This was enhanced a couple of decades later when four bronze lions were added around its base. Nelson has benefitted from the ban on feeding pigeons, as every so often the column had to be cleaned, at great cost, due to the damage caused by droppings. I am sure that he would have hated the thought of losing his life during a crucial naval victory only to be constantly defecated on by pigeons! Incidentally, the image of Nelson always makes me think of the logo and advertisements for the insurance company Admiral. He would probably view this as an even bigger insult!

After briefly admiring the monument, Carol and I navigated our way through the sea of tourists and away from Trafalgar Square, oblivious to our proximity to a quirky landmark. The south-east corner of the square is home to what was once Britain's smallest police station. This may not sound particularly interesting, but it becomes more intriguing when one considers the fact that the station was situated inside an ornamental light fitting! Following the General Strike of 1926, it was decided that a permanent police station was required to keep an eye on events in Trafalgar Square, which had become a popular place to hold protests. Public outcry forced the authorities to change tack, so a more discreet installation was required. Remarkably, a lamppost plinth was hollowed out to provide enough room for a single police officer to keep an eye out for any sign of trouble. The officer could phone a nearby station if help were required. The light would be activated if this were the case, which alerted any passing police officers. I imagine that receiving a solo assignment to watch over a square full of rioters from within the base of a lamppost was regarded as drawing the short straw!

Incredibly, there was once an even smaller station in Florida, where police officers in the quiet village of Carrabelle had to use a phone that was affixed to a building. They would often get drenched during periods of heavy rain, whilst members of the public would sometimes use it for unauthorised phone calls. A solution was found in 1963, when an old phone booth was replaced with one for the exclusive use of the police. It is no longer in operation, but the 'Smallest Police Station in the World' has become a tourist attraction.

The main reason we were in the capital city that weekend was to make use of the Christmas present that Carol had given me: a ride on the London Eye. There was just about enough time to rampage through the area around Leicester Square before making our way over to the huge observation wheel. We walked past a ticket office that has been providing the opportunity to watch a show at one of the numerous West End theatres at a significantly discounted price since 1980. As Carol and I enjoy a trip to the theatre, we could have enquired about what shows were currently on offer, but we did not have the time to squeeze in a musical that weekend. Likewise, we could have checked out what films were being screened at Odeon Leicester Square, where film premieres are often held.

The statue of William Shakespeare in the gardens in the middle of the square underlined the area's association with performing arts. Using this moment to impart some useless trivia, I asked Carol: "Do you know that Shakespeare was married to Anne Hathaway?"

"Don't be silly! What are you talking about?"

"His wife was called Anne Hathaway. Unfortunately, I am not talking about the actress. That would have been far more interesting, as it would mean that she is over 450 years old!"

On our most recent trip, not long before the national COVID-19 lockdown, we admired the latest installations. Statues of some of the nation's most beloved characters and iconic film scenes have been erected, providing visitors a chance to get up close and personal with the likes of Harry Potter, Paddington and Mary Poppins. I posed for a photograph whilst sat on a bench next to Mr. Bean. The childlike character who is accident-prone and seemingly incapable of conversing with others does not seem so far-fetched when sat next to me.

"I don't think we have time to visit Chinatown," I informed Carol.

"That's OK. We will see it another time. You will be visiting a few Chinese towns next month anyway!"

"We don't have time for Covent Garden either. I promise I will buy something for you next time we go."

She held me to that promise, to the detriment of my bank account but the benefit of Hotel Chocolat's takings.

Another short Tube journey took us to Waterloo, close to the London Eye. Situated on the South Bank of the River Thames and reaching a height of 135 metres, it was the world's tallest Ferris wheel until it was surpassed by the Star of Nanchang in 2006. This is in China, of course. I believe that the High Roller in Las Vegas is the current record holder, but someone is bound to build a wheel that is a couple of metres taller at some point.

"It certainly looks impressive!" Carol beamed.

"It seems like we are in store for a pleasant ride. Thank you for my present."

"Did they used to call this the Millennium Wheel?"

"I think that was an unofficial name. The plan was for it to be open to the public by New Year's Eve 1999 to mark the turn of the millennium. This target was missed by a couple of months, which was quite fitting considering that the end of the millennium was actually at the conclusion of the year 2000."

"I bet you would have been fun at a millennium party!" Carol quipped.

"Don't worry. There was no chance of me getting invited to any parties!"

"It looks impressive, doesn't it?"

"It does. Still, I would not want to wait here in the cold for hours, as people do, just so that they have a good view of the fireworks display on New Year's Eve."

"Me neither. I don't like fireworks, anyway."

"You can thank us Chinese for their creation!"

We soon boarded one of the thirty-two capsules, which are numbered one to thirty-three so that the number thirteen can be omitted. I imagine that there are plenty of superstitious people who would refuse to board capsule thirteen and be suspended hundreds of feet above the ground. However, little consideration has been given to the fact that people from China and other Asian countries often have tetraphobia, which is a fear of the number four. This is due to the pronunciation of the word 'four' being similar to that of the word for 'death' in many Asian languages.

The wheel of the London Eye turns so slowly that it does not feel like it is moving. It took around thirty minutes to complete our cycle, which provided ample time to take in the splendid views on offer. It was a rare opportunity for us to admire the landmarks that line the Thames, like Westminster and Big Ben, from such an elevated position. Not even the presence of strangers in our capsule could ruin the experience. One of the must surreal aspects was looking at the other capsules, and the people within them, seemingly floating in the air above London.

Having been treated to such a pleasant half-hour by my girlfriend, and bearing in mind that we were just a few days removed from Valentine's Day, I decided to repay the favour by taking her to one of the city's fine dining establishments: McDonald's. To rub McSalt into the wounds, this appeared to be the busiest and most unpleasant McDonald's in London.

We were so hungry that we were not too bothered by the presence of an army of children running through the restaurant or the mess that was on every table. We were happy just to eat our late lunch as quickly as possible then check into our hotel for the night, dropping off my rucksack in the process. In keeping with our choice of dining venue, I had booked a night in a Travelodge. Not quite The Ritz or the Savoy, but we only needed a place to put our heads down for the night.

As it turns out, we dined in both of these esteemed establishments during a recent stay in London. It was nice to be given a taste of how the other half live, even though we used a Travelzoo voucher for our evening meal at The Ritz. To be fair, the staff seemed to treat us the same as they would have if we were rich celebrities. Perhaps feeling guilty we had dined in a hotel that had been founded by César Ritz, who had been sacked from the Savoy for committing fraud – he was thought to have been involved in the disappearance of thousands of pounds' worth of goods – we decided that it would only be fair to have breakfast in the historic institution on the Strand. The opportunity to tell people we had smoked salmon and caviar for breakfast at the Savoy had nothing to do with it, of course.

Once we had checked in, we began the last leg of our day's sightseeing. The iconic Westminster Bridge provided a perfect spot to observe the grandeur of the Palace of Westminster, which is more commonly referred to as the Houses of Parliament. This rests on the site where Parliament has convened since the thirteenth century. The historic building was reconstructed in the mid-nineteenth century following a fire that destroyed both the House of Commons and the House of Lords. Guy Fawkes and his chums needn't have bothered spending all that time and energy working on the Gunpowder Plot – they just needed an overheated stove.

The building, which was apparently designed using the Perpendicular Gothic style, is one of the most recognisable in the world. Along with its Elizabeth Tower, which houses the bell commonly referred to as Big Ben, it has become a symbol of the nation. We were afforded an unobstructed view that afternoon, but it is currently surrounded by scaffolding due to extensive renovation work that began in 2017. I can empathise with overseas tourists who have arrived in London only to discover that its most iconic structure has been hidden from public view. This has happened to me on numerous occasions, including in Washington D.C. when I was devastated to see that the Lincoln Memorial Reflecting Pool had been dredged as part of restoration plans.

Carol and I wandered through Parliament Square before pitching up at Westminster Abbey. The Gothic building, which is formally titled the

Collegiate Church of Saint Peter at Westminster but mercifully referred to by its shorter name, has been the site of many events surrounding the monarchy. This includes the coronation of William the Conqueror in 1066, the funeral of Princess Diana in 1997, and the wedding of Prince William and Kate Middleton. Many notable figures from British history have been buried or commemorated here, including Charles Darwin and William Wilberforce. This is also where one can find the tomb of The Unknown Warrior. The church had already closed for the day, so we were unable to explore inside. The exterior was certainly impressive though.

We concluded our day by visiting Whitehall, which is the name of a prominent road and surrounding area in Westminster, but it is commonly used as a metonym for the British civil service and government. It is also where the Cenotaph can be found. This was originally intended to honour the lives lost in the name of the British Empire during the First World War, which was on a previously unseen scale, but it now also serves as a way of remembering those who have died in subsequent conflicts. Carol and I paused for a moment of reflection before continuing our path along Whitehall until we were able to see Downing Street. And that was all we were permitted to do: *see* the most famous street in Britain. Or rather, we saw glimpses of it between steel bars. This is because it is gated off from the public and guarded by armed police. Our photographs consisted of a shot of the street sign and a messy image of the security gates and the heavily armed police officers.

Whilst it would have been nice to have been able to wander along the historic street, it was understandable why public access was restricted. After all, 10 Downing Street was subjected to a mortar attack by the Provisional Irish Republican Army in 1991. When considering the current global terror threat, it would be negligent to allow people to approach the home of the highest-ranking members of government.

Incidentally, although Number 10 is the official residence of the Prime Minister of the United Kingdom, it has become commonplace for the head of government to swap living spaces with the Chancellor of the Exchequer at Number 11. This is because the living quarters in Number 11 are more spacious – although recent residents despised the décor so much that they felt the need to spend up to £200,000 on refurbishments. David Cameron was the resident of Number 10 at the time of our trip, although unofficially he lived in Number 11. His Conservative Party had been in an unlikely coalition with the Liberal Democrats since the General Election of 2010; little did we know at the time, but there would be three more elections and two more Prime Ministers by the end of 2019. Then again, it would have been difficult to predict that the United

Kingdom would soon leave the European Union or that a global pandemic would bring the world to a screeching halt. I sometimes forget how much has changed in the past few years..

We returned to our Travelodge after satisfying our appetite at Pizza Express. There was little chance of spotting any famous faces whilst we dined in the moderately-priced restaurant – perhaps we should have gone to the Woking branch.

"I have had a great day," I declared.

"Me too. London is a wonderful city."

"There's slightly more to see than in Wigan!"

"Hey! Don't pick on my home town!" Carol exclaimed.

"We have barely scratched the surface. There are so many more places to see. Hopefully, we will get to visit a few of them tomorrow before we head back to Stevenage."

"You will be roaming around China next month. I hope you will be OK."

"Don't worry; the group will be led by a team of local guides and members of the adventure company. There will also be a doctor on hand."

"I hope you don't need a doctor!"

"Me too!"

We watched some news on television, which focused on the aftermath of the resignation of Pope Benedict XVI and the shocking revelation that Oscar Pistorius had shot and killed his girlfriend, Reeva Steenkamp. He claimed that he had mistaken her for an intruder hiding in the bathroom of his home on Valentine's Night. As we heard about how events had unfolded, his explanation seemed rather implausible. After numerous court cases, he was eventually convicted of murder and is currently serving a prison term of thirteen years and five months. This again highlighted how much things can change over time. Just the previous year, and in the city we had spent the day exploring, he had become the first double-leg amputee to compete at the Olympic Games.

* * *

The following day's sightseeing began, most likely after another unnecessarily complicated Tube journey, with a visit to St. Paul's Cathedral. The latest incarnation of the cathedral was constructed after the previous one had been largely destroyed by the Great Fire of London. Completed in 1710, this stunning building has long been regarded as one of the most iconic sights of the city. The famous dome is amongst the tallest in the world, and the English Baroque architecture is certainly pleasing on the eye.

"The funerals of Winston Churchill and Admiral Nelson were held here," I said to Carol, trying to impress her.

"Prince Charles and Diana were married here," she countered.

"You know your stuff."

"Of course!"

"You will be able to tell me if it is the largest cathedral in Britain then."

"I don't know if it is. Do you?"

"I haven't got a clue!" I confessed. "It must be a contender."

It turns out that it is the second largest cathedral in the United Kingdom when measured by area. Liverpool Cathedral, which I am yet to visit, takes top billing.

You must either purchase tickets online or pay on the door to enter, but we somehow ended up inside the building without parting with any money. I am unsure if the setup was slightly different during our visit or whether we accidentally slipped through the net, but it highlighted the pitfalls, from a business point of view, of allowing the public to enter even a small section before handing over any money. We marvelled at our view of the interior of this wonderful building before baulking at the notion of paying the exorbitant entrance fee. Whilst we would have been happy to pay a reasonable amount, the price of admission made us depart as quickly as humanly possible. I am unable to recall the exact amount that we were asked for, but the 2021 on-the-door entrance fee is an eye-watering £17 per person.

Carol bought tickets for my most recent birthday, so we finally ventured inside. The Whispering Gallery was closed for renovation, of course, but we enjoyed taking in the views from the top of the building and exploring the famous tombs in the crypt.

"Do they have churches in China?" Carol asked me upon leaving the building.

"They have some but not so many. Taoism, Buddhism and Confucianism are historically more prevalent belief systems over there. Missionaries brought Christianity to China but there was a crackdown on religion following Chairman Mao's Cultural Revolution in the 1960s and 1970s."

"Why?"

"Mao wanted to reassert his authority over the Communist Party and kickstart the failing economy. Religious and educational institutions that contradicted the state narrative faced persecution, effectively driving people underground to avoid execution. This did not really help the economy, of course, but it allowed him to eliminate his political opponents. Millions died during this unstable and violent period."

"It's not like that anymore though, right?"

"It's nowhere near as bad nowadays. I saw churches in Macao and Hong Kong. There are some problems though. The Communist Party, which is officially atheist, is known to clamp down on any dissenting voices, including those from religious institutions. Christianity is often viewed with suspicion due to its links to Western society. Muslims are treated worse though."

My words seem rather understated now, but they were spoken before the Chinese government stepped up their persecution of the Uighur population in the Xinjiang region in the West of the Country. Since 2015, it has been estimated that over one million Uighurs have been detained in 're-education' camps. Although the Communist Party have claimed that this was necessary in order to clamp down on terrorist groups in the region, human rights organisations have guided the world's attention towards what has been described as 'cultural genocide.'

The predominantly Muslim population has been subjected to imprisonment, torture, surveillance and intimidation. It has even been reported that there has been an attempt to suppress the Uighur birth rate through sterilisation and forcing women into having abortions. This has coincided with the government's increased investment in industrial and energy projects in this part of the country. The ethnic Chinese population who moved to the area were given most of the newly created jobs, with the Uighurs made to feel like a minority despite being indigenous to the region.

"I am aware that I am hardly providing China with a glowing reference. It just so happens that we have talked about a few subjects that cast a negative light on the Chinese government. There are many aspects of Chinese culture and history that are admirable. I wouldn't want you to think negatively of the people of China."

"I know. Anyway, you are half-Chinese, so I can see that some great things have come out of China!"

We would return to the area surrounding St. Paul's a few years later. Until recently, the television show *First Dates* was filmed in Paternoster Chop House, which was located in the shadow of the cathedral. It felt strange to dine in a restaurant that we have seen on TV so many times. To my wife's dismay, there was no sign of Fred Sirieix. The restaurant has since moved to another location in London and the latest series was filmed in Manchester. Perhaps Carol will have a second opportunity to ambush the French hunk and ask for a selfie!

We walked past London Bridge during our final stroll alongside the Thames. The bridge looked ordinary, with few distinguishing features to indicate its long history. If we had visited during the sixteenth or seventeenth centuries, however, we would have seen a structure covered by shops and houses. There were thought to be around two hundred buildings on the bridge at one point. It is no surprise, therefore, that there were numerous fires and several incidents that resulted in its partial collapse. A more startling nugget of information is that the severed heads of 'traitors' used to be impaled on pikes along the bridge, where they would be displayed for all to see. William Wallace and Oliver Cromwell were amongst those to suffer this gruesome fate. Perhaps the more low-key reincarnation of the bridge is more palatable for tourists!

We were soon admiring the more eye-catching Tower Bridge, which is often confused with London Bridge. This is probably because the former has become a symbol of the city that is often shown on television whenever a story about London is being told. Built in the late-nineteenth century, it has two bridge towers connected by two horizontal walkways 143 feet above the Thames. Vehicles and pedestrians can freely cross the bridge deck, with an estimated 40,000 people doing so each day; whereas there is an admission charge to access the walkways and engine rooms that form part of the Tower Bridge Exhibition.

The most interesting aspect of the structure is that it is a type of bascule bridge, which operates in a similar fashion to a drawbridge. The bascules are raised approximately a thousand times a year to allow river vessels to pass through. There used to be a signal display system in operation during the era of heavier river traffic, but opening times are now published well in advance. The hydraulics used to lift the bascules were once powered by steam. The energy was stored in six accumulators, which meant that the bascules could be lifted at any given moment, which was a process that only took about a minute. Electricity and oil have replaced steam as the driving force behind the hydraulic power. As my knowledge of engineering is almost non-existent, which is most likely demonstrated by my rudimentary description, I recommend that you watch one of the numerous television shows that detail the inner workings of the bridge. I am unable to recall which programmes I have seen, but I know that *Britain's Greatest Bridges* featured an episode dedicated to Tower Bridge.

The bridge is located near the Tower of London. As we did not have time to enter the castle complex, we took a moment to observe it from a distance. Well, as much of it as we could see beyond the defensive walls.

"Have you ever been in?" I asked Carol.

"Years ago, but I can't remember much about it. I think it was built for William the Conqueror."

"Many historical figures seem to have menacing names like that –

William the Conqueror, Ivan the Terrible, Vlad the Impaler. What do you think I would be called?"

"David the Ditherer? David the Timid? David the Cutie Pie?"

"I guess I'm not the most intimidating character!"

"Especially when you're wearing your onesie!"

"Maybe we will visit it next time. I wouldn't mind learning about its gruesome history."

Although the Tower came to be seen as a symbol of oppression and was used as a prison, tales of torture and death were grossly exaggerated for propaganda purposes. This reputation is kept alive by those hoping to earn an income from tourist activity. Apparently, the likes of the then future Queen Elizabeth I and Sir Walter Raleigh were amongst those to have been held captive behind the castle walls. The former was imprisoned for nearly a year due to a suspicion that she was supporting Protestant rebels. Perhaps she was eager to give Raleigh a taste of what she had experienced, as he was later 'sent to the Tower' for marrying one of the Queen's ladies-in-waiting without Her Majesty's permission. King James I had him imprisoned in the Tower again before Raleigh embarked upon a second expedition in search of 'El Dorado.' Following a skirmish with the Spanish, he was executed upon his return to England. If this is how a future queen and a Knight of the Realm were treated, perhaps having a quiet life and being known as 'David the Ditherer' is not such a bad thing!

Carol and I crossed Tower Bridge at road level, which brought back memories of walking along New York's Brooklyn Bridge a few years earlier. There is a sense of wonder that comes from travelling as a pedestrian over one of the world's most iconic bridges. Walking through the archways of the towers and looking up at the walkways above was a delight. Excitement levels were enhanced by the possibility of the bascules rising whilst we were making our way across the Thames – at least in my over-active imagination.

We were provided with a view of The Shard, which had only opened to the public earlier that month. Reaching a height of over one thousand feet, it is the tallest building in the United Kingdom. It is also one of the most recognisable. Its name derived from the criticism the design initially faced, with English Heritage claiming the building would be a "shard of glass through the heart of historic London." It has received a warmer reception since its completion, however, with many people viewing it as one of the new symbols of the city. Tourists can take in a bird's eye view of London from the observation deck or dine in one of the high-end restaurants situated above the floors that house various offices. We did just that in July 2021, once again using a voucher to dine in Ting on the thirty-fifth floor.

"What do you think of The Shard?" I asked Carol.

"I quite like it. It's got a unique look. How about you?"

"I'm not sure. I usually prefer more traditional buildings, but it does stand out from the crowd. I wouldn't say it's ugly...I think it will grow on me over time."

"From what you say, you wouldn't be able to see the top of the building if we were in Beijing, due to the smog."

"I guess I will find out next month. They have plenty of skyscrapers over there."

We did not have time to visit any of the nearby landmarks, such as Southwark Cathedral, where Doorkins Magnificat made home after initially visiting in 2008. This was the name of a stray cat rather than an invader who violently overthrew Britain's monarchy. Even cats are given more impressive names than me! She inspired the children's book *Doorkins the Cathedral Cat* and was even greeted by Queen Elizabeth II and the Mayor of London during their respective visits to the cathedral. Sadly, she died in 2020 – as if the year could not have been any worse.

Despite returning to London several times, we have still not been inside Southwark Cathedral, Shakespeare's Globe or Borough Market. Instead, our attention has been diverted elsewhere, including attending an Elvis exhibition at the O2 Arena and savouring a cup of hot chocolate next to Cutty Sark. We were even given the true Soho experience when a drug dealer tried to sell us some cocaine. This occurred after dining in Bob Bob Ricard, where each table has a 'press for champagne' button.

Aside from the fascinating Natural History Museum, neither of us have visited any of the city's other great museums or art galleries as an adult, but we know that there are plenty of them available to explore in the future and most of them are free to enter. I soon lose interest in museums though – partly due to my short attention span and sometimes because of the knowledge that many artefacts were plundered from countries that the British Empire once occupied. We may well end up exploring such sites at some point, whether that is on our next trip or another occasion. This is the beauty of London: like the other great cities of the world, such as Paris or New York, one can visit numerous times and still leave feeling that there is more to see and experience.

"London has been great. I am already looking forward to coming back here," Carol declared.

"Despite my previous misgivings about London, I must admit that it truly is one of the world's great cities. The red buses and phone boxes, the black cabs, the historic buildings, and the sheer amount of tourist attractions – there is a lot to like about London. It retains so much tradition, but it also embraces the future and is multicultural. Sure, there are problems with racism in Britain but the interaction between people from different cultures helps to slowly move things in the right direction."

"You will be landing in another great city in a month's time."

"I imagine it will evoke a strong sense of history and tradition, but I don't think it will be as multicultural," I asserted, unaware of how much of an understatement that would prove to be.

"Just be careful of the air pollution, as you have asthma."

"I guess that I will soon see the real Big Smoke."

THE BIG SMOKE

BEYOND THE WALL

2: *THE FORBIDDEN CITY*
BEIJING, THE PEOPLE'S REPUBLIC OF CHINA
MARCH 2013

I was soon heading back to London. The company organising the trek, Discover Adventure, had booked tickets for the group to fly directly from Heathrow to Beijing. They had informed me that I could request that a connecting flight be added to my booking, but as this would involve a complicated series of conversations with a stranger, I elected to book my own flight from Manchester to Heathrow. Now stood at the baggage drop-off point in Manchester Airport, I began to panic that all the expensive equipment that I had purchased for the trek would be misplaced en route to Heathrow. When I had signed up for the trek, I had not considered the cost of hiking boots, a waterproof coat, a rucksack, numerous fleeces and whatever other items the staff at Cotswold Outdoor convinced me were essential.

"My luggage will definitely arrive safely at Heathrow, right?" I tentatively enquired.

"It should be waiting for you when you enter the baggage reclaim area, Sir," replied the woman behind the counter.

"That's great. I was just a little nervous because I'm flying from Heathrow to Beijing in a few hours. I'll need my equipment as I'm trekking the Great Wall of China."

"That sounds amazing. I must warn you that there is always a chance that luggage is lost in transit."

I had almost managed to get through to the end of the conversation without adding to my worries. I was aware that although the percentage of luggage lost was low, there had still been over twenty-six million cases misplaced or delayed in the previous year. The prospect of this happening to me and having to trek across the Great Wall of China whilst wearing jeans and a pair of cheap trainers was truly terrifying!

During the short flight, I kept myself distracted from such thoughts by replaying footage of the long-awaited return of David Brent, at least in my mind. The annual Comic Relief show had aired the night before, with Ricky Gervais briefly bringing back the lead character of *The Office*. Watching one of my favourite television characters entertain the nation whilst encouraging people to donate to worthy causes had been a fitting way to spend my final night before the trek. After all, I was about to embark on a trip that would hopefully be a great source of enjoyment and raise a considerable amount for charity.

"Please be there," I muttered to myself as I approached the baggage carousel in Heathrow.

Just to add to the tension, our luggage had not yet been unloaded. After a tense few minutes, the carousel sprang into life and suitcases began to appear. I looked at my fellow passengers as bags continued to drop onto the conveyor belt. Everyone seemed to be wearing the same desperate expression. I wondered if any of us would become part of 2013's lost luggage statistics. One by one, the other passengers displayed a sense of relief and delight as they yanked their case off the carousel. Just as I was resigning myself to a disastrous start to the trek, my expedition bag seemingly descended from heaven.

After navigating through the huge airport and locating the correct terminal, I sat and waited for the others to arrive, not that I would know what any of them looked like. I was wearing my Help a Capital Child T-shirt in the hope that someone would spot me and make the initial approach. I had made significant strides in my quest to become a more socially confident person, but I was still the shy and retiring type. Carol and Mum both sent text messages of encouragement, attempting to make me feel relaxed and happy. I am unable to recall their exact words, but all they really needed to do was inform me that Everton had just beaten Manchester City; thus, practically ensuring that Manchester United would be crowned Premier League champions.

Eventually, I spotted a few members of the group who had also decided to don their charity T-shirts. After taking a deep breath, I gingerly shuffled towards them. My plan worked, as someone greeted me before I had the opportunity to dither. I wondered if any of the five people stood in front of me were friends of one of the managers of the company I worked for. By sheer coincidence, her pals from Liverpool had also signed up for the trek. I am unsure of their names, but I think that one of them may have been called Laura and I am going to guess that the other was called Elouise. As the group introduced themselves, it became apparent that the two in question were yet to arrive.

James, a friendly, well-groomed chap in his early thirties was our contact at Help a Capital Child. He turned to me and asked: "David, what happened to Anthony? He suddenly became uncontactable and failed to pay the balance. Obviously, we had to cancel his place. Have you heard from him?"

"No. He did the same to me. He has not returned any of my messages."

I had only signed up for the challenge after hearing that Anthony had done so. The only member of the group that I was familiar with had disappeared off the face of the planet! I was accustomed to being a lone figure on the periphery of a group, but it meant that I would have to share a room with a stranger for the duration of the trip. Naturally, I assumed that I would be paired with a serial killer who only murdered people called David.

The rest of the group arrived in batches, one of which included two people of a similar age to me who may or may have gone by the names of Laura and Elouise. Along with our itinerary, we had each been sent a list of the names of our fellow trekkers. I remembered that someone had the surname Careless and made a mental note to avoid her whilst making our way past any cliff edges.

"David, this is your roommate, Joshua," James advised.

"Hi, I am David."

"Hi, I am Joshua."

The briefest of introductions had been completed – one which did not last long enough for me to gauge whether he was an axe murderer or not but informed me that he was likely in his late thirties or early forties and, judging by his accent, he was from Birmingham. I am tempted to joke that some people would prefer to share a room with an axe murderer than a 'Brummie,' but that may be taking things too far! It was time for us all to check in. Or at least that was the plan.

James looked sheepish as he told Joshua about the latest development: "There seems to have been a mix up. I feel awful about this, but you have not been booked onto the flight and the plane is full. They can fly you out to China tomorrow if you are willing to stay at the airport hotel tonight. We will cover the cost, of course. Would that be OK with you?"

"Oh. I guess it will have to be."

"You won't miss any of the trek, it just means that you won't be able to join us for our tour of the Forbidden City. The last day of the trip is free for people to do as they please, so you will get an opportunity to see it then. Again, I'm really sorry about this."

Joshua took the news with remarkably good grace and made his way over to the hotel; at least my roommate did not appear to have any anger management issues. I had mixed feelings about this turn of events: on the one hand, I was happy that I would not have to share a room with a stranger on the first night, but it also meant that I ran the risk of becoming isolated from the rest of the group. That would be hard to rectify for someone as shy as I was.

* * *

The probability of failing to integrate with the group seemed to have increased after the ten-hour flight to Beijing had concluded. I had been sat apart from the others for the duration of our journey. Upon disembarkation, it was clear that some of them had broken the ice and become friendly with each other. At least our luggage had arrived safely and our visas had been accepted. This had been another irrational concern of mine. Having sent my passport to the Chinese embassy, paid the extortionate fee and fretted about its safe return for three weeks, it would have been a disaster if it were rejected upon arrival.

After a short coach ride, we were soon sat in a restaurant having a late lunch in Beijing. Forty-plus strangers sat around several tables, sharing food. This was to be my first big test!

"You're quiet."

As expected, it had not taken long to establish myself as the quiet one.

"Look at all of us struggling to use our chopsticks…except him," someone else said, with a gentle nod in my direction.

This was my opportunity to truly become part of the group.

"I am half-Chinese," I declared.

I had assumed that this would lead to a sense of intrigue, but all I got was a half-hearted response of, "Oh, I see."

With our hunger satisfied by ample portions of rice, noodles, chicken and vegetables, we reboarded the coach, which took us to Tiananmen Square. It always feels strange when arriving at a place so strongly linked with a tragic loss of life. Even though most of the deaths and casualties occurred away from the square, many of them outside Beijing, it had been the focal point of student protests; therefore, it understandably became the location most strongly associated with the government-backed massacre. Nevertheless, I was eager to see the square with my own eyes. I believe that, despite the Chinese government's best efforts, it is important to keep the memory of such atrocities in the public consciousness so that the chances of events being repeated are reduced as much as possible. Besides, it is also one of the world's largest and most historic city squares. It was where Mao Zedong, commonly referred to as Chairman Mao, proclaimed the founding of the People's Republic of China in 1949.

Unfortunately, much of the square was off-limits, as it was occupied by some form of official ceremony. We may not have been able to explore freely, but it was certainly an impressive sight to behold, despite the thick layer of smog that had engulfed the area. Occupying 109 acres, the sheer size of it was striking. The grand buildings surrounding the square added to the sense of historical and cultural importance. This included the gigantic National Museum of China and the Great Hall of the People, which is used by the Communist Party to host ceremonial events and to welcome foreign dignitaries. A ten-storey obelisk, known as the Monument to the People's Heroes, is also located within Tiananmen Square. This stands in front of the Mausoleum of Mao Zedong, which houses the embalmed body of the former leader. Incidentally, his wish to be cremated was ignored. I guess that it is easier to disobey the leader of a totalitarian regime after he has died.

We did not visit any of those buildings; we only had time to explore the Forbidden City. This should not come as a surprise, as the 180-acre palace complex is the largest in the world. Tiananmen, which is commonly, although not entirely accurately, translated as 'The Gate of Heavenly Peace,' stands at the entrance of the former Imperial City. The name of the gate, and the square in front of it, seems ill-fitting considering the events that took place in 1989.

As we approached the gate, I heard a voice from behind: "There's Chairman Mao!"

They were referring to the portrait that is on permanent display above the entranceway. The image of Mao, which is replaced in the lead up to the National Day of the People's Republic of China each October, has been a constant feature since 1949. The only exception was when a portrait of Joseph Stalin was temporarily displayed following his death in 1953. It seems that one must be a dictator responsible for widespread persecution and murder to have this honour bestowed upon them.

The Imperial City was once separated from the rest of Beijing by a wall and a series of gates. Several prominent buildings were located within this area, including the former imperial garden Zhongnanhai. This now houses the office of the General Secretary of the Communist Party and the Chinese Premier. Other notable places within the former Imperial City include Jingshan Park, the Imperial Ancestral Temple and Beihai Park, which is commonly referred to as the Winter Palace. The Forbidden City, which consists of 980 buildings, is situated in the centre of the Imperial City. Construction took place in the early-fifteenth century after Beijing replaced Nanjing as the capital city. Apparently, one million workers helped complete the project in just fourteen years. I guess that it is not hard to find the manpower when you are the emperor.

The Palace Museum has been housed in the Forbidden City since 1925. The Last Emperor of China was expelled from the palace complex the previous year after two brief reigns during a tumultuous period that included the 1911 Revolution and the establishment of the Republic of China – which was overthrown in 1949 following their defeat at the hands of the Communists in the Chinese Civil War. Remarkably, Puyi's first reign began when he was just two years old. He was six when he was forced to abdicate. Puyi was restored as emperor by a loyalist general when he was eleven, which also happens to be the number of days his second reign lasted. I was just finishing primary school when I was that age!

Puyi's eventful life continued after his expulsion from the palace. Following the Japanese invasion of Manchuria in 1931, which some regard as the true starting point of the Second World War, he was chosen as the emperor of the new state of Manchukuo. He was seen as a puppet for the Japanese regime, passing any legislation he was presented with, including legalising slavery. There is a tendency to view the war from the perspective of one's home country, but it can be analysed in numerous ways because it was a series of intertwined conflicts from around the world. The fighting in Asia began before European involvement commenced and ended after Victory in Europe had been declared. Whilst the tragic loss of British and American lives, which gives a combined figure in the region of 870,000, is understandably the focus of those in the United Kingdom and the United States, it is often forgotten that over 20 million people from the Soviet Union and upwards of 15 million people from China died as a result of the concerted effort to defeat fascism.

After the fall of Japan, Puyi spent ten years imprisoned as a war criminal. Spared execution for propaganda purposes, he was 're-educated' by the newly established People's Republic of China. The 1987 film *The Last Emperor* won nine Academy Awards, but it has faced criticism that it glosses over the more unsavoury aspects of his character. After all, he was known to have a sadistic streak that resulted in frequent beatings for his servants. Perhaps this should not be too surprising given that he was not allowed to see his biological mother or leave the Forbidden City, and the fact that he wielded absolute power when he was just a toddler.

The Forbidden City was once out of bounds for the general public –

hence the name – with the palace housing twenty-four emperors who were each regarded as the 'Son of Heaven.' Nowadays, the general public are able to walk through the gigantic complex. And there are plenty of people who do so – demand is so high that the authorities have had to introduce an 80,000-person daily limit. Visitors are only permitted to enter from the Meridien Gate, which meant that, if I recall correctly, we had to get back on the coach and make our way over to the south side of the complex.

I was instantly impressed by the sight of the Forbidden City. We almost immediately had to cross one of the small Golden Water Bridges over the moat, which led us to the Gate of Supreme Harmony. Like most of the other wooden structures within the complex, it has two glazed tile roofs, with red and yellow the most prominent colours. There are two statues guarding the stairs leading to the gate. On one side there is a lion with its front paw resting on a globe, which symbolises how the imperial power extended throughout the world. On the other flank, a lioness has her front paw placed on a cub, representing the flourishing imperial family. One of the Discover Adventure guides, who I am going to call Charlotte even though that was most likely not her name, noticed that I was taking lots of photographs but not engaging with other members of the group. She offered to take my photo next to the statues and struck up a conversation.

"So, David, what made you sign up for the trek?" she enquired.

"I am a keen traveller, so when I heard that a friend of a friend was going to trek the Great Wall of China, I could not help but feel jealous. I looked into it and soon registered my interest."

"I didn't realise that you knew someone from the group."

"I don't. Anthony must have had second thoughts, as he cut all contact with me and Help a Capital Child!"

"That must have been disappointing. I'm sure that you will make friends with the others."

"My roommate was supposed to be Joshua, the guy who was unable to join our flight! Not the best of starts!"

It took an hour or so to make our way through the Forbidden City; and we were just sticking to the central sections. Although the architecture was delightful, it all looked similar. The Hall of Supreme Harmony, the Hall of Middle Harmony, the Hall of Preserving Harmony, the Gate of Heavenly Purity, the Palace of Heavenly Purity, the Hall of Union and the Palace of Earthly Tranquillity were all visually impressive; however, the impact of the series of splendid gates, pretty courtyards and grand halls gradually diminished after seeing each one. Mind you, my opinion may have been different if we had seen the Palace of Universal Happiness – at least if it is true to name. I should point out that despite what I have said, the Forbidden City is a wonder to behold and certainly worth a visit if you are in Beijing. The ornate buildings, impressive statues and intricate carvings are a treat for the eyes. It was just unfortunate that mine were bleary after the long journey to China.

Alastair, one of the other Discover Adventure guides, addressed the group: "This place is huge isn't it? A common myth is that there are 9,999 rooms in total, as only the palace in heaven is worthy of having 10,000. I don't believe that's an accurate number, but it makes for a nice story."

Alastair seemed to be an extremely confident person who was entirely comfortable within the world of exploration.

Before leaving the Forbidden City, we noticed that couples were queueing up to have their photograph taken in front of some trees. Upon closer inspection, it was apparent that the branches of a couple of 400-year-old Lian Li Cypress trees had become intertwined. Once regarded as a symbol of the everlasting harmony between the emperor and empress, it is now popular with young couples who appreciate the romantic sentiment.

As we waited for our coach to return, a couple of young Chinese women asked to have their photograph taken with me. "They obviously want their picture taken with a handsome fella," I told myself. My ego was soon deflated when I noticed that people were asking for photos with other members of the group.

Alastair explained: "This always happens. Many of the people visiting Beijing from the more remote places in China have never seen a non-Chinese person before. The sight of a coachload of mostly white people is a novelty to them. The culture is different where they are from, so they will think nothing of asking for your photograph just because of the colour of your skin. It's weird but they are not trying to be rude, even if it comes across that way."

I looked to my left and noticed that the blonde women in our group were especially popular, with groups of Chinese people queueing up for photographs as if they were pop stars. As Alastair had said, I do not believe that they were ill-intentioned; rather, it underscores the impact of interacting with people from diverse cultures. In this case, the people in question had most likely never met anyone with a different ethnic background. Having been born in Greater Manchester, I had been raised in a multicultural society and from a young age I had attended school with people of various ethnic and religious backgrounds. This was normal to me, but it was something alien to the people who were posing for photographs alongside members of our group.

Whilst the coach set off for our hotel for the night, I flicked through the photographs I had taken. My favourite image was of a lone guard stood at attention whilst looking across a square at one of the grand halls within the Forbidden City. The smog seemed to add a mysterious element to the photo. We had hardly covered any ground in the ten minutes that had elapsed since our departure. It was clear that the traffic in Beijing was not conducive for travelling from one point to another without spending an eternity in transit. Not only were the roads congested, they were also hazardous. Drivers reacted to traffic jams by ruthlessly cutting across other vehicles, weaving in and out of traffic, albeit often at crawling pace. The Highway Code was certainly not in operation out there – it was every person for themselves! I was thankful that I was not the one tasked with safely guiding a coach carrying over forty people to our hotel.

At one point during our journey, a drunk man decided to add to the chaos. He stumbled across four lanes of traffic before spinning around and lying on the floor. He was obviously not settling down for a nap or wishing to end his life under the wheels of our coach, as he was grinning from ear to ear. He was just extremely drunk. And stupid. It made me wonder what a friend of my family, who we refer to as Uncle Sydney, would think of this. He is often less than complimentary when referring to people from mainland China, complaining that they spit and urinate in the street, in addition to showing a general lack of manners when they venture into Hong Kong territory. His comments were perhaps a little harsh, but it highlights the tension that exists between the two regions. There have been protests in Hong Kong about the number of visitors from mainland China who often arrive by the coachload in order to purchase consumer goods. By comparison, it makes the North-South divide in England seem rather genteel.

In addition to the sea of cars and the occasional drunk lying in the road, I noticed that there were plenty of bicycles weaving in and out of traffic. I was not in a position to count them all and test Katie Melua's claim that there are "Nine Million Bicycles" in Beijing, but the number seemed to be within reason. When I had heard there had been criticism about the accuracy of her 2005 song, I had assumed that it was to do with the number of bicycles, but it was actually directed at the lyric: "We are twelve billion light-years from the edge. That's a guess, no one can ever say it's true." Some scientists were apparently in uproar, partly in relation to the inaccurate number quoted, but more to do with her verse seemingly undermining a century of dedicated research into the subject. Simon Singh wrote a piece in *The Guardian* suggesting she adjust her opening verse so that it read: "We are 13.7 billion light-years from the edge of the observable universe. That's a good estimate with well-defined error bars." Melua took the criticism with good grace, as she re-recorded a humorous version with the proposed amendment.

As usual, I have gone off on a tangent. The point I intended to make about the song was regarding the line: "There are six billion people in the world, more or less." The world's population was approximately 6.5 billion in 2005. It had already increased to around 7.2 billion by the time of the trek; this has since risen above 7.8 billion. The rapid expansion of the human race over the past century is highlighted by estimates that place this number at just 1.9 billion back in 1920. This is, of course, placing a huge strain on the planet. We have encroached onto the habitat of various wildlife around the world, threatening certain species' existence, and damaged the planet through pollution, deforestation and an increase in the earth's temperature.

China took the most extreme approach of any nation in the world when it came to population planning. In order to curb the rapid increase in its populace, the government stated that couples should only have two children. Then, in 1979, the infamous one-child policy was introduced. Severe fines were dished out to those who disobeyed and financial rewards were given to couples who stuck to the guidelines. As parents in rural areas relied on the labour of their male offspring, the policy was amended to allow another child if their firstborn was female. It did not stop struggling parents sometimes abandoning female babies or putting them up for adoption. This led to a higher-than-expected male population within China.

There were many exemptions, however, which has led to some analysts claiming that the effects of the policy have been overstated and that much of the population was in fact permitted to have more than one child. The policy had been strongly criticised by human rights groups for decades but was still in place at the time of our trek. With China becoming alarmed at the prospect of the steep decline in the birth rate impacting the economic growth of the nation, the policy was relaxed in 2016 to permit a second child, before being amended again in 2021 to allow three children.

Thinking about this policy makes it clear that our fates are often defined by which side of a man-made border we were born in. If my mother had been born in mainland China rather than Hong Kong, she would not have been able to leave the country to start a new life in the United Kingdom. She would almost certainly not have met my father in China, and even if she had, she would not have been allowed to have a second child after giving birth to my elder brother; therefore, I would not exist. On a broader scale, many people are condemned to an extremely difficult life in which they are fleeing persecution and are deprived of safety and the means to support themselves. Where we are born has a significant bearing on our life prospects. This makes it all the more disappointing when a large percentage of the people living in prosperous countries are determined to slam the door shut on refugees who were dealt a much tougher hand.

As the coach crawled through the gridlocked traffic towards our hotel, it became clear why the Chinese authorities had been so keen to build the Shanghai Maglev Train. Since the service opened to the public in 2004, the fastest commercial electric train in the world has shredded the transit time between Shanghai Pudong International Airport and the city centre. Severely congested roads often lead to huge delays for car journeys to and from the airport, but the thirty-kilometre trip takes less than eight minutes on the magnetic levitation train. Using powerful electromagnets, the train is elevated a fraction above the track; thus, removing the tremendous amount of energy required to overcome friction. This allows the vehicle to reach a top speed of 431-kilometres-per-hour. If only they had built a maglev train between the forbidden city and our hotel!

Incidentally, the world's first commercial maglev system was in operation between Birmingham International Airport and Birmingham International Railway Station from 1984 to 1995. Despite a track length of just 600 metres and the train travelling at a much lower speed than the Shanghai Maglev, it was closed due to issues with its reliability.

Upon arrival at our hotel, there was unanimous agreement that we were in need of an early night before we began our trek the following day. The hotel seemed nice enough. It occupied a large building, looked clean and modern, and would certainly be of a higher standard than what we would be exposed to over the course of the next week. Part of me was relieved to have a room to myself, but it made me feel more isolated from the others and I was aware that I had been deprived the opportunity to form a bond with at least one member of the group.

A more pressing concern was that I had no roommate to wake me up if I overslept! As I was tired due to the long journey and an afternoon of sightseeing, I was not confident of waking up in time for our first official briefing in the morning. I took the overly cautious step of setting twenty different alarms on my phone, each spaced a few minutes apart, and another on my travel alarm clock. After sending text messages to Mum and Carol to let them know that everything had gone smoothly up to that point, I turned out the lights. It was time to get some much-needed sleep before the adventure began in the morning. I would finally be trekking the Great Wall of China! Providing that I woke up in time.

BEYOND THE WALL

3: HEAVEN'S LADDER
HUANGYAGUAN, THE PEOPLE'S REPUBLIC OF CHINA
MARCH 2013

After being woken up by the sound of both my alarm clock and the furious beeping of my mobile phone, I lay in bed thinking about the adventure that was about to commence. The next week would be spent walking along the Great Wall of China whilst being surrounded by breathtaking scenery. My thoughts were soon interrupted by the sound of the alarm on my phone again. I took this as my cue to get out of bed and prepare myself for the day ahead. Moments after stepping into the shower, the alarm went off again. I had forgotten that I was a lunatic who had set twenty alarms! After turning them all off, finishing my shower and making myself half-presentable, I gathered my belongings and headed down to breakfast.

I sheepishly walked past some of my fellow trekkers and exchanged a cursory greeting. Despite their friendly faces, it still felt awkward. There was only one course of action – and this can be applied to many situations in life: I piled gigantic portions of fried noodles, rice and dumplings onto my plate and told myself that everything would sort itself out.

"Do you mind if I sit here?" I asked a group of four or five trekkers already sat at one of the restaurant's many tables. If they had answered, "No, f**K off," then I think that would have been enough for me to have packed my bags and flown home. There was still no sign of Joshua – I wonder what he would have thought if he had finally arrived only to find that his roommate had already abandoned the trek!

"Yeah, sure. Take a seat, mate. I'm James."

Not to be confused with our Help a Capital Child guide, this was another James, who was a burly bloke I estimated to be in his mid-twenties. I shall refer to him as James G from this point.

"Big question to start with: which footie team do you support?" he asked whilst wearing a beaming smile.

"Manchester United. How about you?"

"Me too. I'm half-Chinese and I'm from London, so of course I support United!" he answered, accompanied by a booming laugh.

I was unsure whether I should be pleased that we had quickly found common ground or disheartened that he had met the criteria for the stereotypical United fan that is ridiculed by supporters of rival teams.

Another couple of my fellow trekkers introduced themselves. Phil and Farhad, who were both bald and appeared to be in their mid-thirties, were former members of the British Armed Forces, as well as good friends. As I began to fret about the prospect of being left trailing in their wake on the Great Wall, I eased my concerns by noting that our group included people in their late-fifties and some who had considerably larger abdomens than mine.

One interesting aspect of the group was the high proportion of females. Excluding the guides, there were just eight males. Judging by photographs of other treks that I had seen when browsing the Discover Adventure website, an overwhelming female majority seemed to be a common theme. I am not sure why this is the case; perhaps women in Britain are more involved in charity fundraising activities or the advertising campaigns are more effective with their demographic. Either way, the sample size was too small to draw any definitive conclusions. I just know that most male characters in pretty much any teen movie would have been thrilled by the gender ratio! This was not the case with me, as I was just worried about somehow becoming a social pariah.

Our first team meeting of the trip was headed by Alan, another Discover Adventure guide who had flown out from his home country of South Africa to join us overnight. He was tall, bald and suntanned, and I assumed that he was in his early forties. Perhaps it was because he had consumed a copious amount of caffeine, but he seemed to be a larger-than-life character who was likely to be the most energetic member of the group.

"We will use today as an opportunity to acclimatise ourselves to the task at hand. We will be driving to Huangyaguan, where we will join a well-kept section of the wall that will not be too taxing. A few hours of walking will get our bodies used to covering long distances and steep inclines. This will allow you to become comfortable with your trekking gear. Make sure you wear a durable pair of socks, tie your shoelaces properly and fasten the straps on your rucksacks around your chest and waist. This will ensure the weight is evenly distributed."

I had only brought a small backpack with one strap that fastened across my chest. Fortunately, I found this adequate for the trek, but this was the first indication that most of my fellow trekkers had invested in better quality trekking gear and had taken a more serious approach to the whole thing. Some of them had rucksacks that were bigger than me! Others had walking sticks and had spent weekends hiking up mountains in preparation for the trek. All I had done was walk to and from work each day.

"There is a toboggan ride that takes you down one of the mountains. We will have the opportunity to do this towards the end of our trek. You can all decide on the day, but who reckons they will be interested?" Alan asked the group.

My heart skipped a beat as I imagined a dangerous and frightening ride down a mountain designed for adrenaline junkies rather than a wet blanket like me. After all, I do not even like rollercoaster rides, and I feel uneasy when I am in a car doing more than fifty-miles-per-hour whilst the windows are down. I anxiously surveyed the room, desperately hoping that none of the others showed any enthusiasm. Seven or eight people stated that they would definitely want to ride the toboggan, whilst most seem undecided. This was not enough to quell any fears that the majority of the group would take part, causing me to feel obliged to join them. No decisions would be made until later in the week, which meant that this worrisome thought would linger in the back of my mind for the next few days.

It took around three hours for our coach to reach our starting point in Huangyaguan, which is located in the Tianjin municipality. Upon arrival, I noticed that Joshua was still absent. I felt bad for him – imagine spending over a year fundraising and preparing for the trip, then to be told that you could not fly to China with the rest of the group. Not only that, but he had missed out on visiting the Forbidden City and was now going to be absent during the group's first encounter with the Great Wall. I began to wonder whether he would take any part in the trek.

Before we joined the wall, we all posed for a group photo in front of a large statue of General Qi Jiguang. We had no idea who he was, but the combination of the statue and the wall provided an impressive image to mark our starting point. It turns out that this section of the wall had been rebuilt under his watch in the sixteenth century and was renovated following former Chinese leader Deng Xiaoping's rallying call to 'Love China and Build the Great Wall' in 1984. This is now one of the most accessible sections of the wall for tourists. As Alan alluded to, this segment was not going to be the most challenging or authentic that we would experience over the coming week, but it would provide a pleasant introduction to the wall.

The sight of the imposing figure of Qi Jiguang against the backdrop of the Great Wall of China made me think of a quote I had read the previous week. Chairman Mao famously uttered a phrase that can be loosely translated as: "He who has not climbed the Great Wall is not a true man." I already knew that I was not a true man in the eyes of traditional members of society – I was unassertive, I had never driven a car, and I sometimes used a knife and fork when eating a burger or a pizza – but at least I would have the opportunity to fool people into believing I was!

Before beginning our day's trek, Alastair invited us to use the public toilet. Several people were shocked at the basic facilities on offer, which amounted to little more than a hole in the floor. He seemed to take great pleasure in informing us: "That will be the nicest toilet you use this week. It will seem like a luxurious palace in comparison to the horrors you encounter!"

The reality of what we had signed up for was beginning to sink in: the prospect of spending hours on end trekking the Great Wall was nothing compared to the thought of having to use stomach-churning toilets for a week! An unexpected dilemma now revolved around the volume of water I should drink during each day's trek. I obviously needed to drink enough to avoid dehydration but taking in a large amount of liquid would require more visits to the ghastly toilets!

Although I joke about it, access to decent toilets and clean water is not something that should be taken for granted. Millions of people across the globe are faced with the prospect of drinking dirty water, risking their wellbeing in the process. Others must walk several kilometres each day in order to access clean water for their families. Having a functioning toilet and decent sanitary conditions is rarely given consideration in the 'developed world,' but many disadvantaged communities across the planet are deprived of such facilities.

There was a fair number of tourists posing for photographs on this section of the wall. On previous trips that I had taken, I would have been one of them, but now they somehow felt like an inferior form of traveller. We brushed past them as if they were a nuisance obstructing our noble quest. It is ludicrous how wearing some hiking gear can instantly transform you into a travel snob! The number of tourists dwindled as we covered further ground. There may have been more people gathered on the wall than was desirable, and the renovation work may have left this historic structure looking a little too polished, but the epic scale and accomplishment of this ambitious project was clear to see.

After spending our first day in Beijing, it was a delight to be surrounded by the natural beauty of undulating hills and mountains in every direction. Watchtowers were positioned on the most elevated positions along the wall, further enhancing the extraordinary panoramas. Humans have a habit of destroying such scenery, but this appeared to be a rare example of a man-made structure that enhanced the aesthetic quality of its setting. Perhaps this was because I was aware of the colossal feat of engineering that had taken place and the fact that the Great Wall is frequently described as one of the wonders of the world.

The weather was more agreeable than I had anticipated. The sun was unobscured by cloud, the sky was a brilliant blue and the temperature was pleasant. I soon removed my fleece and my jacket, placing both items into my backpack, feeling relieved that there was room for both. I was wearing a tight T-shirt, which prompted Alan to pass comment on my physique: "You've got some impressive biceps there."

With Chairman Mao's words about being a man rattling around in my mind, I began to feel more confident. Despite standing at just five feet, five inches tall and having asthma, I appeared to be in better shape and of a younger age than most of my fellow trekkers. Being so quiet and shy, having a relatively muscular physique and numerous tattoos has often proven to be useful in preventing myself from becoming a social misfit, as people will often strike up a conversation with me about these subjects.

We had been joined by another guide. This time it was a Chinese man, who may have been called Jin, with in-depth knowledge of the areas we would be travelling through. He was similar in stature to me, although at least ten years older. Jin soon utilised the other icebreaker that I have become accustomed to: "I see that you have some Chinese tattoos. Are you Chinese?"

"I am half-Chinese. My mum is from Hong Kong and my dad is from England."

"So, you speak Cantonese then? I know a little, but Mandarin is my main language."

"I don't speak much Cantonese. I wish I had paid more attention to the language when I was younger. I can have some basic conversations with my mum but nothing more than a few sentences."

Jin had brought up an interesting subject: there are hundreds of different languages and dialects in China. Before the country was unified, there were a variety of dynasties and tribes that had their own languages. Hakka Chinese and Jin Chinese, which I would love to tell you was Jin's mother tongue, are examples of the many languages still spoken by millions of people in China. Standard Chinese is a dialect of Mandarin that has been adopted by the Communist Party as the official language of the nation, with over seventy per cent of people in China regarding Mandarin as their first language. The basis for the written form of most of the languages in China is similar, with characters generally having the same meaning; however, some use traditional characters whilst others have embraced simplified Chinese. Although the mainland government regards simplified characters as the standard script, Hong Kong and Macao still use traditional versions.

It can be difficult to explain the differences, but simplified Chinese characters use less brushstrokes. I am tempted to compare it to American English; after all, words such as 'thru' have replaced the likes of 'through' when used informally in the United States. The American dialect omits the letter 'u' from many words ending in 'our' and removes the use of the double 'l' in many words. They replace the 's' with a 'z' in words that end in 'ise,' not that this shortens it. It can be infuriating when software on computers and phones attempt to correct my sentences because they are set to American English by default. For this reason, it will often be suggested that I should write something along the lines of: 'As a keen traveler, my neighbor would regularly organize trips…'

I spend enough time worrying about making mistakes; I do not need any false 'errors' pointing out to me! Having said all that, I frequently stray from many of the rules of traditional English, so many of you are no doubt infuriated by my writing style by this stage!

I soon regretted my conversation with Jin, as he began to pose questions to me in front of the group. For example, he asked me why the Chinese often favour the number six. I had an inkling that the answer was to do with good fortune, but I was aware that the number eight was regarded as the most auspicious number. My indecision meant that I failed to even answer the question. Jin handed me multiple opportunities to impress the group with my knowledge of Chinese culture, but I invariably made a mess of them all.

When he was not inadvertently embarrassing me in front of the others, he made sure that he was providing us with a general overview of the history of the wall. For example, he informed us that the Great Wall of China was in fact a series of walls built as far back as the seventh century BC. The different dynasties that ruled parts of China in the following centuries added new sections and joined existing ones to form border walls. It was the Ming Dynasty that made a concerted effort to establish a more extensive and robust wall with watchtowers to help repel any invading Mongolian tribes. Unfortunately, the 13,000-mile wall was only effective if it was manned by disciplined troops. This proved to be a significant problem, as the remote location and the harsh conditions resulted in a lack of morale and motivation. The wall was breached several times, most notably by Genghis Khan's army.

"The Great Wall looks fantastic, but it was not effective. Guards would sometimes abandon their posts, rendering it useless," was Jin's rather downbeat verdict. "Some of the older sections of the wall were built by soldiers and convicts. It is thought that around 400,000 people died during its construction, with many buried in or under the wall itself. They say it is the longest cemetery on the planet."

Jin struck a more cheerful tone when he informed us of the ingenuity regarding its construction: "They used sticky rice to build the wall! This was added to the mortar, which proved to be durable. This was also employed during the construction of pagodas, tombs and city walls. Apparently, it is strong enough to withstand earthquakes!"

"Is it true that you can see the Great Wall from space?" was one of the questions that a member of our group asked Jin.

"No. Although the total length is over 21,000 kilometres, it is far too narrow to be seen from space, at least not without specialist equipment. Look around you; the wall has a similar width to a normal road. This myth has long been debunked. Some astronauts have said that under the right conditions it is possible to see it from low Earth orbit when you are one or two hundred miles above the surface, but many have said that they failed to see it even in favourable conditions."

As we had been warned, some sections of the wall were steep, which put more strain on our joints. Thankfully, it was not testing enough for me to rue my decision of undertaking the trek without the aid of a walking stick. Mind you, we were only on a heavily-renovated section. Although the view was essentially the same throughout, I did not tire of taking photographs whenever there was a brief pause to allow those at the rear to catch up. Despite knowing that I would be treated to such views for the next week, I felt a burning desire to capture as many images as possible. This is often the case when I visit somewhere for the first time, possibly due to an irrational fear that something will happen that brings the trip to a halt.

I had thoroughly enjoyed our gentle introduction to the trek. Our surroundings had been picture-perfect, although maybe a little too polished, and it boosted our collective confidence for the week ahead. Walking for a few hours had also re-energised my body after spending the last couple of days sat on a plane or a coach.

Another short coach journey took us back to our accommodation for the night. With a courtyard surrounded by single-storey red buildings, I thought that our pretty 'mountain hotel' resembled a monastery that had been converted into an American motel. Not that I had ever seen such a thing. The most pleasing aspect was that we could see the Great Wall on the mountains just a few hundred yards behind our accommodation. It is not often that you can see such an awe-inspiring sight from your hotel!

I took my backpack and my expedition bag, which had been stored in the bowels of the coach, to my room and inspected my new lodgings. As expected, there was no heating, so it was likely to be a cold night in the shadow of the mountains. The toilet was a hole in the ground. We had been told not to put any toilet paper down the hole as this could cause a blockage. Instead, all used paper was to be placed in a bin next to the toilet – I felt sorry for the staff who would have to empty the bins the following day! There were two single beds but still no sign of Joshua. Perhaps I would be a loner for the duration of the trip. Just as I considered this possibility, James from Help a Capital Child entered the room alongside Joshua and informed me: "Your roommate has finally arrived! You already met at the airport, so I'll leave you to get reacquainted."

"Hi Joshua. I bet you're glad to be here at last."

"Yeah, I'm excited now. It was not ideal to have been left behind! It's just one of those things, I guess. I can't do anything about it now, apart from enjoy the rest of the trip."

"You have not missed much anyway," I lied. "We had a quick tour of the Forbidden Palace when we were jet-lagged and today was just a gentle introductory walk."

I was impressed that Joshua had shown such good grace, so I was trying my best not to enthuse about anything he had missed.

The group reconvened for our evening meal in a communal area within the hotel. A spread had been laid out for us, including chicken and beef, boiled rice, and steamed vegetables. It was time to conquer another of my fears: the dreaded buffet! Whilst I like sampling a variety of food, I cannot help but fret about the hygiene standards of other diners. Would they touch anything with their hands then put it back? Would they sneeze or cough near the food? I also worry about the portion sizes – is it acceptable for me to take three florets of broccoli or should I just take two? Anyway, it was time to face the buffet. Having been relieved that no one committed any of the aforementioned sins, I gave myself small portions of chicken and vegetables, then loaded up on rice as there was so much of it on offer.

Packets of instant noodles were a rather surprising inclusion in the spread. I suppose that this cheap, long-lasting food is ideal for groups of trekkers in remote locations. Noodles are thought to have originated from

China; however, the modern version of instant noodles were introduced in Japan, where they are often called instant ramen. Dried blocks of pre-cooked noodles only take a few minutes to prepare for consumption but have a shelf life of up to a year.

Surprisingly, packets of instant noodles have become the most popular item to exchange within American prisons in recent years. A decline in the quality and quantity of food provided has led to an increased demand for extra grub. This cheap and versatile item, which is easy to store, has overtaken tobacco as the most sought-after commodity for those behind bars. It seems strange to think that inmates will even do other people's laundry in exchange for instant noodles! Gustavo 'Goose' Alvarez contributed to a book about the subject. Having spent a decade incarcerated, he details some of the creative recipes involving instant noodles and provides some insight into their role in prison life. Apparently, there was an occasion in the aftermath of a prison riot in which tensions between rival factions were only resolved after a shared meal involving ramen. This provided the inspiration for *Prison Ramen: Recipes and Stories from Behind Bars*.

Jin smiled as he held up a bottle of alcohol: "You all have to try some *baijiu*. The Japanese have *sake*, but this is stronger! It is sixty-per-cent alcohol!"

He poured a small amount into each of our plastic cups and instructed us to raise a toast to the Great Wall before downing our shots. As expected, it was not the type of drink to savour. My throat felt like it was on fire. Still, I felt compelled to accept another couple of shots, as the high alcohol volume seemed to aid the bonding process within the group. We each spoke about why we had signed up for the trek and gave some insight into our personal backgrounds. A couple of trekkers, who I think were called Gwaenelle and Claire, spoke about how they would miss their young children over the next week or so. Many people explained how cancer had inflicted misery upon their friends and family.

We discovered that Geoff and Lisa, which are probably not their actual names, were a father and daughter who had undertaken a series of challenges after Lisa had been diagnosed with cancer. The father appeared to be in his early sixties, whilst his daughter was probably in her late thirties. Thankfully, her cancer was in remission. One of their recent high-octane challenges, all of which raised money for cancer-related charities, was a tandem wing-walk.

"Trekking the Great Wall will be a gentle affair in comparison to walking along the wing of a plane flying high above the ground!" Geoff declared.

"After my cancer scare, we decided to live life to the full. I want to experience everything life has to offer and be daring," Lisa added. "Plus, we get to raise lots of money for charities close to our hearts."

We all felt inspired by their story. It underscored how fortunate I was to be in good health and on a once-in-a-lifetime journey. Feeling at ease around my new roommate, I managed to get a good night's sleep. The baijiu probably helped in that regard.

* * *

The following morning, we were provided with a rather different breakfast than what we had been treated to at the hotel in Beijing. There was no cooked food in sight; instead, we were each handed a couple of cereal bars. They were not as tasty as the noodles I had enjoyed the previous day, but they were probably more appropriate in terms of nutrition. After all, we would be exerting a considerable amount of energy during the course of the day.

I was grateful that we were each given a couple of bottles of water to keep us hydrated during the next leg of our trek, but less thrilled about the instruction to take part in various exercises that would prepare our bodies for the day ahead. The gentle stretches and aerobic routines were not particularly unpleasant, and the opportunity to warm up in the shadow of the Great Wall of China was a rare one, but I have always hated the idea of exercising as part of a group. The prospect of forty strangers stood in a circle watching each other flail around and generally look silly was less than appealing.

Undeterred by this daunting task, I showed the courage of a lion by flexing a few muscles and following the self-appointed boxercise instructor. Elouise worked in the fitness industry, so she had taken it upon herself to help the group prepare for our first proper day of trekking. I had become a qualified gym instructor a few years beforehand, but of course I kept quiet. The only thing less enticing than taking part in group exercise would be standing in front of the others and feigning enthusiasm whilst demonstrating how to perform some star jumps and burpees! For this reason, it is perhaps unsurprising that I have never made use of my qualification.

Having been caught out by the unexpectedly warm weather the previous day, I decided to leave my fleece and jacket in my backpack. Typically, the weather had completely changed since we were last on the wall; it was now covered with a light dusting of snow and ice, the sky was overcast and there was a chill in the air. It was remarkable to think that sunshine and a vibrant blue sky had accompanied the same scenery less than twenty-four hours ago. The weather in northern China was evidently as unpredictable as it is in Britain! Despite the cold weather, I made the hard-headed decision of not putting on additional clothing until we had ascended Heaven's Ladder.

This involved a steep climb of over three hundred narrow steps leading up a cliff face. Whilst this activity was taxing on the joints, it was certainly not beyond the capability of a bunch of average Joes like us. The tricky conditions under foot were the more pressing concern. We had to be careful not to slip on any icy steps and potentially sweep the other forty members of the group back down Heaven's Ladder! Bordered by a multitude of barren trees, our careful ascent did not offer any meaningful view of the surrounding area. Instead, we had tunnel vision during our long climb.

Once we had reached the top, however, we were blessed with impressive panoramas of the neighbouring mountains and the landscape below. I used the short drinks break to capture a series of photographs and take in the views we had been afforded. This was an example of what the trek entailed: a period of physical exertion followed by a moment to savour the breathtaking beauty around us. Although it may not have been a death-defying trek through the wilderness on a Bear Grylls-style expedition, it was to be a challenging yet immensely satisfying adventure for our group of office workers and shop assistants.

I finally put on my fleece and jacket, to the undoubted amusement of some of the others. During our climb, I had batted away several questions regarding my decision to persevere without remedying my unsuitable clothing. Now I was getting a few nods and smiles to indicate they were pleased that I had eventually come to my senses. I guess the prospect of someone suffering with hypothermia on the second day of the trek was something that everyone wanted to avoid.

The next section of our route took us through a forested area as we continued to climb higher and higher. As Alan had explained to us during our introductory meeting, large parts of the trek would take place away from the wall. This was partly because some segments were in poor condition, and due to the stated intention of devising an interesting course. We had already experienced a variety of terrain and weather, which meant that we were not just following a monotonous path along the wall.

It was not long before my inexperience of trekking came to the fore. Alastair warned us that the ground was slippery, but we had to trust the grip on our footwear.

"This is why you all spent your hard-earned money on those expensive hiking boots!" he advised.

What he said made sense, but my instincts duly took over during the first tricky patch I encountered. We had to negotiate a bend whilst being mindful of a slope on one side leading to a section forty metres below.

"Just trust your footwear," I told myself.

The first bit of lateral movement resulted in me diving headfirst into full-blown panic mode. Before I knew it, I had resorted to clambering onto all fours and holding onto the ground for dear life. This was counter-productive, as it deprived me of the advantage of the sturdy grip on the soles of my boots. I was now lying face down on the muddy path whilst my arms and legs were frantically scrambling around in an illogical manner. This seemed to make the ground even more slippery, so I decided to remain perfectly still. As I was at the rear of a small sub-group at the time, nobody had witnessed my pathetic display. This promptly changed as the next few members of the group caught up.

"Are you OK, David?" asked James G.

It was probably for the best that I could not see his facial expression from my position. God only knows what he thought when he saw me sprawled out face down in the dirt.

"Yeah, I am fine," I lied.

I saw several pairs of hiking boots stroll past, indicating that Alistair was correct when he stated that things would be much simpler if we trusted our footwear. I just had to lift myself off the floor and return to an upright stance. The trouble was that this was much more difficult than the initial task of walking that I had failed so miserably. With James G and the others marching on, I finally summoned the courage to return to my feet. After a little wobble and a slide, I was once again upstanding, at least in terms of posture, if not in character and reputation.

In keeping with this theme, a few members of the group were quick to abandon any façade of respectability once they saw the state of the public toilets. I chose to stay well clear whilst I waited for the initial reports from those brave enough to enter. I obviously did the right thing, as several people soon came rushing out with a look of horror written all over their faces. It must have been bad in there if it caused people to literally run away from the toilets! Given the remote location, I guess that there is little to no maintenance. I decided to wait until we arrived at the homestay before relieving myself, but some of the others could not hold it in. Instead, they did their business off the mountainside. It must speak volumes about the state of the toilets if people would sooner drop their drawers by the edge of a mountain than use the public facilities. I kept my distance, but I can only imagine what the sight of a group of women squatting over the mountain edge, attempting to keep their balance and their safety intact whilst they relieved themselves, would have looked like!

Once we had made our way through the forested area and reached the top of the ridge, we re-joined the wall. In contrast to the well-preserved section we had scaled the previous day, this part of the Great Wall was in terrible condition. It was so run-down that it looked little more than a dirt path. If someone had shown me a photograph of this crumbling portion, I would not have thought that it belonged to the Great Wall of China. However, this somehow felt more authentic than what we had seen the day before. Jin explained that most of the wall is in a similar condition, with a few sections preserved for tourists.

It was trickier under foot though, and the several-hundred-metre drop on either side was rather unnerving. It felt like we were starring in a film in which a group of survivors must make their way across a barren land in a dystopian future. In our case, the destination was our homestay in a remote mountain village, as opposed to somewhere that was critical for humankind's survival. I took as many photographs as I could whilst we made our way through this awe-inspiring scene above any sign of civilisation. Other than the remains of an old wall.

Snow began to fall as we started the descent to our accommodation for the night. This added to the feeling that we were plotting our way through a desolate land. It also increased the group's desire to reach the homestay. Parts of our route were quite difficult to negotiate, with the combination of the gradient and the snow testing the much-lauded grip of our footwear. Some resorted to running down the trickier sections, reasoning that they felt like they would fall if they continued their cautious approach. I declined the opportunity to follow suit, as it had once ended badly for me when I had attempted something similar in Norway. Still, we all made it back in one piece. Aside from a few blisters and weary limbs, we had completed our first challenging day of the trek without suffering any significant damage!

The homestay in the mountain village was as basic as I had expected: there was no heating and the toilet was another hole in the floor. Our kind hosts offered all that was required though: a place to put our head down for the night and somewhere to shelter from the elements. I was thankful that I was not one of the people who had to share a giant bed with five others. I believe that a group of women who were on friendly terms with each other were the chosen ones, whereas I was once again paired with Joshua. Thankfully, we were given twin beds.

There was a celebratory atmosphere as we gathered for our evening meal. Although the trek was still in its infancy, it felt like we had truly immersed ourselves in the experience over the course of the day. We were a long way from our home comforts, we had faced several relatively challenging sections during our seven-hour trek and we had bonded as a group. Admittedly, I had probably formed fewer connections than most of the others had, but I could still appreciate the communal spirit. It was what I imagine the contestants of *I'm a Celebrity...Get Me Out of Here!* experience during their three weeks in the jungle. Except that we were not getting paid hundreds of thousands of pounds to take part. Mind you, I was glad that the food we were given was considerably nicer! We enjoyed a barbecue of various meats and vegetables as we sat around the outdoor firepit.

There was not any baijiu on offer that night, but several bottles of vodka and a seemingly endless supply of booze was made available to purchase from our hosts. Each bottle of beer cost a handful of yuan, which worked out at less than one British pound, so most of us overindulged. I am not saying this just because we were sat around a firepit, but it was a warming scene. A group of strangers were becoming friends, delicious food had been devoured and alcohol was being consumed liberally. All whilst we sat in picturesque surroundings beneath the night sky.

As the group continued to bond, I soon encountered a situation I always dread: the others began taking part in drinking games. I declined the opportunity to join in, but I can clearly remember some of the group playing a variation of the 'Have you ever...?' game. This apparently involved someone saying 'I once...' followed by something highly inappropriate or rude. If any members of the group had ever taken part in the stated activity, they were required to take a sip of their beer. In most cases, people seemed to use this as an opportunity to confess something naughty that they would not have otherwise brought up in conversation. Before long, people were detailing their most outrageous drug- or sex-related deeds whilst the rest of the group was left in shock. I drank my beer as normal throughout the proceedings and attempted to make it clear that I was not taking part. Hopefully, this was evident to the rest of the group – otherwise I will have come across as the most debauched and depraved man in history!

HEAVEN'S LADDER

BEYOND THE WALL

4: *THE LEDGE OF DEATH*
JINSHANLING, THE PEOPLE'S REPUBLIC OF CHINA
MARCH 2013

Despite needing several layers of clothing and my sleeping bag to keep me warm throughout the night, I had a surprisingly decent kip. A heavy night of drinking, at least by my standards, seemed to once again help in that regard. I must have gone to bed under the influence of alcohol, as I had forgotten to remove my disposable contact lenses. I woke up aware of their presence but not feeling any discomfort. As we did not have a mirror in our room and because I had doubts about my ability to keep a fresh pair of contact lenses uncontaminated by my surroundings, I made the bold decision to keep them in for another day. Although I knew that my eyes would undoubtedly feel dryer than the Sahara Desert by the day's end, I did not want to risk being unable to put a new pair in; thus, being unable to see the Great Wall, let alone walk along it. I did have a pair of glasses, but I was far too self-conscious to wear them in those days. All in all, I was a bit of an idiot!

Upon leaving my room, I was appreciative of my ability to survey the scene in front of me. There had been heavy snowfall overnight, leaving our mountain village looking even more spectacular than it had the previous day. It resembled what I had always imagined an idyllic skiing resort in the Alps to look like. The prospect of looking daft and potentially endangering my health due to my ineptitude had always put me off skiing, but photographs of Alpine resorts had always looked spectacular. This unexpected vista was enough for me.

Our morning exercise routine was kept brief due to the weather conditions, so we were soon trudging our way through several inches of snow. The glorious sunshine that had accompanied the first day of our trek seemed a distant memory as we slowly moved along our route. The initial part of the day's trek took us through farming terraces, not that we could tell what type of ground lay beneath the snow.

We then joined a road that seemed to go on forever. Each step that I took involved pushing a boot through the crisp yet soft white layer resting on top of the ground beneath my feet. Whilst some of the others discussed last night's shocking revelations, I detached myself from the group and enjoyed a period of solitude. It was becoming clear to me why so many people wax lyrical about the virtues of walking and running. When you are hiking or jogging for a prolonged period, it is easy to clear your mind of all the nonsense that usually keeps it unnecessarily occupied. You become solely focussed on the task at hand. With the crunching sound of each step, my mind became clearer. I just had to keep moving, one step at a time. Before long, I had become so accustomed to walking that it had become second nature. This meant that my mind was completely free to truly take in the beauty of the snow-topped mountains surrounding our path. I felt extremely fortunate to be able to experience something like this. The simplicity of the task had allowed me to enjoy the moment rather than worry about what comes next. I had even forgotten about the potential toboggan ride.

The bliss of solitude was eventually broken once we reached a main road. 'BEEEEEEPPP!' A lorry driver who was heading in our direction, but still several hundred metres away, was sounding his horn. In fact, he kept his finger pressed on the button until he passed us twenty seconds later. This seemed a rather odd thing to do but Jin explained the logic behind it.

"It is common for drivers to blast their horn as they travel along roads where there are people walking about. It is basically a warning they are coming and people should get out of the way because they may be unable to stop in time. Better to make a little extra sound than run over forty tourists!"

The snow was less prevalent here due to the traffic that was occasionally passing though. After a few more beeping lorries whizzed past our group, we reached a petrol station. This seemed out of keeping with our beautiful surroundings, but passing vehicles still needed to ensure that they had enough juice in the tank to complete their journeys. I believe it was here that James from Help a Capital Child advised us was a good place to purchase some additional snacks. Most of us bought things we craved from back home; some opted for chocolate bars, but crisps have always been my guilty pleasure. When Alan Partridge once mentioned that his fictional radio show discussed important issues such as, "What happens if you just eat crisps?" I was desperate to know the answer!

We eventually re-joined the wall, once again stepping onto an unrestored, crumbling section. This was one of my favourite parts of the Great Wall. It was in distinct contrast to the portion we had walked on during the first day of the trek. The sight of the disintegrating wall snaking along the undulating ridgeline was spectacular. It was clearly no match for Mother Nature. Hiking up and down the steeper sections was more taxing on our muscles and joints, but we had become accustomed to it by this stage. The sheer drop to the valley on either side was now a normal aspect of the trek. The fear of falling to our death had been pushed to the back of our minds – we felt like true hikers!

However, I doubt that many seasoned hikers attempt to sing a medley of all the Spice Girls' hit singles! That is what I had to endure, as a dozen or so female members of the group decided this would be the best way to keep spirits up during hours of trekking. Despite knowing more lyrics than I probably should admit, I declined the opportunity to join in. It was a surreal experience to listen to vocally-challenged women belting out a series of 'girl power' hits from the 1990s whilst marching along the Great Wall of China.

Following a winding path down the hillside, we had to negotiate our way through a series of fields. Maize, walnut and fruit trees lined our route as we ended our day's exertions on more favourable ground. With my mind free of distraction, the five-hour trek had been my most contented period of the trip so far. I was now looking forward to the remaining days with relish rather than apprehension.

A three-hour scenic drive took us to Jinshanling and our accommodation for the next two nights. Our lodgings were certainly a step up from the homestay in the mountain village. With a well-preserved section of the Great Wall visible from the complex, it had a similar feel to the mountain hotel that we had stayed in after our first day of trekking. There was a small village nearby with a selection of shops selling food, clothing and all manner of trinkets. We did not have time to inspect what was on offer, but we were assured that we would be able to do so the following day. After the long drive, I was too tired to show much of an interest anyway. As so often is the case, five hours of physical activity did not feel half as tiring as a three-hour coach ride. A prolonged period as a passenger on any type of vehicle has a way of making me sleepy that cannot be achieved by other means. For this reason, I can understand why Mum used to drive me around in her car in the middle of the night when I was a baby.

Having consumed another pleasant meal consisting of shredded pork, chicken, vegetables and rice, we were informed that the hotel's main hall would be playing music and was offering a range of games, including badminton and table tennis. I was reluctant to join in, but did so once there were less people around to witness me making a fool of myself. Not long after my game of badminton had commenced, I noticed that the hall was virtually empty. Apart from a few of the more reserved characters like Joshua and Geoff, most of the group had left.

It transpired that the others had made their way over to one of the hotel rooms for another round of drinking games and general merriment. Even though I knew that I would have hated every second of taking part in the likes of 'truth or dare,' it brought back memories from my school years: I was standing in a pitifully empty hall with a handful of fellow outcasts, aware that I had not received an invite to the real party where all the cool kids were hanging out. After staying in the hall until it no longer seemed impolite to leave, Joshua and I headed back to our room, passing the rowdy room en route. Apparently, the party raged on well into the night and a fun time was had by all.

* * *

Following our usual breakfast and exercise routine, we re-boarded our coach. Thankfully, this time the journey only lasted twenty minutes. There was no sign of the heavy snow that accompanied the previous day's trek, but there were some hazardous patches of ice in sight. We began our exertions by walking through the village of Gubeikou. Forty-odd Westerners carrying lots of hiking gear probably looked rather out of place in this quiet Chinese village, but judging by their lack of notable reaction, they must have been used to tour groups passing through on a regular basis. Nobody approached us to request photographs of these strange white people anyway!

We walked through some nondescript farmland before reaching an unrestored yet well-preserved section of the wall. This once again differed to what we had previously experienced. The basic brick-like construction dates back to the Qing Dynasty that once ruled this land. We walked alongside the wall for a while before climbing onto it for the first time that day. The differing conditions of each section helped to avoid any feeling of monotony, if it is even possible to feel such a way about something so arresting.

After a brief period on the wall, Jin advised us that we would take a path down to the valley in order to avoid a military post. He warned us not to take any photographs of it, as the Chinese authorities do not like people doing this. We followed a series of dirt paths before beginning our ascent to another section of the wall. The icy conditions had meant that Jin and Alastair had adjusted our route due to safety concerns, but we still had to overcome some steep, challenging terrain. Our guides often provided a helping hand, in the literal sense, as they pulled us up to higher ground. We eventually ended up in a spot that worried them. The group would either have to turn back and more or less abandon our route, or negotiate a risky passage.

Alastair remained calm as he addressed us: "Listen up, guys. We are going to have to walk along this ledge in order to continue the day's trek."

We looked on with horror as he pointed to a narrow, icy ledge on the mountainside. There was a fifty-metre drop to our left.

"Jin and I will go first, to make sure that it is safe," he continued. "You will have to walk across, one at a time, then we will lift you up once you reach the other side. I know it looks scary, but we are confident that it will be OK. It's only about ten metres in length. You just have to hold your nerve."

The problem was that we had all lost our nerve the moment we caught sight of the ledge. There was a genuine sense of terror reverberating through the group. The ledge was just about wide enough to accommodate a single person, whilst the ice meant that we would have to be extremely careful with our footing. A fall would almost certainly cause serious injury or death. Paralysed by fear, we stood completely still as we watched Jin and Alastair make their way across the ledge. Part of me had hoped that they would turn back and call it all off, but they soon reached the other side and signalled that we were good to go. There was a notable absence of volunteers when it came to the decision of who would be the first to attempt the crossing. After an agonising period of silence, Phil and Farhad announced that they would go first.

"I guess with our background, we would look rather silly if we did not put our names forward," Phil stated.

"Your careers in the Armed Forces have prepared you for this very moment," someone from our group joked, with a shaky voice.

The rest of us collectively held our breath as we watched our two intrepid friends make their way across the ledge in single file. Slow and steady, they made it to the other side before climbing up to higher ground. The next person to cross used a different technique, where they faced the mountain and shuffled sideways, one step at a time. Every person that followed adopted the same method.

"Please make sure my family know I enjoyed the trip!"

"Even if I fall to a gruesome death, at least we got to see the Great Wall of China."

"Just make sure they fly my body back to England rather than leaving it down there."

"If we survive the Ledge of Death, I will appreciate every remaining day on earth!"

These were the type of comments being made as we nervously took it in turns to edge across. Terrifying situations such as this often result in people adopting a form of gallows humour. I am unable to recall exactly what was said, as I was too busy clinging on for dear life. I had not trusted my footwear when I was walking through slippery, forested terrain, but a similar mistake on the 'Ledge of Death' could prove catastrophic. To illustrate how ridiculously self-conscious I was back then, I remember worrying about how feeble I would look to the rest of the group as I slowly made my way to safety. With my nose and palms pressed against the mountainside, and my boots cautiously inching across the icy ledge, I not only feared for my life, but I worried about what people thought of my attempted crossing. Upon making it to the other side, the feeling of relief was palpable. As Jin lifted me to higher ground, I felt like an earthquake survivor being rescued from the rubble. Everyone made it across. We had survived the Ledge of Death, which left us feeling exhilarated and happy to be alive.

The military post was just about visible from the section of the Great Wall that we joined. I instinctively started taking photographs. It was so far away – probably a couple of kilometres – that I could not make anything out. James G stared at me, as if to say, "What are you doing?" The fear, relief and exhilaration that I had recently experienced must have made me forget about our instruction not to take photographs. Either that or I had felt invincible after surviving the Ledge of Death.

I put my camera away and told myself that nobody would be able to see me taking photographs from such a distance. Then I began to worry about being in a country with a questionable human rights record and a tendency to imprison anyone who angers the regime, without fair trial. This prompted an irrational decision to hide behind a crumbling wall of the watchtower that we were huddled in.

I shook off the paranoia by casting my eye over the sight of the wall snaking high across the landscape. The views were as magnificent as ever; the perfect reward for conquering the ledge. The remainder of our day's trek took place on a restored part of the wall. It seemed to rise and fall more frequently than any section we had previously seen. Steep climbs were soon followed by dramatic descents. To conclude our eight-hour trek, we were given some free time to travel in any direction we wanted before the group made its way back to Jinshanling. I savoured this opportunity to roam along the wall and capture the beauty of my surroundings, both with my eyes and my camera. Eventually, I found myself standing on an open section of a watchtower with three other members of the group. Mohammed persuaded me to pose for a photograph alongside Lee, a quiet guy who had been recording much of the trek on his camcorder, and my roommate Joshua.

"I have an idea – I will set the timer on my camera and when it is about to take the photo, we will all jump in the air. It will be a fun action shot," Mohammed suggested.

Several attempts later, we ended up with a great photo of the four of us in mid-air with the majestic sight of the Great Wall of China behind us. As this photograph does not belong to me, I have not included it in the book. I can assure you that it is a great image, as are many of the group photos that were taken by others. The memories of this once-in-a-lifetime trip come flooding back to me whenever I look at them.

Unlike the previous evening, we were given time to have a browse in the shops belonging to the small village near our hotel. Many of the women purchased an item of Chinese clothing that became popular in Shanghai in the 1920s. The *cheongsam*, otherwise known as the *qipao*, is typically a one-piece, high-necked, body-hugging dress that is usually made from either silk or cotton. Judging by the prices that our group paid, I would suggest that the latter was used for their garments. The eye-catching turquoise, red and gold outfits seemed to be popular with tourists. As with most cheongsam, the sleeves were extremely short, barely beneath the shoulder, and there was a partial slit partway up the skirt. You will have to forgive my inability to eloquently describe women's fashion!

I admired some calligraphy but did not buy any souvenirs. Instead, Geoff, Mohammed, Joshua and I had a cup of tea and some cake in a small café. It is not often that you can savour a cup of tea whilst looking out of the window at a view of the Great Wall of China!

After our evening meal, we settled down for a quiet night in the main hall. This time there were no secret parties taking place. Instead, we all took part in a quiz. I am not sure who won but, unsurprisingly, it was not my team. It was apparent that scaling the Great Wall had given us all a feeling of elation that we were desperate to experience again once the trek was over. I mentioned that I would love to follow the Inca Trail to Machu Picchu, Mohammed spoke about his desire to sign up for a Mount Kilimanjaro challenge, and Joshua stated his intention to take part in a Grand Canyon trek the following year. The administrative blunders that had deprived him of the first couple of days had obviously not put him off! One of the numerous women called Leanne, which seemed to be an unusually common name within the group, pondered whether she should board a flight to Vietnam instead of immediately returning to England. She had been encouraged by a couple of our fellow trekkers who had spoken fondly about previous trips to Southeast Asia. Leanne knew that her boyfriend back home would disapprove but Alan suggested that she should go for it, as we only have one life. This was fanciful talk, of course, as it was impractical to embark on another trip at that time. She flew back to London with the rest of us, but the general sentiment being expressed was that the trip had excited our souls. This was an addictive feeling that we did not want to relinquish.

* * *

After spending some of the morning on deteriorating parts of the wall, the majority of the final day of our trek took place on a restored section that was popular with tourists. This became more apparent as we marched to the finish line. Not only was the quality of the wall improving, but we were encountering more and more people. This was a shock to the system since we had become accustomed to having the Great Wall to ourselves. A member of our group jokingly said, "Hey! Get off our wall!" to a bemused passer-by. It was clear that the trek was winding down and we were re-joining the masses. If there were any doubts about this, it was confirmed by the presence of vendors selling water and snacks along the wall.

Our seven-hour trek did not seem particularly taxing. This may have been because our bodies had become used to the daily grind, or simply due to the more friendly terrain and weather conditions. The sky was overcast but the temperature was mild. There were certainly no icy ladders leading to heaven or any deadly ledges in sight. It was our final chance to take in the beauty of this wonderful landscape. I would miss being treated to the almost constant sight of the historic wall and the rolling hills. It would feel strange not to spend my days walking for hours on end and calculating distances based on the watchtowers dotted along the wall.

During one of our brief moments of respite, one member of the group made a suggestion that almost caused me to have a panic attack. Lottie, who was in her early twenties and most likely not actually called Lottie, said that she had seen a video of another group of trekkers doing the 'Harlem Shake' on the Great Wall of China. Although I had no idea what she was referring to, I instinctively knew that it would be something that would strike fear into my heart. I was out of touch with pop culture, but it was apparently the latest viral sensation. Not to be confused with the original dance from the 1980s, this involved people posting short videos that began with a lone figure, often masked, dancing to Baauer's "Harlem Shake" song whilst everyone else in shot either ignored them or was supposedly unaware of what was happening. Around fifteen seconds into the video, the bassline drops and it cuts to a scene of everyone in the group dancing with feverish enthusiasm. The online craze had only begun the previous month, but an average of four thousand 'Harlem Shake' YouTube videos were being uploaded each day in the weeks leading up to our trek. Everyone was trying to outdo each other, with a variety of outlandish versions surfacing, including those featuring army units, passengers on a plane, underwater participants and generally ridiculous outfits. Others chose a spectacular backdrop like the Great Wall of China.

As the trendier members of the group explained the premise, I was overcome by a sense of dread. I would sooner have walked back to England than take part in such an enthusiastic group dance! Especially if it were to be filmed for the entire world to see. Along with some of the older members of the group, I practically ran away from the chosen spot for our video shoot. I am unsure of who volunteered to be the lone dancer for the opening segment, but as I watched the others jump around in a silly fashion on the wall, I remember feeling incredibly relieved that I had managed to avoid participation. I recently searched the internet for the offending video, but I could not find the one belonging to our group. In case you have a burning desire to see what this spectacle looked like, there are numerous versions that were filmed on the Great Wall.

At some point in the afternoon, we crossed the finish line that had been set up by our guides. This evoked mixed emotions for me. On the one hand, there was a sense of satisfaction and achievement that the entire group had successfully completed our trek; however, the knowledge that it was all over filled me with sadness. It had been the most incredible week I had ever experienced. After witnessing breathtaking beauty at every turn, walking across challenging terrain and overcoming moments of genuine fear, our mission had finally been accomplished.

Deducting the money used to fund the trip, we calculated that we had raised over £65,000, which would be used to improve the lives of teenagers and young people affected by cancer. It had been the primary purpose of our trek, so this knowledge helped banish any negative emotion. We had raised a considerable amount of money for a good cause and we had been fortunate enough to have been provided with such a wonderful experience. With this in mind, we all wore beaming smiles as a series of group photos were taken.

The feeling of elation within me was enhanced by the news that the toboggan ride had recently been closed to the public. I was relieved that there was no longer any possibility of feeling pressured into taking this high-octane ride. Mind you, the closure was due to a recent accident, so it was not exactly a reason to celebrate. Having captured my final photographs of the wall and taken in the views of our spectacular surroundings for the last time, we began making our way back to the coach. This involved walking past an endless row of stalls selling tacky souvenirs. There were T-shirts depicting Barack Obama in communist attire and 'I walked along the Great Wall' ornaments, but I did not purchase anything. One of the younger women in our group, Hayley, boarded the coach clinging onto a bag of nuts.

"How much did you pay for them?" Alan asked.

"Fifty yuan," she cautiously responded.

"Fifty! That's about six quid!" Alastair interjected. "Did you not barter?"

"No, that was the price. I didn't know I could barter."

"You could have got that bag for about fifty pence!" Alan concluded.

The whole coach was roaring with laughter. It was a good job that I had not bought anything, as I hated the thought of bartering. Like Hayley, I probably would have paid whatever ludicrous price was first quoted. Only I would also have tipped the vendor. It was a light-hearted way to conclude the trek and it bode well for our collective spirit heading into the final two nights in Beijing.

THE LEDGE OF DEATH

BEYOND THE WALL

5: A RELUCTANT STRIPTEASE
**BEIJING, THE PEOPLE'S REPUBLIC OF CHINA
MARCH 2013**

After a long coach journey that sent me to sleep, we arrived back at the same hotel in which we had spent our first night in Beijing. This time my roommate Joshua was present, so I would not have my own lodgings. As I had rarely been able to receive a mobile phone signal during the past week, I made the most of the opportunity to contact Mum and Carol for the first time in a few days to let them know that I was still alive. Hopefully, they would regard this as good news!

Our guides had arranged an evening meal in the city centre in order to celebrate the completion of the trek. Unfortunately, this involved another coach ride through the gridlocked streets of Beijing. There are over twenty million people who reside in the nation's capital, and it seemed as though they had all taken to their vehicles at the same time. The coach inched along towards our destination as cars ruthlessly changed lanes at a second's notice and bicycles weaved in and out of traffic.

Sarah, the doctor that Discover Adventure had arranged to accompany us throughout the week, had seemed like a quiet and sensible person. Possibly feeling a sense of relief that she had completed her duties without having to attend to any significant medical emergencies – unless you count blisters and aching muscles – she chose this moment to reveal her more eccentric side. As Coolio's "Gangsta's Paradise" began playing on the coach radio, she leapt out of her chair and excitedly declared that she knew all of the lyrics to the song. To prove her point, she rapped along to the 1995 hit with gusto. The rendition of the Spice Girls' greatest hits that I had been exposed to earlier in the week seemed like a musical masterpiece in comparison. Still, I could not help but be entertained by the unexpected and bizarre performance of a middle-class white woman yelling: "Fool, I'm the kinda G the little homies wanna be like; On my knees in the night, sayin' prayers in the streetlight!"

I wonder what the restaurant workers made of the arrival of a group of white women wearing *cheongsam*. Some may consider it to be an example of cultural appropriation, but I do not think that anything untoward transpired. The women in our group had wanted to show that they were at least trying to embrace an aspect of Chinese culture, and the vendors had made some much-appreciated money from tourists. Besides, the charge of cultural appropriation is usually made when a dominant ethnic group adopts elements of a disadvantaged minority's identity for entertainment or business purposes. This was not the case here, as white people are the ethnic minority in China. It is more likely that the restaurant staff were amused rather than offended!

We had the downstairs section of the restaurant to ourselves, which turned out to be for the best. When discussing my tattoos throughout the week, I had let slip that I had a map of the world and the Universal Declaration of Human Rights tattooed on my back. I had managed to fend off several requests for me to show my ink to interested parties by stating that they would see it by the end of the trip, but I was no longer able to hold off the group. My plan had backfired, as I was now sat in a restaurant with around forty other people asking me to take off my top. If I did not strip off, there was a chance that they would tear off my clothing! That may be a slight exaggeration, but it had become apparent that I would have to undress to appease the group.

To wolf-whistles, hollering and rapturous applause, I cautiously took off my T-shirt. For a shy, self-conscious person like me, this was the stuff of nightmares. I tried my best to smile through the ordeal and do my best to hide any unease. Several people took photographs as I paraded my half-naked body, spinning around so that everyone would get a chance to see the artwork. I guess this serves as a cautionary tale for any introverts who decide to get tattooed! It is also one of the many reasons why I would not cut it as a Chippendale; with the most notable being that there is not much demand for a balding five-feet, five-inch stripper!

After the ordeal was over, and another delicious meal consumed, we moved on to a riverside nightclub. It was similar to a typical club in Europe, or so I believe, with loud music blasting out English-language songs through the speakers, a dancefloor and a couple of rooms dedicated to karaoke. Basically, it contained all the things that I hate about nightlife. I spent most of the night sipping bottles of Tsingtao beer and avoiding the dancefloor and karaoke rooms as if my life depended on it.

There were some fleeting moments when I could just about hear what people were saying to me, but most of the night remains a blur. One thing that I do remember is being stupid enough to go out without a coat. Standing outside shivering in the cold whilst we waited for taxis back to the hotel was not much fun. Still, we decided to let the female members of the group take the first few taxis that arrived. Alan and I ended up being the last two to depart. During our taxi ride, we discussed the splendour of the trek that we had just completed, and he once again encouraged me to follow the Inca Trail to Machu Picchu.

"Judging by what I have seen this week, you would easily cope with the trek," he assured me.

"It's certainly near the top of my bucket list."

"You should do it. Not many of the people who have said they will do this or that after our trip will actually do so, as 'real life' tends to get in the way. But if you are in a position that allows you to follow your dreams, then you should. That is what life is all about."

"This has been the perfect experience: we have explored one of the wonders of the world whilst raising lots of money for a good cause."

"We are definitely amongst the lucky ones able to do things like this. I say make the most of it."

*   *   *

Our last day in Beijing kicked off with an optional trip to the Summer Palace. I believe that everyone in the group decided to pay the small fee to join the tour, which involved a coach journey to the Haidian district. The UNESCO World Heritage Site covers 2.9 square kilometres and is comprised of lakes, imperial gardens and palaces. The sixty-metre-high Longevity Hill and 540-acre Kunming Lake certainly dominate the landscape. The Summer Palace, which has a history dating back to the twelfth century, was looted by French and British troops in 1860 at the conclusion of the Second Opium War. The nearby Old Summer Palace was completely destroyed. It reportedly took four thousand British troops three days to burn it to the ground. This was in response to the imprisonment of the British delegation sent to negotiate the surrender of the Qing Dynasty.

The elevated, lakeside position of many of the buildings within the palace complex enhanced its aesthetic quality. Most of the ornate pavilions and gates were impressive, but not dissimilar from what one finds throughout China. They were just on a larger scale. The same can be said about the lion statues and courtyards. There were some unique features though, such as the Marble Boat. Situated at the northern edge of the lake, this decorative stone pavilion resembled a paddle steamer. It had been destroyed by Anglo-French forces in 1860 but was restored in 1893.

The eighteenth-century Seventeen-Arch Bridge was another delightful sight. The 150-metre-long bridge arcs over Kunming Lake, connecting the east bank with Nanhu Island. There are fifty-nine lion statues on the columns of the white marble parapets.

One of my favourite parts of the complex was the aptly-named Long Corridor. Stretching 728 metres along the northern shore of the lake, this covered walkway is splendidly decorated with paintings on the beams and ceilings. There are over 14,000 pieces of art depicting various scenes throughout history and many that feature in Chinese folk tales. Although there were too many of my fellow tourists knocking about for my liking, I thoroughly enjoyed this stroll by the lake.

Not content with having spent a week trekking the Great Wall of China and then walking along the Long Corridor, I climbed the many stairs up Longevity Hill. The Tower of Buddhist Incense is its crowning glory. Overlooking the lake, this three-storey octagonal tower has become the symbolic structure of the Summer Palace. Standing outside the tower, I took a moment to look out over the lake and the surrounding area. The cityscape of downtown Beijing was visible from my position, highlighting how traditional structures and modern buildings are often simultaneously in view in the Chinese capital.

Following our trip to the Summer Palace, we visited the centrepiece of the 2008 Summer Olympics and Paralympics. The Beijing National Stadium, commonly referred to as the 'Bird's Nest,' has a capacity of 91,000 and is set to be used during the 2022 Winter Olympics and Paralympics. Interestingly, its most distinguishing feature was born out of what appeared to be a pressing need to solve a problem that eventually became irrelevant. It was decided that a series of steel beams would surround the stadium in order to disguise the support for the retractable roof; however, the plan to install the roof was eventually scrapped altogether. The roof that never was led to its iconic design that featured a concrete seating bowl and an outer steel frame that were independent structures separated by a distance of fifty feet. As the nickname suggests, it was soon pointed out that the design resembled a bird's nest, which is seen as a treasured item in China.

The Chinese artist Ai Weiwei was an artistic consultant on the project. His contribution to the creation of the National Stadium was not enough to prevent him facing persecution by the Chinese government though. As an outspoken critic of the Communist Party's stance on democracy and human rights, he has regularly faced the wrath of the authorities. In 2011, he was accused of 'economic crimes' and detained for 81 days without charge. This came a couple of years after he had stated that he was suffering from headaches due to a beating handed out by the police following his investigation into substandard construction that succumbed to the 2008 Sichuan earthquake. He eventually left China to live in Germany for a few years, before recently moving to the United Kingdom.

Almost five years had passed since the Olympics had taken place in Beijing, so there were no sports fans occupying the empty space outside of the impressive stadium. Like many venues throughout the world that were erected for the Olympics or the Football World Cup, it faced the distinct possibility of becoming an unused reminder of excessive spending. Beijing Guoan Football Club backed out of an agreement to play their home matches in the stadium after stating that it would be humiliating to occupy such a vast arena when they only attracted an average attendance of 10,000 spectators. Fortunately, the authorities have managed to avoid further embarrassment by securing the rights to host a variety of prestigious sporting events and music concerts from time to time. We were not permitted to enter the stadium, but the exterior was an impressive sight to behold.

Like most tours, it included a visit to a place that was hoping to entice tourists into spending their money on souvenirs. In our case, this came in the form of a silk factory and outlet. Our visit concluded with us having to fend off persistent attempts to convince the group to spend all of our remaining yuan, and more, on expensive silk garments. Incidentally, I was alarmed to learn about the traditional method in which silk is made. Recently-hatched silk moth larvae, known as silkworms, are fed mulberry leaves before they form a silken cocoon. This is then placed in boiling water, killing the silkworm pupa, so that the silk filament can be extracted. Around five thousand silkworms are required to make a pure silk kimono. Gandhi was an advocate of Ahimsa silk, which does not require any living creature to be harmed, although the quality of this alternative material may not be quite so good. This employs a method that allows the pupa to hatch, with the leftover cocoon used to make the silk.

Upon returning to our hotel, we were free to do whatever we pleased for the rest of the day. Although I would have liked to have returned to Tiananmen Square in order to wander around this vast public space, observe groups of people practicing Tai Chi by the Temple of Heaven and have a look at Chairman Mao's embalmed body, I felt obliged to accept Phil and Farhad's invitation to tag along with them to Beijing Zoo. I do not even like zoos. To add to my discomfort, this required using a metro system heaving with commuters and tourists who were committed to disregarding the principle of queueing. All because I did not feel like I could turn down their friendly invitation! Joined by a couple of Londoners from our group called Danielle and Kika, we survived the ordeal.

As with many zoos, I felt uncomfortable with the lack of space provided for the animals. There were no obvious signs of ill-treatment, but it did not exactly look like a happy life for the elephants, monkeys and tigers. Unsurprisingly, the animals native to China are the star attractions. Red pandas often leave the biggest impression with visitors, but Phil had been particularly keen to see the giant pandas. As a couple of them slouched against the wall of their enclosure and munched on bamboo, I could not help but think they looked remarkably like humans wearing panda outfits. Their mannerisms seemed to match those of a couple of tired blokes who had decided to have a break from work! Rather than the majestic sight of pandas roaming around in their natural habitat, it all looked a bit sad really.

We wandered around the zoo, having a look at some of the hundreds of different animals before calling it a day. Our little group decided to indulge in some Western food before heading back to the hotel. The metro system had been hectic, but McDonald's was downright chaotic! There was not a hint of a queue nor any pleasantness from the members of staff behind the counter. Mind you, I doubt that any of us would have been wearing our best smile if we were being inundated with throngs of hungry people who had just alighted a crowded train. Frustratingly, there did not seem to be any logic in the order in which meals were being processed. We eventually received our food and devoured it as if we were pandas stuffing our faces with bamboo.

The group split up into smaller factions for our evening meals. I joined a dozen or so others in a restaurant opposite the hotel, which I was pleased to discover served Chinese food. Our last evening meal in Beijing was a pleasant one. Although I was as quiet as always, it was nice to spend some time with the people who had shared this wonderful experience. We discussed the highlights of the trek and spoke about the other challenges that we could sign up for. It felt like a life-changing week; whether that would really turn out to be the case was another matter altogether.

* * *

We flew back to London the following morning. There were no issues going through security or passport control, which relieved my paranoia about being arrested for taking photographs of the military post or criticising the Chinese government. Several members of our group were vocal for much of the flight, all in good spirit but undoubtedly annoying for the other passengers. The cabin crew kindly made an announcement over the public address system, congratulating us for completing our fundraising mission. This only added to the celebratory mood in the air – no pun intended.

We all said our goodbyes at Heathrow before going our separate ways. Some were greeted by friends and family at the airport, whilst others boarded coaches bound for their home cities. I watched as my fellow trekkers seemed to instantly slip back into their regular lives. Would they forget about how the week had stirred feelings deep within their souls? Would they even attempt to fulfil their stated intentions of breaking free from their old routines? More importantly, would I? I had mixed feelings during the flight back to Manchester: I was looking forward to being reunited with Carol and my family, but I knew that I would miss spending my days trekking through such a beautiful landscape. Could I possibly lead an existence that combined the stable structure of work and family life with this newfound sense of adventure?

BEYOND THE WALL

6: DRUG DEALERS, A MERMAID AND A DEAD DUCK
COPENHAGEN, DENMARK
MARCH 2013

Just four days after arriving back in Manchester, I was venturing overseas again. As much as I would like to tell you that I had impulsively decided to quit my job and travel the world, this was arranged many months beforehand when Carol and I had decided to spend the Easter holidays in the Danish capital. We did not need to book any days off work, so we snapped up some cheap flights as soon as they had become available, even though we had first-hand experience of the astronomical costs we were likely to incur in Scandinavia. Our plan was to limit our spending by visiting attractions that did not require an entrance fee and avoiding any expensive restaurants. I was a seasoned cheapskate, so this would not require much effort on my part!

As Copenhagen Airport is only seven kilometres outside of the city centre, getting to our accommodation was a straightforward task. This was made even easier by the fact that there are excellent transport connections, including a regular train service to Copenhagen Central Station. I had booked three nights at Absalon Hotel, which was less than a five-minute walk from the station. The train was one of the most expensive forms of transport but by far the most convenient, given the location of our hotel. The plan to keep costs as low as possible had not got off to the best of starts. At least we had not taken a taxi!

We had spent more Danish krone than anticipated by this point, but we made up for it by having our evening meal in an all-you-can-eat pizzeria next to the station. Although the food may not have been up to Gordon Ramsay's standards, the prices were most agreeable. For the equivalent of around ten British pounds, we could satisfy our hunger for the remainder of the day. With our luggage in tow, we piled as many slices of pizza onto our plates as possible. After devouring a few slices, Carol suddenly remembered something that made her sport a worrisome look.

"It is Good Friday and we have eaten pizza with meat toppings," she said with a regretful tone.

"I am not bothered by that anyway, as I am not religious."

"I am, though."

"Are you? You don't go to church."

"I used to, and I still regard myself as a Christian. Besides, I like following some of the traditions. We usually have fish instead of meat on Good Friday."

"Oh well, it can't be helped now. Don't worry about it. I doubt that God will strike you down for eating some pizza!"

Carol seemed to lose her appetite, but I went back for seconds.

It was noticeable how there was a huge volume of bicycles parked next to the station – row upon row of bikes were docked outside the building. It brought back memories of Beijing! There may not be nine million bicycles in Copenhagen, but it is regarded as one of the most cycle-friendly cities in the world. A whopping sixty-two per cent of the population is said to use this method of transport to travel to and from their place of work or study. The Danish authorities encouraged its citizens to cycle as much as possible by introducing cycling routes that pass through green areas and quieter roads; thus, increasing the safety of cyclists. This has had a positive effect on the Danish population, with the health sector benefitting from less people suffering from obesity and other issues related to a lack of exercise. This is also believed to have resulted in economic advantages, as bicycle shops and wholesalers provide a boost to the private sector. The most noteworthy impact is on the environment, with lower carbon emissions an obvious benefit to the planet. The city's air quality is amongst the highest in Europe - perhaps this knowledge swayed my opinion, but the air did seem noticeably cleaner. Either way, it was a far cry from the smog of Beijing and the air pollution of London.

We only had to walk a few hundred metres along Istedgade before we reached the Absalon Hotel, which was located within a Neo-Classical building. A sign affixed to an establishment further along the street seemed to be an ominous sign of the seedy image of the Vesterbro district, which was once the favoured haunt of drug dealers and prostitutes. It simply read, 'Spunk.' To our relief, it turned out that it was just a regular bar.

* * *

Following a good night's sleep in our pleasant hotel room, we ventured into the dining area for our first breakfast of the trip. Carol had some cereal, fruit and yoghurt, whilst I opted for bread rolls, cheese and, of course, some Danish pastries. After all, the country is renowned for these sweet treats. It is worth noting, however, that they were introduced by Austrian bakers who had moved to Denmark; therefore, the pastries are referred to as *Wienerbrød* or 'Viennese bread' by the Danish population. As we took our seats, a large man walked past with a plate almost stacked to the ceiling with pastries. We had never seen so many buns on one plate! There must have been a dozen of them piled on top of each other.

"I guess they must be good," I said to Carol.

"He hasn't tried them yet!"

"Maybe he has – that could be his second lot!"

"Like you in the pizzeria yesterday!"

I took a bite of my pastry.

"Yep, they are good. I can see why he was so keen!"

Even with our thick coats, hats and gloves on, there was a chill in the air as we walked towards Tivoli. There was also a smattering of last night's snow on the ground, which I guess is to be expected in Scandinavia in March. Having launched in 1843, Tivoli is the world's third oldest amusement park still in operation. Unfortunately for us, it was not open during our stay in the city. This is because it closes for most of winter before opening its doors again in April. We had just missed out on seeing this magical old place. Part of me was relieved that I did not have to endure any high-octane rides, but I had a genuine interest in exploring this historic site. I would have been willing to have a ride on Rutschebanen. Given that it is one of the world's oldest wooden rollercoasters, built in 1914, I think I would have been able to handle it. Just about. Maybe.

Although we were unable to enter, it provided the perfect backdrop for a photograph. I captured a delightful image featuring a statue of Hans Christian Andersen looking across to Tivoli on the other side of the boulevard that bears his name. The nineteenth-century Danish author is best known for his collection of fairy tales that became immensely popular throughout Western society. His work, which has been translated into at least 125 languages, includes "The Emperor's New Clothes" and

"The Ugly Duckling." He was also a traveller who wrote about his journeys around Europe.

His statue borders Rådhuspladsen, or City Hall Square, which, unsurprisingly, is the location of Copenhagen City Hall. Opened in 1905, this delightful red-brick building features a golden statue of Absalon. My guidebook confirmed that the statue had not been erected in honour of our hotel; it actually paid homage to a twelfth-century Danish statesmen and a key figure within the Catholic Church. The Danish flag, which is apparently the oldest national flag in the world still in use, was flying high above the building. As the City Hall's clock tower is one of the tallest buildings in Copenhagen, this would at least provide a handy landmark if we got lost.

The square is also the home of the Palace Hotel and the headquarters of the national newspaper *Politiken*. It was the statues of the square that I was most interested in though. We had already seen Hans Christian Andersen, but there were several others situated around the square. The Dragon Fountain, which reaches a height just shy of seven metres, features a bull fighting a dragon. It was not the prettiest thing to look at, but it made my photographs of the City Hall more interesting.

The Weather Girl is a quirky golden sculpture perched high upon the Richshuset. This features a girl with a bicycle – well, it does if the weather is clear. If rain is expected, it is replaced by an alternative installation in which she is holding an umbrella and walking her dog. I found this unusual weather forecasting system to be charming, regardless of its effectiveness. Thankfully, the girl with the umbrella was out of sight! Given that nobody wants to see her, I imagine that she suffers from extremely low self-esteem!

Another unique statue is adjacent to the City Hall, where the *Lur Blowers* stand on top of a terracotta column. Legend states that these two musical men sound their horns whenever a virgin walks past. It would appear that the residents of Copenhagen enjoy an active sex life, as the *Lur Blowers* did not once sound their horns during our visit. Perhaps the unsavoury side to Vesterbro was still thriving after all!

The walk to Rosenborg Castle was much easier than what I had experienced over the previous couple of weeks. The ground was flat and there were no hazardous obstacles to overcome, other than what was now just a dusting of snow. I could not help but relay this information to Carol.

"Are you going to be one of those people who go on about walking and hiking all of the time?" she playfully asked.

"I hope not! It may take a while to switch back to normal life though."

"Give over! You only spent a week or so in China. You seem to have settled back into your 'normal life' already!"

Maybe she was right. Other than occasionally thinking about the trek, our trip to Copenhagen felt like any other city break we had been on.

"Anyway, take my photo as I stand behind this tree," Carol requested.

"What's the point in that? I won't be able to see you if you are stood behind it."

"I will peer out from one side. It will be a cute photo, especially with the snow."

"I won't fit behind the tree if I eat as many Danish pastries as that guy had this morning!"

We passed the Rundetaarn, or the Round Tower, on our way to the castle. Unsurprisingly, this is a round tower. There is an observation platform just under thirty-five metres above street level, but we declined the opportunity to check it out. It was constructed in the seventeenth century, with its primary purpose to serve as an astronomical observatory, which is now open to the public.

"Apparently, the spiral ramp inside the tower was designed to allow a horse and carriage to transport items to and from the Library Hall and the observatory at the top," I informed Carol.

"Are you making that up? I can't imagine horses trotting up and down that tower!"

"It's true. It seems a bit strange today, but people relied on the old horse and carriage method back then. It is hard to picture it though."

Both the Rundetaarn and Rosenborg Castle were built at the behest of King Christian IV of Denmark, who was the country's longest serving monarch. He is regarded as a leader who brought stability and prosperity to the nation, even if he overindulged in alcohol. More interestingly, albeit on a much sadder note, he had an obsession with witchcraft that led to dozens of people being burnt to death. I am going to go out on a limb here by stating that this was slightly unfair on the 'witches.' He also fathered over twenty children with several different women, which makes Boris Johnson's philandering seem rather tame in comparison.

We were soon entering Kongens Have – the King's Garden. This thirty-acre park originally served as the private gardens for Rosenborg Castle but is now open to the public. Despite the bareness of the trees, it was a lovely park. There seemed to be the perfect amount of people strolling along the paths, with enough to make it seem like an amiable place but not too many that it became overcrowded. The castle was built in a Dutch Renaissance style that reminded me of Amsterdam Centraal. It is surrounded by a moat, which is where we saw something rather sad.

"Oh no! Look at that duck!" Carol said with a sorrowful tone.

The water must have frozen overnight. Some sections had thawed but a dead duck was trapped in some of the remaining ice. The sight of its head lodged in the ice, beak down, was jarring.

"It was probably swimming along, unaware that it was going to become trapped and freeze to death. I can't look any longer!" Carol said whilst turning away.

"It was probably already dead, but it is a sad sight."

It is an image that still haunts Carol.

We did not enter the castle. Organised tours can be arranged but we assumed that ticket prices would be dear. Besides, we did not feel in the mood for a guided tour. Having turned down the opportunity to have a look at the Crown Jewels, we strolled around the gardens for a while. Rosenborg Barracks and the Hercules Pavilion can be found here, whilst the David Collection is located just outside the grounds. I briefly considered paying the latter a visit until I discovered that it is an art museum focused on C. L. David's collection, rather than an exhibition hall dedicated to me.

Frederiks Kirke, often referred to as the Marble Church, was our next port of call. Boasting the largest church dome in Scandinavia, it is reminiscent of the green copper-domed grand buildings that I have seen protruding from the streets of Paris or Rome. Indeed, St. Peter's Basilica is thought to have been an inspiration for its design. It took nearly 150 years to build and was involved in a trial at the Court of Impeachment in 1877, after the Finance Minister Andreas Frederik Krieger sold the unfinished church in a controversial deal that included the acquisition of the rights to subdivide neighbouring plots for development. He was eventually acquitted.

We admired the building's imposing columns and statues before opting to have a look inside. Our decision was made considerably easier by the absence of an entrance fee. The dome looked even more impressive from inside the church. The intricately-decorated features of the nave were enhanced by the relatively compact layout, which sees the congregation sit directly beneath the dome. I am not religious, but if I were, I imagine that this would be the type of church I would attend. Just being able to look up at the magnificent dome would make it worthwhile.

Upon exiting the building, we continued walking along Frederiksgade, occasionally turning around to look back at the view of the Marble Church, until we reached Amalienborg. This is the winter home of the Danish Royal Family. They have twice as many residences as there are seasons though! There are even four palaces within Amalienborg. The four identical buildings surround a large plaza with an equestrian statue in the centre. This was no surprise, as you can find a statue of a bloke on a horse in virtually every European city. Apparently, this one honoured King Frederik V, who founded Amalienborg. It is where the public can watch the changing of the guard, but it was unexpectedly quiet when we passed through. We did not fancy visiting the museum, which would have required us departing with precious Danish krone in any case, so we continued travelling along our route until we reached the waterfront. Carol and I briefly regarded Copenhagen Opera House, which opened in 2005, on the opposite side of the harbour. The roof resembled a sheet of metal that had been balanced upon the building, jutting out above the space in front of the entrance. That is as far as my architectural knowledge extends!

We turned left and began walking towards *The Little Mermaid* statue. The docks on the other side of the water were an indicator of the city's rich maritime history. Before I had an opportunity to pass comment, Carol pointed at a statue of a naked man and shouted, "It's you!"

I paused for a second, inspecting the size of the sculpted genitalia and pondering whether I should take offence, before realising that this was a replica of Michelangelo's *David*.

Gefionspringvandet was the next point of interest we encountered along the waterfront. This is a large fountain that depicts oxen pulling a plough and being driven by the Norse goddess Gefjon – which is sometimes spelt Gefion. Given that it was donated to the city by the Carlsberg Foundation, I am tempted to say that it is probably the best fountain in the world. For what it is worth, it is certainly the finest Gefjon-themed fountain that I have ever encountered. Legend states that King Gylfi promised Gefjon any territory she could plough in one night. Gefjon promptly transformed her four sons into oxen and turned over enough land, which was thrown into the sea, to create the island of Zealand. This is where much of Copenhagen is now located. I am glad that Gylfi did not put a similar proposition to my parents!

St. Alban's Church is situated just behind the fountain. As the name suggests, this is an Anglican church built for the sizeable English inhabitants of the city in the late-nineteenth century. Indeed, it is often referred to as the 'English Church.' The Gothic Revival building, with its single tower, would look at home in a quiet British town, where it would serve as a focal point for a small community.

Carol and I were soon stood behind a group of fellow tourists on Langelinie Promenade, waiting for our turn to spend some time with *The Little Mermaid*. The bronze statue, which has become the symbol of the city since its unveiling in 1913, was evidently still able to attract large crowds. In keeping with the mix-and-match aspect of the story, Edvard Eriksen's four feet-tall creation was modelled on a ballerina's head and his wife's body. Apparently, this was because the ballerina did not want to pose in the nude, rather than any perverse fantasy.

The statue was, of course, inspired by Hans Christian Andersen's fairy tale in which a young mermaid is willing to exchange her voice, and potentially her life, for legs and the chance to gain an eternal soul. This ambition was driven by her love for the human prince whose life she had recently saved. She agrees to a deal that will either see her marry the prince or die from a broken heart. Unfortunately for her, the prince elects to marry another woman who he had incorrectly credited with saving his life. Carrying a broken heart, the Little Mermaid is given the opportunity to return to her former life in the sea if she kills the prince and lets his blood drip on her feet. She cannot bring herself to do this though. Andersen initially crafted an ending in which her body dissolved into foam and she ceased to exist, but eventually adjusted this so that she became an ethereal spirit after her body dissolved. As a reward for her selflessness, she is given the opportunity to earn her soul by doing good deeds for humankind for three hundred years. Unsurprisingly, the Disney adaptation has a happy ending in which she and the prince get married.

We patiently waited a few minutes before taking it in turns to pose for photographs next to the statue that was sat on a rock by the water. It looked nice enough, but not necessarily awe-inspiring.

"If you were a mermaid, would you have sacrificed your life to be with me?" I asked Carol.

"Probably."

"I must be your chosen prince then."

"Mostly because I would not want to spend my life underwater," she concluded. Her wink reassured me that this was said in jest and there was hope for me yet. Either that or she had something in her eye.

Despite its symbolic value to the city, or perhaps because of this, *The Little Mermaid* has been the regular target of acts of vandalism. It has had its head decapitated a couple of times, its arm chopped off and it has been covered in red paint. On one occasion it even had a sex toy affixed to its hand. A statue that need not worry about such incidents is *The Genetically Modified Little Mermaid*. Bjørn Nørgaard's sculpture is part of 'The Genetically Modified Paradise' he created as a humorous take on postmodern society. It features elongated skeletal legs and a head that has been distorted beyond recognition. Vandals would not know where to start with that! We were unaware that this bizarre artwork was located just a few hundred metres away.

Carol and I crossed the moat in order to have a quick wander around the pentagon-shaped citadel known as Kastellet. The seventeenth-century fortress now serves as a public park, although there are military barracks on site. It was a pleasant area to walk around, with green spaces and well-preserved pastel-coloured buildings. We admired the Citadel Church, the windmill and the Dutch Baroque Gates before moving on.

The sun had come out to play by late-afternoon. The buskers on Strøget, which is one of Europe's longest pedestrian-only shopping streets, must have appreciated this. There was a steady stream of people ambling along the 1.1-kilometre car-free route through the city centre. Carol took a photograph of me alongside a statue of Robert Wadlow outside the Guinness World Records Museum. Stood next to the tallest person in recorded history, I looked like one of the tiny characters featured in *The Borrowers*! The American man was eight feet, eleven inches tall when he passed away aged twenty-two. Due to hypertrophy of his pituitary gland, he was believed to be still growing at the time of his death.

Like many others, we departed with some Danish krone after taking in a few street performances. Perhaps we were watching a pop star of the future? After all, the band Lukas Graham, famous for their global hit "7 Years," are from Copenhagen. The lead singer, Lukas Forchhammer, was raised in Freetown Christiania – we would visit this unusual commune later in the trip.

After a busy day of sightseeing, we had the choice of either shopping in the abundance of designer stores or going for a drink in a pub. It is not often that I drink alcohol in the afternoon, but this was certainly preferable to spending a fortune on clothes that I did not need. Being typical tourists, we had a couple of *smørrebrøds*, which are the open-faced sandwiches that Denmark is famous for, accompanied by pints of Carlsberg whilst we discussed our first impression of Copenhagen.

"It seems a clean city," Carol began.

"Even the air seems clean," I added. "I am not sure if this is because the thought was already in my mind prior to our trip though."

"I think the air is clean. There are less cars around, and it is a pleasant city to walk through."

"The Danes have a word called *Janteloven*, which is basically an unwritten rule stating that people should aim for what is good for the collective rather than the individual. I suppose we have not spent enough time here to form a conclusion about that."

Carol paused before changing the subject: "The worst part was seeing that duck. It was so sad!"

"I wonder if we will mention it years from now."

"Rather than the duck, I hope that we will hold on to memories of *The Little Mermaid*, the City Hall and whatever we see tomorrow."

"I wish we could quit our jobs and do this all the time. You know, just travel the world as we please," I mused.

"I think everyone wishes they could do that. Unfortunately, there are bills to pay!"

"We'll have to plan how we'll combine ordinary life with travelling," I said fancifully.

A couple of hours later, we returned to Strøget for our evening meal. We decided to play it safe by ordering one Danish dish and one portion of something we knew that we would like. Our logic was that sharing both dishes increased the chance of at least enjoying part of our meal. We opted for one of the nation's most popular dishes, *stegt flæsk med persillesovs*, which consisted of fried pork belly, potatoes and parsley sauce. Our other choice of burger and chips provided the safety net. Carol was not a fan of the traditional dish, although I enjoyed everything apart from the parsley sauce. I ended up having most of the Danish option whilst Carol tucked into a chunky burger. Our first full day in Denmark had been every bit as enjoyable as suggested in the song "Wonderful Copenhagen," performed by Danny Kaye in the 1952 film *Hans Christian Andersen*.

* * *

After consuming a healthy breakfast consisting of fruit, yoghurt and a porridge-like dish known as *Grød,* we began our second full day in Copenhagen by revisiting City Hall Square. The weather was more favourable than it had been the previous day, so we decided to take a new set of photographs, this time featuring bright-blue skies and sunshine. Typical tourists!

Amalienborg is not the only palace complex in Copenhagen. The latest incarnation of Christiansborg Palace is not as old as one may expect. Completed in 1928, it replaced the two previous versions that were both destroyed by fires. Prior to that, two castles were situated here at various points in history. Both were demolished. It seems that building a castle or a palace on this site may not lead to a long shelf life! Christiansborg now houses the Danish Parliament, the Danish Prime Minister's Office and the Danish Supreme Court. The Royal Family still make use of part of the palace, including greeting dignitaries and hosting banquets in the Royal Reception Rooms.

Christiansborg is only a few hundred metres from the City Hall, so we were soon approaching the palace grounds. This involved walking over the beautifully-decorated Marble Bridge that spans Frederiksholm Canal, and then passing between the two rococo pavilions. It was certainly an entranceway befitting a palace. Tours were available, but as we had done at Amalienborg, we just pottered around the grounds for a while and inspected the grand architecture. The viewing platform in the palace tower would not open to the public until the following year, so we were unable to look out over Copenhagen from one of the city's highest viewpoints.

We did get to see another equestrian statue though; this time it portrayed King Christian IX, who is often referred to as the 'father-in-law of Europe.' This is because the children he fathered with his second cousin, Princess Louise of Hesse-Kassel, married into various royal families across Europe. Likewise, Queen Victoria of the United Kingdom is known as the 'grandmother of Europe.' Remarkably, King Willem-Alexander of the Netherlands is the only reigning European monarch who is not a descendant of either of these historical figures. Queen Elizabeth II of the United Kingdom, for example, can trace her family tree back to both.

"It's strange that the royal families of so many nations are interwoven," Carol said to me as we looked at the statue.

I relayed a somewhat dubious claim: "That's nothing compared to Genghis Khan. A guy from work told me that he has around sixteen million descendants!"

The nearby Børsen was next on the agenda. This seventeenth-century building once housed the old stock exchange but is now home to the Danish Chamber of Commerce. It is another of the city's Dutch Renaissance buildings, but it has a unique 56-metre spire that resembles four intertwined dragon's tails. Carol and I took a few photographs but did not hang around too long. Instead, we paid a visit to yet another palace.

The site for Charlottenborg Palace was given to Ulrik Frederik Gyldenløve by his half-brother, who happened to be King Christian V. Gifts handed out by royalty tend to be rather good! Gyldenløve had a mansion built there in the late-seventeenth century, but later decided that it was too big for him to spend his final years in. Ownership was transferred to the Royal Danish Academy of Art, who still occupy the building, and he had a smaller mansion built for himself. I am sure we can all relate to the problem of having a mansion that is too big! For what it is worth, I thought that the building looked less extravagant than the name suggested and is more in keeping with the current occupants.

We were soon admiring the Royal Danish Theatre, which is an attractive building flanked by two imposing statues. The first one we approached depicted the poet Adam Oehlenschläger, who penned one of the Danish national anthems. Interestingly, Denmark is one of only two countries in the world to have two official national anthems of equal status – the other being New Zealand. Canada has both English and French versions of their national anthem, but I am not including that in this exclusive club. We briefly inspected the second statue, which portrays the influential playwright Ludvig Holberg, before moving on to one of the most attractive areas in Copenhagen.

Nyhavn is a historic canal-side district best known for its colourful townhouses. Hans Christian Andersen lived in three of them at various stages of his life, including when he wrote "The Tinderbox" and "The Princess and the Pea." Most of these buildings are now occupied by restaurants and bars that have become popular with tourists due to their picturesque setting. Although we had no intention of spending a fortune in these establishments, it appeared that all of the seats overlooking the canal were occupied.

We enjoyed taking our time strolling along the canal, inspecting the numerous wooden boats and taking in the view from the small bridge spanning the water. Different shades of yellow, red, blue and green coloured the buildings on either side. It was so pretty that we could not stop taking photographs, including a selfie that we still have on display in a snow globe in our living room. Perhaps we should have visited the previous day, as the photo would have had more of a winter look to it. At least we had our woollen hats on.

Long before it became a tourist attraction, Nyhavn was a popular jaunt for sailors. Heavy consumption of alcohol and prostitution once thrived here – I was getting the impression that the Danes were more promiscuous than their reputation would suggest.

Having avoided paying the inflated prices in the restaurants of Nyhavn, we ordered a couple of hot dogs from one of the many vendors in the city. The red sausage that we had, known as *rød pølse,* is the type used in traditional Danish hot dogs. Smothered in ketchup and mustard, I did not notice much difference from the versions I had previously tasted. We enjoyed them anyway!

We were soon heading towards Freetown Christiania. Commonly referred to as Christiania, it is a notorious commune in the borough of Christianshavn. In 1971, people from the surrounding neighbourhood broke down the fencing that encircled the abandoned military barracks. Not long after that, the creation of Christiania was declared. It was stated that: "The objective of Christiania is to create a self-governing society whereby each and every individual holds themselves responsible over the wellbeing of the entire community."

This resonated with hippies, squatters and anarchists, who soon moved into the newly-established commune. The residents of Christiania came up with a set of rules that were independent from the rest of

Denmark. Although hard drugs are forbidden, cannabis has long been openly used and sold in Christiania. The national government have tolerated this, but there has been increasing friction since an apparent clampdown in the early-2000s. Many Danes view this self-declared semi-autonomous district as a successful social experiment, but the stance from the government has varied with each administration. Prior to our trip, I had read that not much effort was being taken to disguise the fact that drugs were still on sale.

"Is it safe?" Carol asked.

"I think so. It's popular with tourists, so it can't be that dangerous. There is the odd murder here and there, but I'm sure we will be fine."

"Thanks! That's really put my mind at ease!"

A sign by the entrance informed us that it was forbidden to take photographs, confirming what I had read in my guidebook. Perhaps feeling emboldened by my decision to take forbidden photos of the military post in China, I brazenly captured a few images on my camera. This immediately caught the attention of an aggressive-looking man whose demeanour suggested that he would take great pleasure in dismembering me.

"No photographs!" He barked. "I'm not joking. If they see you taking photos, they'll take it off you and smash it into pieces."

I wondered whether he was referring to the camera when he said that they would "smash it into pieces." I also feared who "they" were.

"Put your camera away!" Carol snapped. She had a worried look on her face.

"Sorry, I won't do it again," I apologised with a whimpering voice. My rebellious streak had vanished, never to be seen again.

"We have barely stepped foot in Christiania, and you have nearly got us killed."

Many of the buildings were covered in colourful street art, and the flag of Christiania, which features three yellow circles on a red background, was proudly on display. There were no cars in sight. This was officially a car-free zone until the Danish authorities demanded that the few residents who owned vehicles parked their cars within the boundaries of the commune. Around one thousand people live within the nineteen acres belonging to Christiania. This underlines another reason why photography is forbidden: it may look fascinating to tourists, but this is where many people call home. As the name suggests, Pusher Street is synonymous with the cannabis trade. It is where stalls line the street, offering people the opportunity to purchase the drug. Nowadays, the Danish authorities enter the commune and take action against this, but it still goes on. Another sign by Pusher Street read, 'Green Light

District' and underlined the rules once again.

"No photos, remember!" Carol warned me.

"Don't worry. I plan on walking out of here alive."

There were a few shifty-looking characters knocking about – although my paranoid mind may have unfairly painted them in this light – but overall, the area was fairly quiet. I had read that the locals are willing to chat to tourists as long as it is not about drugs, but I did not feel like hanging around much longer. I was too jumpy to delve deeper into this unusual place and gain an understanding of the community that went beyond the drug trade. We only caught a glimpse of the artistic subculture, which includes a vibrant jazz scene, and we did not explore the outdoor spaces that celebrate the beauty of the natural world. This was all my fault, of course, as I had broken the social contract stating that tourists should respect the culture and the residents of the places they visit. My worries were the result of a selfish, albeit not all that terrible, act that I had committed.

A few years after our visit, a dealer shot two police officers and a bystander. This led to a further crackdown on drug activity and an increased police presence. Christiania residents were also fed up with how the easy-going drug trade had been taking over by organised gangs who did not even live in the commune. They were filmed tearing down the cannabis stalls and pleading for people not to sell or buy from the area. The feeling seems to be that outsiders have exploited the commune to sell their drugs, whilst the community has simultaneously been subjected to the national regulations that it tried to escape. I guess that an increase in tourists like us hardly helped to maintain the original ethos.

Looking for redemption for my sins in Christiania, we headed to the nearby Church of our Saviour. The building is in keeping with the Dutch Baroque style prevalent throughout the city, but it is the helix spire that is the star of the show. The black and gold spire features an external staircase that wraps around it four times. A commonly told myth states that the architect committed suicide by jumping from the top of the spire after realising that the spiral turned anti-clockwise rather than in the intended direction. However, he actually died in his bed several years after it was completed and there is no record of him expressing any dissatisfaction about the project.

It was a fascinating spire that enhanced the aesthetics of an otherwise ordinary-looking church. The figure of 'Our Saviour Himself' keeps a watchful eye over the city from its position on a golden globe resting on top of the spire. We were unaware of this at the time, but visitors can ascend the 400 steps to the top of the church. The final 150 of these are on the narrow external staircase of the spire, providing a view from a height of ninety metres. If I had known that it was possible, I may have been tempted to climb this 'Stairway to Heaven' – then again I had already ascended 'Heaven's Ladder' just a week or so earlier.

Carol and I had completed our sightseeing for the trip. We did not have time to visit the National Museum of Denmark or the 'Black Diamond' extension to the Royal Library, which was given its nickname due to its black granite cladding and its angular shape. Nor were we able to see Frederiksberg Palace, the former summer residence of the Royal Family, but we had already had our fill of palaces for the weekend in any case.

Employing a marginally more daring dining strategy to what we had used the previous evening, we ordered chicken and asparagus puff pastry tarts known as *tarteletter* for our starter. Our main-course selections of Danish meatballs, known as *frikadeller*, and breaded pork patties called *karbonader* represented a safer bet. They proved to be excellent choices that satisfied our appetite for the evening.

* * *

Upon our arrival at Copenhagen Airport, I declared: "Everything has gone smoothly. It has been the perfect trip."

I appeared to have tempted fate, as after we had gone through security to the departure lounge we were informed that our flight back to Manchester had been delayed. Initially, the departure board stated that our plane would take off an hour later than scheduled. This soon turned into two hours. Then three. We eventually departed six hours later than planned. It transpired that the delay had been due to a security scare at Manchester Airport, with the alarm raised due to a suspicious image on the baggage scanner. The terminal was evacuated and the bomb disposal squad was brought in. They eventually deemed that the package was safe – it turns out that a bottle of contact lens fluid had been tightly packed alongside a mobile phone.

"OK, it was nearly perfect," I said with a chuckle.

"I have to say that Copenhagen is a lovely city. There were lots of interesting things to see and it was easy to get around."

"Don't forget about the clean air!"

"You're obsessed with the air!"

"Shame about the duck though."

"Why did you have to remind me about that?!"

I felt content after a wonderful long weekend in the Danish capital. Maybe I could cope without some of the grand voyages I desired if I squeezed lots of short trips into my ordinary routine. Then again, would this really satisfy my appetite to embark on adventures in far-flung destinations around the world?

DRUG DEALERS, A MERMAID AND A DEAD DUCK

7: A MODEL CITY
BASEL AND LUCERNE, SWITZERLAND
MAY 2013

A few months before trekking the Great Wall of China, I had booked a father-and-son trip to Basel. As flights were less than fifty pounds each, I had decided to pay for Dad's ticket for his Christmas present. I must admit that there was a selfish element to this, as it ensured that I would spend the Early May Bank Holiday in a country I had not previously visited. Dad is notoriously difficult to buy presents for and I knew that he would enjoy the trip, so I was effectively killing two birds with one stone.

As the name suggests, EuroAirport Basel Mulhouse Freiburg serves cities in Switzerland, France and Germany. Situated near the tripoint of the three nations, it is one of the rare airports operated by two countries – in this case, Switzerland and France. Although the entire building is on French soil, it is split into Swiss and French sections. There is a customs road connecting the airport to Basel, meaning that passengers do not need to clear French customs.

Given its proximity to these other nations, it is unsurprising that German and French are the main languages in Switzerland, with most people speaking a variation of the former. Italian and Romansh are the less prevalent national languages.

Our accommodation also had a slightly unusual set-up. If I recall correctly, it was about nine o'clock on Friday evening by the time our taxi reached Apaliving Basel. The budget hotel had contacted me to state that there would be no one on reception when we arrived, as they do not have anyone on site during weekend evenings. I had been given a code to enter the building and would need to check in using a self-service kiosk. I had feared that the code would not work, meaning that we would be locked out late at night in a foreign city with nowhere to stay, but everything went smoothly.

Our room reminded me of a university dorm, not that I ever resided on campus whilst I was studying; instead, I lived at my parents' house. Most teenagers cannot wait to leave home and enjoy their first taste of independence, but I did not possess the social skills to live with a group of strangers in a building with hundreds of others. This meant that my university experience consisted of all the boring bits of student life without much of the fun. Each morning, I would take the tram from the family home in Timperley to Manchester Metropolitan University, attend a few lectures and seminars then return home. University is supposed to be about parties, drinking, socialising and living away from your parents for the first time, is it not? I managed to make a few friends and join them on the odd night out in the city, but it was hardly the lifestyle that university alumni usually describe as the best years of their lives.

The room was clean and possessed all that we needed: we had our own bathroom, television, fridge, kettle and safe. The plain décor and the presence of a desk added to the feeling that we were staying in a student dorm. Thankfully, we had been given twin beds as requested, as there would not have been anyone on site to remedy such a nightmarish scenario! After unpacking our cases, we ate the food we had purchased at Manchester Airport. Knowing that we would arrive late at night, we had decided to purchase a couple of Boots meal deals. Devouring pre-packed sandwiches and crisps with my dad in a dorm-like room was about as close as I was going to get to the hedonistic university experience!

* * *

Having been aware that breakfast was not available in our hotel, we had also purchased some cereal bars from Boots. I had eaten muesli in many places around the world, but I did not do so in the country where it was first created. Incidentally, it was developed at the start of the twentieth century by the physician Maximilian Bircher-Benner for patients in his hospital. Who says hospital food must be awful? People who hate muesli, I guess.

Cereal bars consumed, we headed out onto the streets of Basel. With the dark clouds looking ominous, we donned our jackets but the rain never materialised. The short walk to the city centre took us past the Basel SBB railway station, which I am sure you are fascinated to learn is

Europe's busiest international border station. The two clock towers and impressive architecture of the Neo-Baroque building, completed at the beginning of the twentieth century, enticed me to use my camera for the first time during the trip.

Although there are numerous cultural institutions in the city, we declined the opportunity to explore the likes of the Kunstmuseum Basel, which houses a substantial public art collection, or Theater Basel, which hosts operas, ballets, plays and musicals. I may have given Dad little option but to travel to Switzerland, but I could not, in good conscience, force him to spend a few hours wandering around museums and art galleries that he had absolutely no interest in. We decided to have a quick look at the Tinguely Fountain though.

"Are you Tingueling with excitement, David?"

"I'll file that one under 'dad jokes!' I suppose I set that up with my woeful pronunciation."

The Swiss artist Jean Tinguely created this modern landmark in 1977 by installing a series of iron sculptural machines in a shallow fountain. Powered by a low-voltage current, they are in constant motion.

"What do you think of it?" I asked.

"It's quite interesting. Although it looks like someone left some old machinery in a fountain."

"With the wheels and pulleys, I can see what you mean. It's as if a factory just dumped all their equipment here when they were forced to close. It is something different, I guess."

If this was the level of our artistic analysis, it was probably for the best that we did not spend the day passing comment on the works of art in the city's museums and galleries!

We enjoyed walking through the Altstadt, which has a reputation for being one of the most pleasant Old Towns in Europe. There is a mixture of architecture dating back to the fourteenth century, with narrow cobbled streets and French windows adding to the charm. This is also where many of the city's most famous landmarks can be found.

Basler Münster, or Basel Minster as it is known in English, is the symbol of the city. The two towers of the red sandstone building dominate the skyline. Named after Saint George and Martin of Tours, Georgsturm and Martinsturm provide a point of reference throughout the city.

"We can just look for George and Martin if we get lost," Dad suggested.

"I read that Martin is almost two metres shorter than George – I can relate to always being the short one of the group!"

There was no charge to enter the Münster, although we did donate a few Swiss Francs. I have never seen a *Harry Potter* film in its entirety – shocking, I know – but the interior of the church, which was constructed using Romanesque and Gothic styles, reminded me of Hogwarts. I could certainly picture Harry and his friends sat on the rows of wooden chairs whilst the stained-glass windows brightened up an otherwise dark interior. I have either made a good comparison or underlined the fact that I am one of the few people on the planet not obsessed with the little wizard. Incidentally, my father-in-law is called Herbert Potter. My wife tells me that he used to receive prank calls because his number was listed in the phonebook as 'Mr. H. Potter.'

We had the opportunity to climb the 250 steps to the top of one of the towers, but for some reason we declined. The views are supposed to be splendid and it only costs a few Swiss Francs. Perhaps we were put off by the gloomy weather.

Marktplatz was our next port of call. There were numerous stalls selling groceries in this busy market square, but it was the red sandstone façade of Basel Town Hall that held our attention. It is known locally as *Roothus*, which means 'council house' but sounds like 'red house.' It was not only the colour of the building that was striking, as the walls were adorned with colourful frescoes and unusual statues. The multi-coloured ceramic tiles on the roof also caught the eye. There are a handful of guided tours offered on Saturdays, but we had not made the necessary arrangements.

At least we were able to wander through the courtyard, which was decorated with more colourful frescoes, and admire its marvellous exterior. Town halls, churches and towers often look similar to their equivalents in other cities, but that cannot be said about this unique 500-year-old building. It is not just a tourist attraction though – the Cantonal Parliament regularly hold meetings within the assembly hall.

Switzerland is renowned throughout the world for one thing: having the most expensive Big Macs. OK, I may be exaggerating the extent to which people pay attention to The Big Mac Index published by *The Economist*, but I was intrigued to see if they somehow tasted any better here. This was probably an excuse for indulging in fast food because the index is designed as a light-hearted way of analysing the purchasing-power parity between countries and potential exchange-rate movements, rather than a reflection of the quality of the burgers.

I had consumed a Big Mac in Norway in 2012. One could have purchased thirty Big Macs in India for the amount that would have been required to pay for seven of them in Norway that year. Switzerland was the only country that was marginally more expensive. As it turns out, Norway had moved to the top of the chart by the time of my visit to

Basel, meaning I had once again missed out on sampling the reigning champion. This did not dampen my spirits, however, as it still meant that I would soon have consumed the two most expensive Big Macs around.

Dad and I handed over the appropriate number of Swiss Francs for our meals, but I am unable to recall the exact amount. I am sure that you are all fascinated by the revelation that the price of a Swiss Big Mac worked out at around one pound more expensive than the standard price in the United Kingdom that year. Unsurprisingly, the Big Macs tasted like any others produced by this global franchise. This paragraph probably sheds some light on the type of characteristics that typically belong to someone who stayed at their parents' house during their university years!

Following our traditional Swiss meal, we walked a few hundred metres to Mittlere Rheinbrücke. Aside from the Münster, no structure in Basel is more synonymous with the city. The Middle Bridge, as it is known in English, was given this name because it was the centremost of three bridges spanning the Rhine in Basel at the time of its reconstruction at the start of the twentieth century. The original bridge had been built nearly seven hundred years earlier.

At the bridgehead, we saw another statue of a horse and its owner, but this time the former was being led by a striding Amazon. It is an unfinished piece, as Carl Burckhardt died before it was completed. The 192-metre-long granite bridge, which has seven arches, has managed to retain an authentic appearance that does not differ greatly from the original version. For this reason, it complements its surroundings near the Old Town. A recreation of the old bridge chapel, known as Käppelijoch, is situated midway along the bridge.

"In the Middle Ages, convicted criminals were sentenced to death here," I informed Dad.

"Is that why you have brought us here? What crimes have we committed to warrant this fate?"

"We're actually here as witnesses in the trial of the individuals responsible for charging a king's ransom for a Big Mac."

"To be fair, the pricing is probably in line with the cost of living in Switzerland."

"Don't ruin my joke with sensible comments!"

There was a model of the Old Town on the Kleinbasel bank of the Rhine. I took far too much pleasure in capturing photographs of the 1:500-scale model with the real thing in the background. I could not help but be charmed by the sight of the Münster's towers on the other side of the river looming large over the miniature version in front of me. You have to get your kicks somehow, I guess.

We spent a couple of hours strolling along the riverbank, admiring the view of the city on the other side of the Rhine. I believe that we also wandered through a park, but nothing in particular sticks out from my recollection of the walk. Although the Pfalz viewing terrace by the Münster is heralded as the ideal spot to observe the beauty of the river and the surrounding area, it was pleasant enough by the riverbank.

It was late afternoon by the time we returned to the Old Town. Feeling at a loose end, we walked up and down Freie Strasse, where the main shopping area can be found. We had no interest in browsing the stores for clothes and other consumer goods, but it killed a bit of time.

The spirit of the Great Wall trek seemed to be a distant memory. We were in a charming European city winding down for the day rather than excitedly plotting our next move. I am not entirely sure why this was the case; it may have been because Dad and I had never been the type to go to a bar together or treat ourselves to an upmarket meal. We could have had a few drinks, tried some local food, or simply enjoyed the moment. This did not seem to fit in with the type of activities that I associate with my father, which often have a sports theme. It was a shame that Fussball Club Basel did not have a home game that day. Instead, they were playing 250-kilometres away in Sion. We did not know it at the time, but Basel, who would go on to win that season's Swiss league title, fielded a future English Premier League star named Mohamed Salah.

"I think we have seen most of the main sights in Basel. Do you fancy catching the train to Lucerne tomorrow?" I asked Dad.

"Yeah, that sounds good. Lake Lucerne is supposed to be nice."

"We may as well go to the train station now…"

"Does it take that long to reach Lucerne?" Dad joked.

"I just think it would be best to make sure we know our way around the train station, so we are not caught out tomorrow."

We entered through one of the Basel SBB station's clock towers and made a note of the layout. The ticket hall and the train shed were located under the high ceiling of the steel-arch building. Despite the cavernous nature of the station, it was a hive of activity, with passengers darting about in all directions. Basel SBB is known for its significant length, but we were thankful that the layout seemed easy enough to grasp. Despite the presence of twenty-three tracks, there were only nine platforms. Having allayed any concerns about the following day's mission, we purchased our evening meal. Our final sin for the day was to decline the opportunity to try some *raclette, fondue* or *rösti*. Instead, we bought some more packaged sandwiches, crisps and cookies to take back to our hotel room. It was another wild night!

* * *

The train to Lucerne was due to depart in just over a minute. People were already making that exaggerated action of checking their watch, as if to say: 'The train is not here yet. How strange!' This gives an idea of the punctual nature of the Swiss rail network. Only bettered by a handful of countries such as Japan, it is rare for a train to be late in Switzerland. By contrast, I come to expect tardiness when commuting in the north of England. I usually opt for a train scheduled to arrive at my desired destination an hour earlier than necessary, as the risk of being late is just too high if I take the seemingly more appropriate service. Even then, I am often late. Trains run behind schedule so frequently in the Greater Manchester region that you still have hope of catching your required service even if you arrive at the station long after it was due to depart. Sometimes you end up taking an even 'earlier' train that turns up at the station twenty minutes after the train you intended to take was supposed to set off.

A few seconds later, our train rolled in. It is not just the punctuality of the service that is impressive: the trains are newer, cleaner, faster and more spacious. It is costlier to travel by train in Switzerland than in most places, but this is unsurprising, given the fact that everything in the country costs a fortune. At least you get a good service in return, rather than the abysmal trains that I have often travelled on in England. Pacer trains sum up the state of British railways in recent decades. Converted from old buses, they were introduced in the 1980s as a stop-gap measure. They ended up trundling along the tracks of Great Britain for decades, only retired from service by Northern Trains at the end of 2020, with Greater Western Railway and Transport for Wales set to follow suit. A pacer train has been donated to the National Railway Museum – I can barely imagine what a Japanese tourist would make of it!

It took just over an hour to reach Lucerne. The current train station only opened in 1991, exactly twenty years after the previous building had been destroyed by a fire, so it did not have much character or sense of history. A grand arch, topped by a statue called *Zeitgeist*, which roughly translates as 'Spirit of the Age,' is all that remains of the old station. As Dad had intimated the previous day, the city is located beside Lake Lucerne in Central Switzerland. It is also in the shadow of Mounts Pilatus and Rigi in the Swiss Alps. These geographical features have long made Lucerne a favoured tourist destination. It certainly created a positive first impression on us.

We passed Lucerne Theatre on our way to the Jesuit Church that stands by the side of the River Reuss, which meets Lake Lucerne a few hundred yards away. The bulk of the construction of this Baroque building took place in the seventeenth century, although its onion-topped towers were not completed until 1893. I had read that the church had been built in line with the Counter-Reformation goal of re-establishing the prominence of the Catholic Church in Europe following the Protestant Reformation; therefore, I was prepared for a lavish, over-the-top interior. I have to say, however, I thought that the immaculate white marble and the ceiling artwork were visually impressive, without appearing garish.

As people seemed to be preparing for Sunday Mass, we did not spend too much time inside before heading to the symbol of the city. The Kapellbrücke, or Chapel Bridge, is the world's oldest surviving truss bridge. Originally built in the fourteenth century, the wooden covered bridge spans the Reuss. Its unusual diagonal direction and the 34.5-metre Wasserturm, or Water Tower, give it a distinctive appearance.

"The tower once served as a prison and torture chamber," I informed Dad.

"At least they were provided with a beautiful setting for their ordeal."

"I am not sure the prisoners will have paid much attention to their surroundings when they were being subjected to unspeakable horrors!"

"There are paintings in the triangular panels above our heads. It looks like they are present all the way along the bridge."

"They remind me of the Summer Palace in China. I did not expect to be saying that during our visit to Lucerne!"

The paintings appeared to depict various scenes throughout the history of Lucerne and Switzerland. There were originally 158 paintings, but many of the pieces were ruined during the devastating fire of 1993, which almost destroyed the entire bridge. Looking up at the paintings, and thinking about the bridge at the Summer Palace, caused me to ponder why other pedestrian bridges did not display such artwork. Mind you, I wonder how many tourists collide with each other whilst their focus is fixed above their heads!

A muddled walk through the Old Town's cobbled streets, where we regarded a series of small public squares, fountains and pastel-coloured townhouses, led us to the seventeenth-century Town Hall back by the Reuss. The Renaissance building has a more conventional appearance than its equivalent in Basel. The Kornschütte on the ground floor was once used as a trading hall, but it now hosts exhibitions and concerts. The flags of Lucerne and Switzerland were proudly on display over the open arcades that serve as a weekly marketplace. It was a stark contrast to Basel Town Hall; both were aesthetically pleasing in their own way, but this building conformed to a more typical image of a town hall.

Hofkirche St. Leodegar was the next notable building we visited. The previous basilica on this site had burned down during the Thirty Years' War that is estimated to have claimed up to eight million lives across Europe between 1618 and 1648. With the conflict raging on, the church that replaced it was one of the few that were built during this period. Having climbed the considerable staircase to reach the Renaissance building, I was pleased to discover that the scene in front of us looked almost identical to the images I had seen online. A white stone section was flanked by twin towers that had been saved from the previous structure, whilst vibrant red and yellow flowers provided the perfect frame for my photographs. We did not venture inside, as there was a service being held at the time. After all, Sundays are viewed as a sacred day in Switzerland.

The *Lion Monument* was the next item on our itinerary. We passed something called the Bourbaki Panorama en route, but we were oblivious to what it was. If I had known that it is a circular painting, 114 metres in length and 10 metres in height, I may have been tempted to pay whatever entrance fee was required. Apparently, it portrays an epic scene in which 87,000 soldiers of the defeated French Bourbaki army arrived in Switzerland after fleeing the Prussians during the harsh winter of 1871. The artist, Édouard Castres, was a Red Cross volunteer who had witnessed how the Swiss government had looked after the men upon their arrival. It was a moment that reflected the country's humanitarian image – indeed, the Red Cross was founded in Switzerland. Prior to the advent of cinema, a visit to the panorama would have been regarded as a truly immersive experience. I imagine that it still is.

The powerful imagery of the *Lion Monument* was evident as soon as we caught sight of it. Carved into the cliff face of a former sandstone quarry, the ten-metre-long sculpture depicts a mortally-wounded lion slumped over a shield bearing the mark of the French monarchy. The sad expression of the lion, particularly in its eyes, is most haunting. I could not understand the inscriptions above and underneath the sculpture, but it apparently commemorates the Swiss Guards who were massacred as a result of the Insurrection of 10 August, 1792 during the French Revolution. It is estimated that around 760 soldiers died after revolutionaries stormed the Tuileries Palace that they were defending. The monarchy, headed by King Louis XVI, was overthrown and a Republic was established. Karl Pfyffer von Altishofen was a Swiss Guard on leave in his home of Lucerne at the time of the insurrection. Determined to honour his fallen comrades, he commissioned the memorial. Thanks to the artistry of Lukas Ahorn, Bertel Thorvaldsen's design came to fruition in 1821.

"It's such a moving memorial. The lion looks so sad. It's almost as if his tears have accumulated in the pool below," I commented.

"It's an effective way of honouring the victims and it certainly evokes an emotional response."

We moved on from this poignant memorial to the intriguingly-titled Glacier Garden, or Gletschergarten as it is known locally. I could not help but feel underwhelmed by what we encountered. It resembled a quirky garden centre that had a few boulders positioned beneath a large tent. Perhaps my expectations were too high, but the geological site was not exactly the most spectacular place I had ever seen. Although it was interesting to examine some fossils, peer down a few large potholes that were apparently formed during the last ice age, and learn about the history of the land going back twenty million years, there was something strangely anticlimactic about our visit.

Perhaps this was due to the rather jumbled composition of the complex, with an old manor house, a museum, and a modest tower offering a view over Lucerne. Each element had its merits, but it all seemed rather strange when put together. Bizarrely, there was a nineteenth-century mirror maze that would not have looked out of place in a fairground. We manoeuvred our way through the maze, which had a lavish design inspired by Granada's Alhambra, whilst I displayed my cowardice by constantly holding my arm out in front of me to eliminate the possibility of walking face-first into glass. As to be expected in such places, there was a collection of novelty mirrors that distort one's appearance. I saw multiple versions of myself in one display, and a single image of me that resembled Stretch Armstrong in another. There was even one that made me look five stone heavier. At least I hope that was a novelty mirror and not an indication that I had eaten too much junk food during the trip!

After devouring another expensive McDonald's meal, we visited Museggmauer, which is part of the fourteenth-century ramparts that once protected Lucerne. As Dad enjoys outdoor pursuits, I knew that he would sooner walk along the well-preserved wall and climb some of its nine towers than visit a museum. Not only did this allow us to get a close look at the historic structure, but it also afforded us a stunning view over the city, Chapel Bridge, the Reuss and Lake Lucerne. All against a mountainous backdrop.

"Does this bring back memories of your trek?" Dad asked.

"It may not be as spectacular as the Great Wall of China, but it's beautiful in its own right. I am glad people see the value in preserving historical sites, even as progress marches on. This once helped protect the city; now tourists can walk along it whilst locals play football," I commented, pointing towards the football pitch to our right.

Over the course of the next forty minutes or so, we walked along the entire wall, burning off the junk food we had consumed in the process, and visited the towers that were open to the public. The façade of the Zyt Tower features two giant figures carrying the face of its famous clock. To this day, the stroke of the clock tower is one minute ahead of the chime of the church bells, keeping alive the tradition of allowing it the first stroke in the city.

We used the Spreuerbrücke to cross back to the other side of the Reuss. Less celebrated than Kapellbrücke, this is another covered wooden footbridge with a series of triangular paintings. It provided a delightful passage over the river before we returned to the train station.

I spent the journey reading up about Switzerland, before relaying some of the information to Dad: "Did you know that according to Swiss Law, anyone of sound mind can request an assisted voluntary death as long as they have consistently voiced this wish over a period of time? Euthanasia organisations have been widely used by foreigners who have a terminal illness or suffer from a painful, debilitating condition. This has led to the coining of the term 'suicide tourists.' I am not sure how many…"

"Is that why you have brought me here?! To finish off your Dad?!"

"Don't be silly…we could never afford the fees! Seriously though, I am generally in favour of this practice. Why should someone endure prolonged suffering and be denied the opportunity to end their life on their own terms?"

"I would hate to spend the final years of my life in constant pain as I physically and mentally deteriorated."

"I also read that Switzerland is amongst the countries best prepared for nuclear war. Regulation in the 1960s stated that all residential buildings must contain a nuclear shelter. This is no longer required, but there is a law that dictates that everyone should be assigned a place in a shelter near their home."

"So, we're here to protect ourselves from an imminent nuclear war rather than for assisted suicide? That's reassuring."

"Unless there is a sudden escalation in tension between the United States and Russia, or Kim Jong-un completely loses the plot, I think we will be OK."

Dad and I were soon back in our room in Basel, eating more sandwiches and chocolate during another raucous evening in Switzerland. Incidentally, I would not try any traditional Swiss food until I visited the country again in 2018. That is unless you count the small bar of Toblerone I ate that night.

After checking the football results, I discovered that Manchester United had lost to Chelsea. United had already clinched the title, so it did not seem too important at the time. Little did I know, but this would turn out to be Sir Alex Ferguson's penultimate home game in charge, as he soon announced his retirement. Thankfully, the club appointed 'The Chosen One,' David Moyes, and have gone on to achieve an even greater level of success in the years that have followed.

* * *

Our flight back to Manchester was scheduled to depart in the early evening; therefore, we had another few hours to explore Basel. As we had seen most of the main points of interest, we used this time to aimlessly wander around the city, hoping to keep ourselves entertained. It is a shame that I ended up almost willing the time away. Then again, this was quite fitting, given that Switzerland is renowned for its watches.

Despite my lack of enthusiasm, we managed to stumble across some interesting attractions. Spalentor is one of the three remaining gates once belonging to the city walls. Its main rectangular tower is flanked by two round towers, which for some reason made me think of a mini-Disney castle. It was once the entrance point for people arriving from France.

We walked past St. Mary's, but I had already seen enough Roman Catholic churches for the weekend. The Synagogue of Basel was more interesting, as the architecture was different to the other religious buildings we had seen in Switzerland. First opened in 1868, there was clearly an Eastern influence on the design. The red and white striped façade and the two domes topping the building were an indication of this. As the synagogue only accommodates visitors who have booked an organised tour, we had to find something else to keep us occupied.

Desperately seeking anything that sounded remotely interesting, we headed over to the University of Basel's Botanical Garden; however, it merely resembled an allotment, with a series of small greenhouses displaying various tropical plants. This was a place for garden enthusiasts rather than a couple of lost souls wandering around the city. It had been my last hope.

During our final walk through Basel, we encountered a giant figure repeatedly swinging his hammer. Thankfully, we were looking at an unusual art installation rather than being subjected to a horrific attack. Part of Jonathan Borofsky's *Hammering Man* series, which includes similar pieces in Frankfurt, Seoul, New York and various other cities, this 13.5-metre-tall, two-dimensional steel sculpture has been hard at work on Aeschenplatz since 1989. The kinetic sculptures are intended to celebrate workers throughout the world; more importantly, it provided some much-needed mental stimulation. There was still a couple of hours to kill though.

Feeling defeated, we sat down on a bench in a small park. At least it was sunny. I had bemoaned the fact that my structured life was preventing me from travelling around the world, yet I was wasting the final hours of our stay in a foreign city. It was becoming clearer that the spirit of travelling is more important than the destination or the length of the visit. Perhaps it was my mindset that was holding me back rather than the lack of opportunity to travel more extensively?

BEYOND THE WALL

8: *THE CITY OF A HUNDRED SPIRES AND CONSTANT RAIN*
PRAGUE, THE CZECH REPUBLIC
MAY 2013

During our travels across the world, Carol and I have been remarkably lucky with the weather. When we visited Brazil during the wet season, my weather app indicated that there would be heavy rainfall and thunderstorms for hours upon end every day; as it turned out, we escaped with just a brief downpour each evening. We have regularly been blessed with temperatures hovering above thirty degrees when staying in European cities in early-Spring. Even when we woke up to stormy conditions in the Caribbean, it cleared up in time for us to take a speedboat to another island.

Neither Zeus, Jupiter nor any of the other gods capable of effecting the weather have ever inflicted misery upon us. Except in Prague. It rained from the minute we arrived in the Czech capital until the moment we departed. It was the type of unrelenting fine rain that saps the life out of you. I am pleased to say that it did not completely ruin our trip – we still had a great weekend – but it made it difficult to truly appreciate the beauty of the city. Although I am sure that Prague is as picturesque as most visitors describe, the damp and dreary weather gave it a rather gloomy appearance.

I am unable to recall the finer details, but I know that we travelled from Václav Havel Airport Prague to the city centre by a combination of bus and metro. Having chosen our accommodation due to the low price, I just hoped that the condition of our room was acceptable and that we would have enough time to explore the city. We were only staying for two nights during the Spring Bank Holiday, and it was already mid-morning.

"Hello, welcome to our small hotel. I wish you a safe stay in my city. Breakfast is served in this room," the slim, balding, moustachioed man behind reception informed us.

There was something slightly odd about his demeanour, although I could not quite pinpoint why. He was friendly, but he seemed like the kind of guy nobody would be surprised to discover was a serial killer.

"We've chosen a cheap, tiny hotel that belongs to Norman Bates," I whispered to Carol as the man disappeared into a small room to photocopy our passports.

"You're the one who chose this hotel! It's on you if we get murdered!"

"And he has copies of our passports."

The man returned our documents then paused for thought.

"We have a nightclub in the basement that will be open until 6 am. I will be on duty tonight. It's just down there," he said whilst pointing towards an unmarked door at the bottom of some stairs that would have you screaming at the television when a crime thriller showed the next potential victim approaching it.

We quickly collected our key and headed up to our room.

"There's no way in hell that we're going down to that basement!" I said with a chuckle.

I will not mention the name of the establishment just in case Norman takes offence and makes it his mission to hunt me down. Our room was clean enough and was about as good as one can expect when charged such a small amount. Leaving our luggage behind, we headed back out into the rain to explore Prague. We had no time to spare, as we were scheduled to fly home in just over forty-eight hours. Carol and I could have walked to the main attractions in less than twenty minutes, but that would have been a miserable experience that would have left us looking like drowned rats. We decided that taking a tram would be a more sensible idea. I cannot remember how many Czech koruna this required, but I do not think it was much. There seemed to be the standard European honour system in place, where you purchased tickets before boarding and validating them yourself.

"This type of system relies on the good morals of travellers. I wonder how many people abuse it?" Carol asked.

"I imagine there are plenty of fare-dodgers. I always find it strange how people justify this behaviour back home. I've heard lots of people boasting about how they never pay for a Metrolink ticket. It's the same as someone walking out of a restaurant without paying for their meal or nicking something from a shop."

We alighted near Prague's most famous landmark. Charles Bridge was completed in the early-fifteenth century, providing the only route across the Vltava River for over four hundred years. We passed a couple of notable churches close to the bridge – the magnificent dome of the St. Francis of Assisi Church dominates the skyline, whilst the St. Salvator Church belongs to the Klementinum.

"The historic complex of the Klementinum includes the library featured in a famous short story," I began, referring to "The Secret Mile" by Jorge Luis Borges. "The main character dreams of going to the library, where he is told that God can be found within one of the letters on one of the pages of the 400,000 books. Shall we try and find it?" I asked Carol.

"No."

"It would keep us out of the rain for a bit."

"I would sooner stand in the rain."

"I read that Father Koniáš is buried here. He is known as the 'Destroyer of Czech Books' because he burned thousands of them. I guess everyone has a different attitude towards books – you can either search for God's salvation or burn them all!"

The fourteenth-century Old Town Bridge Tower guarded the entrance to Charles Bridge. The Gothic tower looked dull and dreary, in keeping with the weather. In that regard, it reminded me of the Scott Monument in Edinburgh. From a distance it looked old and dirty, and it was impossible to appreciate its merits until viewed from close quarters. Umbrellas were out in full force as crowds made their way across the uncovered pedestrian bridge. Unfortunately, we were the only fools not equipped with such a device, so we had to rely on our 'water-resistant' jackets to prevent us from getting soaked. They did not.

In addition to those selling fridge magnets and model churches, there were optimistic individuals offering to draw caricatures of passing tourists. Given the atrocious weather, it was hardly surprising that they were struggling to tempt anyone to sit down in the rain for ten minutes. Despite the gloomy sky and unrelenting rain, I could still recognise why the 516-metre bridge, with its sixteen arches and thirty marvellous statues, was a UNESCO World Heritage site. There was a religious theme to the statues, with various saints and biblical scenes depicted, including *The Crucifix and the Cavalry*.

Some tourists had decided to brave the weather and take a boat ride along the Vltava. It was perhaps more likely that they had purchased their tickets in advance and had been caught out by an inaccurate forecast. Either way, it looked most unappealing.

Charles IV reportedly laid the first stone at 5:31 am on 9 July, 1357 due to his obsession with numerology. He believed that selecting this specific time, which formed the palindrome 1357 9/7 5:31, would provide the bridge with additional strength. The various disasters that have occurred here, such as the flood of 1432 and the fighting that took place during the Thirty Years' War, can be viewed as evidence that this superstitious time and date offered little protection. Alternatively, it can be pointed out that the bridge was never entirely destroyed by such incidents. I just wish that Charles IV had chosen a time that had ensured that no rain would fall over the city during Spring Bank Holiday weekend in 2013!

Another interesting tale about the bridge states that egg yolk was mixed into the mortar in order to strengthen the construction. There has not been any evidence found to support this claim, but it certainly makes for a good story. Given that sticky rice was used to hold the Great Wall of China in place and egg yolk may have helped strengthen Charles Bridge, I wonder if any builders have ever considered using treacle.

Upon reaching the end of the bridge, I asked Carol whether she wanted to continue our path towards Prague Castle.

"I think it would be best to visit there tomorrow and just stick to the Old Town today. The narrow streets may provide us with some protection from the rain," she suggested.

"Yeah, it looks like we would be exposed to the elements near the castle. The weather will surely be better tomorrow," I stated, tempting fate in the process. "Shall we attach our 'love lock' to the bridge?"

"That will be nice."

I was referring to the well-intentioned but impractical romantic gesture of affixing a padlock to a bridge or a gate then throwing the key into the river. Couples have decided to express their eternal love in this way in various cities around the world – I had first come across this practice in Cologne. Although the notion of adding a lock adorned with the names of a loving couple sounds heart-warming, it has infuriated many disapproving citizens. Bridges soon become overwhelmed by the presence of so many locks, causing them to be regarded as an eyesore or, in some cases, result in structural damage.

We used a felt-tip pen to write 'Carol + David, May 2013' on our padlock before deliberating who should attach it to the steel fence by the bridge. Carol soon worked out that we would be stood in the rain for hours if I were handed the task, as I would worry about the Czech police appearing out of nowhere to arrest us. Or throw us into the river instead. Therefore, she took it upon herself to fasten the padlock and chuck the key into the Vltava. I immediately regretted our actions – we had simply wanted to follow a romantic tradition, but I felt incredibly guilty. We had not only disfigured part of a historic bridge, but we had also thrown some metallic litter into the river. That was the last 'love lock' we ever made. At least Carol and I are still together!

Having returned to the Old Town side of the bridge, we began to explore the historic centre. The Old Town Square has served as one of the focal points of the city since the twelfth century, when it started life as the central marketplace of Prague. It is the location of one of Europe's most celebrated annual Christmas markets, although there was a more modest offering during our Spring visit.

A statue of the religious reformer Jan Hus, who was burned at the stake for heresy against the doctrines of the Catholic Church, stands proudly in the square. Executing a vocal opponent of the Church only galvanised his supporters, however, eventually leading to the Hussite Wars. The statue was erected in 1915 to commemorate the five-hundredth anniversary of his martyrdom. Twenty-seven leaders of the Bohemian Revolt were executed in the square in 1621. A variety of gruesome methods were used to kill the men: some were beheaded, a few were hanged, whilst others were quartered. Tongues or hands were cut off prior to execution if it was deemed that their crimes warranted such a fate, and twelve heads were apparently affixed to the Old Town Bridge Tower. Attaching our 'love lock' does not seem quite so terrible in comparison!

Twenty-seven crosses mark the pavement in front of the Old Town Hall, honouring those who were executed. The building consists of a series of once-separate houses that were added to the original structure. They may not look particularly important on their own, but they form an administrative complex that has existed since the fourteenth century. Despite the rain, we were not tempted to enter the Old Town Hall or climb to the top of its seventy-metre-tall tower; instead, we stood outside getting even more drenched. At least for another five minutes or so, anyway.

We had not gone insane; rather, we were simply waiting to take in the infamous show provided by the Prague Astronomical Clock, otherwise known as Prague Orloj. Built into one side of the tower, the fifteenth-century creation is one of the world's oldest astronomical clocks. It still impresses tourists with its hourly procession of the Twelve Apostles. On the hour, a door opens for Jesus to lead his disciples into view whilst a skeleton representing Death tolls the bell. The small crowd that had gathered by the tower seemed to enjoy the intricate mechanics as much as we did. The knowledge that this hourly show has been performed for hundreds of years only adds to the charm. According to legend, bad fortune will strike the city if the clock is neglected. As it seemed to be in working order, I could not blame the citizens of Prague for the incessant rain.

In addition to this unique display, there is much to admire about the clock. The astronomical dial displays a plethora of information that is difficult to decipher with the untrained eye. Unsurprisingly, I did not have a clue what each element represented. Apparently, the background symbolises the Earth and the sky, with the surrounding Roman numerals indicating local time. The signs of the zodiac are displayed in the outer circle, with the positioning of the sun and the movement of the moon shown in a manner that is beyond my descriptive capability or understanding of astronomical clocks. The old Czech timescale is also present, indicating the time of sunset. Beneath the clock, there is a calendar plate with medallions representing the twelve months of the year. This is flanked by the figures of a philosopher, an astronomer, a chronicler and the archangel Michael. The outer circle lists the names of 365 saints and the fixed holidays according to the Church calendar. I was unaware of what any of this information related to, but I found it fascinating nonetheless.

After the show concluded, a woman with a dog in her handbag walked past. She seemed to love the attention from curious onlookers – I am referring to the woman rather than the dog. Although I am unsure of the breed, it was white, fluffy and small enough to comfortably fit into a handbag. We found it strange that someone would want to do that, but it seemed as though animals were now being used as live fashion accessories. Judging by her attire – I am once again referring to the woman rather than the dog – it was evident that she had just attended a wedding. Perhaps this was held in one of the churches surrounding the square. The Church of Our Lady before Týn has been one of the most notable buildings in Prague since construction began in the fourteenth century. The Gothic church's eighty-metre-high towers loom large over the Old Town. Interestingly, one of the towers, Adam, is wider than the other, Eve.

"I am not sure if this is intended as a compliment of the female form or an assertion of masculinity…" I mused.

"I'm not bothered," Carol replied.

"Me neither. I just wanted to say something impressive but got a bit muddled."

"Nothing new there then!"

The eighteenth-century St. Nicholas Church is another notable religious building bordering the square. Constructed in the Baroque style, the stunning façade we were now admiring was obscured by the Krenn House until the latter was demolished in 1901. The sad sight of horses resigned to their fate of pulling a carriage of tourists always makes me feel uncomfortable. Here, the horses were stationed in front of the church waiting in the rain for the next set of people to pay a fortune to be carted around the Old Town.

We had a brief look at the Kinský Palace, which now houses an art museum, and the Stone Bell House. The name of the latter relates to a stone bell that is embedded into the outer corner of the building. It was reportedly the former temporary residence of Elizabeth and John of Bohemia but is now under the administration of the National Gallery.

The Powder Tower was the next tourist attraction we visited. This Gothic tower was inspired by the Old Town Bridge Tower; therefore, it was unsurprising to see that it had a similar appearance. This was intended to serve as a grand entrance point into the city, but its name was derived from its later use as a storage space for gunpowder. It was another structure that was difficult to appreciate due to the gloomy weather. Although it is possible to ascend the 186 steps to the viewing platform, a day of travel, sightseeing and punishing rain had left us lacking the energy or will to do so. The Municipal House, built in the Art Nouveau style, is situated next to the tower. This celebrated concert venue provided a greater contrast against the grey sky, but by this point we felt defeated by the rain.

I got the map out to have a look for any nearby attractions, only to discover that it was quickly becoming a soggy mess. Bizarrely, the Sex Machines Museum was one of the locations still visible on the map. We did not visit, but years later I recall my brother enthusiastically telling me that it was one of the only places that he and his fiancée spent time exploring during their stay in the Czech capital. John found it hilarious that there was a three-storey museum dedicated to all manner of erotic contraptions.

As I tried to make sense of the map, we were approached by an intoxicated man. He appeared to be a local who was, understandably, attempting to communicate in Czech. Although he was almost certainly trying to provide us with some friendly assistance, his lack of balance caused him to stumble into me. I instinctively moved the map away from him and began to walk away. This seemed to offend him, as he then shoved my shoulder.

"Hey!" Carol yelled at him.

I had visions of a scene from an episode of *Red Dwarf*, in which Cat repeatedly speaks out of turn to Caligula, yet each time it is Lister who ends up getting slapped as punishment. Fortunately, the drunkard showed little appetite for taking his grievance any further and I was spared a vicious beating! Aside from this incident, we did not encounter anything to disprove Prague's reputation as a safe city with a low crime rate.

I was unaware of this at the time, but my ability to see clearly in the rain was partly due to the work of a Czech chemist. Wearing glasses can be a pain when it is raining, so I am always thankful that I have the option of wearing contact lenses. Otto Wichterle is best known for inventing soft contact lenses whilst living and working in Prague. I doubt that I would ever have worn contacts if I had to rely on the old-fashioned hard lenses that my father uses.

Feeling as if we had just climbed out of a swimming pool, we decided to forget about visiting the historic Estates Theatre or any buildings belonging to the Charles University, which is one of the oldest universities in Europe. A return to our hotel was the only thing that appealed to us at that moment.

Another tram ride took us back to our modest accommodation, where we encountered Norman lurking in the corridor near our room.

"Hello, my friends. You should dry yourselves, as you look very wet."

"Even Norman is having a laugh at our expense," I muttered to myself after returning to our room.

As we dried off, I became aware of the rather disturbing positioning of a tiny window in the bathroom. It must have been designed to let some light in from the corridor as there was no external window, but I had visions of Norman getting excited as he peered in.

"If someone crouched down from the staircase leading to the corridor, I reckon someone would be able to get a glimpse of the bathroom," I stated.

"By someone, you mean Norman."

"Yes. To be fair, I don't think anyone could see anything other than the top corner of the room, but it's a worrying thought!"

"Stop picking on Norman!"

"Are you going to his nightclub in the basement then?"

"Definitely not!"

A couple of hours later, we were enjoying our first meal in the Czech Republic. We did not want to venture too far due to the ongoing rain, so we entered the first place that served hot food. This was a smoky pub that certainly could not boast any Michelin stars. It appeared to be a place where locals enjoyed no-frills traditional Czech food. We ordered a couple of portions of *vepřo knedlo zelo*, which is widely regarded as the national dish. The version we were given consisted of roasted pork, dumplings and sauerkraut. Pilsner Urquell is the most well-known Czech beer, so our choice of beverage was an easy one. The food was delicious, and the drink was much appreciated after a gruelling day in the rain.

"All of our food and drink only cost just over ten pounds. No wonder why Prague is a popular choice for stag weekends," I commented.

"It's not just tourists who indulge in alcohol. The people of the Czech Republic consume more beer per capita than any other country in the world. Also, the price of beer is often cheaper than bottled water."

"You've been reading my guidebook, haven't you?!"

"I'm tired. Let's go back."

We resisted the temptation to visit Norman's basement.

* * *

Having consumed a few stale croissants and some cereal in the hotel, which was not being overseen by Norman on this occasion, Carol and I stepped back out onto the streets of Prague. It was still raining. We crossed Charles Bridge again, where we saw that our 'love lock' was still in place. I am sure that the authorities will have removed the offending item not long after our visit, but it remained there for the duration of our stay. We soon crossed Čertovka, the 'Devil's Canal,' which is connected to the Vltava. It was unclear why it was given such an ominous name, as it appeared to be a delightful body of water lined with picturesque buildings that inevitably leads to comparisons with the canals of Venice.

We took a few photographs of the canals before moving on to the Lennon Wall in Malá Strana, the Lesser Town. Given the country's communist past, I had assumed that there was an error on my map, and that the wall was dedicated to Lenin. In fact, it is adorned with John Lennon-inspired graffiti and song lyrics. Much to the annoyance of the communist regime, Lennon was a symbol of freedom, Western culture and political causes. Consequently, there were frequent clashes between the authorities and those who valued the wall as a way of rebelling against their oppression.

Long after the Velvet Revolution and the move away from communism, the wall is still regularly updated with artwork honouring Lennon and the causes he believed in. At first glance, it looked like just another messy, graffiti-riddled wall, but upon closer inspection, the messages had an anti-war, pro-democracy theme. Multiple Lennon Walls have recently been created in Hong Kong as a form of protest against the local and national governments. People have affixed post-it notes to various walls to express their desire for true democracy, but the Chinese authorities rarely tolerate such actions.

We could have visited the nearby KGB Museum, but we did not feel like delving further into the city's communist past. We also declined the opportunity to visit the celebrated Infant Jesus statue in the Church of Our Lady Victorious, the Wallenstein Palace, or the Petřín Lookout Tower, which is basically a 63.5-metre observation tower that was designed to resemble the Eiffel Tower. There was another St. Nicholas Church, but we did not bother with that either. Instead, we wandered through the pretty streets of the Lesser Town before making our way over to Prague Castle. The complex is recognised as the world's largest ancient castle, occupying just under 70,000 square metres. This should not come as a surprise, given that the Czech Republic has amongst the highest concentrations of castles in the world.

The view of the castle complex from Charles Bridge had provided an indication of its size, but it did not look particularly beautiful from afar. The gloomy weather may have been to blame, as the sheer number of sightseers it attracts indicates otherwise. Many of the 1.8 million annual visitors watch the changing of the guard; however, we had not timed our arrival to coincide with this ceremonial showpiece. The rain would probably have spoiled this spectacle anyway. Due to the number of different buildings that form the castle complex, Carol and I often struggle to recall the details of our visit.

St. Vitus Cathedral is the most prominent structure and is regarded as the most important church in the country. Positioned by one of the main courtyards, the fourteenth-century Gothic cathedral reaches a height of 102.8 metres. The imposing building was a magnificent sight to behold – this is one aspect that has stuck in our minds. It is one of several churches within the castle complex. With so many spires dominating the skyline, it was becoming clear why Prague is often referred to as the 'City of a Hundred Spires.' There are, however, thought to be more than five hundred – perhaps a thousand – spires, towers and turrets. Despite the high number of religious buildings, the Czech Republic is known for having a large proportion of its population identify as non-religious. This may be due to the religious conflicts the country has endured or a reaction to the oppressive regimes that once restricted personal freedoms.

I often try to retrieve memories of our visit to the castle, but I struggle to recall anything of substance. We must have roamed around the complex taking photographs of the churches, including the colourful St. George's Basilica, the various gardens and the numerous palaces. I believe we may have paid a visit to the New Royal Palace and Queen Anne's Summer Palace, otherwise known as Belvedere, but it is all a bit of a blur. I remember that the rain continued to fall though. Walking around the castle complex did not seem too different from exploring the grand buildings of the Old Town. Although there were plenty of historic structures, it did not have the typical feel of an ancient castle.

After leaving the complex, we crossed back over the Vltava and headed towards the Old Jewish Cemetery. We paid the modest entrance fee and put on the skullcaps we were given – I believe that this is known as a *kippah* or *yarmulke* and is predominantly worn by Jewish men – whilst we waited in the long queue to enter the grounds. It soon became apparent that there were lots of people buried here.

"How many graves do you think there are?" Carol asked.

"I read that there are around 12,000 headstones, but as there are multiple bodies buried in each grave, there could be up to 100,000 people here."

"That is a lot. So, are the high numbers due to the Nazis?"

"I thought that may be the case, but the history of the cemetery goes back much further. It was first used in the mid-fifteenth century or earlier, with the final burial taking place in 1787. The persecution of Jews pre-dates the Nazis, with Jewish people forced to live in the former Jewish Ghetto, as they were banned from residing anywhere else in the city. The ruling authorities often restructured the area and flattened buildings, and there was little that the Jewish community could do about it."

We paid our respects to the dead whilst examining the thousands of headstones, some of which were ornate whilst others were basic and nondescript. The most striking thing we noted was the lack of available space. The headstones were crammed in as close together as possible, with bodies often piled on top of each other, which was partly due to a section of the cemetery being displaced for a new road and because of the Jewish custom forbidding the removal of old graves.

Prague had been the home of many Jewish scholars prior to the Nazi occupation of Czechoslovakia. I was surprised to learn that the Old Jewish Cemetery and much of the Jewish Quarter was spared by the Nazis; however, it appears that there may have been a horrifying reason for this. It has been suggested that the Nazis were planning to preserve these items for a 'Museum of an Extinct Race.' Thankfully, this did not come to fruition, but it is a chilling thought that this may have been created if there had been a different outcome to the Second World War.

Our next port of call was also intertwined with Nazi history. Reinhard Heydrich, who was a key figure in the formulation of the planned genocide of Jews in occupied Europe – known as the 'Final Solution to the Jewish Question' – was assassinated by soldiers sent to Prague by the government-in-exile in London. After Heydrich was killed during Operation Anthropoid, the soldiers and those who assisted them fled to Saints Cyril and Methodius Cathedral in the New Town. Cornered by the

Nazis, it soon became clear that there was no escape. Those not already killed by opposition forces committed suicide. Sadly, the subsequent Nazi retaliation resulted in many deaths and the complete destruction of the village of Lidice. The museum in the church crypt pays homage to the people now regarded as national heroes. The building itself did not look particularly significant, which underlines how it is only when you know the history of a place that you can understand its importance.

Carol and I then paid a brief visit to something more light-hearted. The Nationale-Nederlanden Building is commonly referred to as 'The Dancing House' due to its unusual shape. In contrast with the surrounding Art Nouveau buildings, it has incredulously curvy outlines. It made me think of a wax candle that had been melted and distorted beyond recognition, but Frank Gehry, who provided assistance to Vlado Milunić's project during the 1990s, apparently named the house 'Fred and Ginger' due to it resembling a couple of dancers.

The last President of Czechoslovakia and the first President of the Czech Republic, Václav Havel, was one of the project's biggest supporters. Having lived next to the site, which suffered significant damage during the American bombing of Prague in 1945, he had shared Milunić's enthusiasm for the creation of a modern building that would have cultural and social significance. Prior to his ascension to national leader, Havel had been a playwright and political dissident. He played a key role in the Velvet Revolution that peacefully toppled the communist regime. Since his death in 2011, he has been honoured in numerous ways: Prague's airport was named after him, the square by the National Theatre now bears his name, and the Václav Havel Award for Creative Dissent was established by the Human Rights Foundation.

We wrapped up our day's sightseeing by visiting Wenceslas Square, which at 750 metres in length, is more of a boulevard than a square. The National Museum is the crowning glory at the upper end of the square. Unsurprisingly, we encountered an equestrian statue of Saint Wenceslas, the former Duke of Bohemia, in front of the museum. Apparently, his younger brother was complicit in his murder in 935 AD. I think it is clear who people view more favourably, given that the older sibling was made a patron saint of the Czech state and is referred to as 'Good King Wenceslas' in a famous carol recited on Saint Stephen's Day. Meanwhile, his murderous brother is known as 'Boleslav the Cruel.'

"This is where Jan Palach set himself on fire in 1969 as a form of political protest following the Soviet invasion of Czechoslovakia," I informed Carol.

"I hope you are not planning something similar!"

"Don't worry, self-immolation is not part of our itinerary! Do you

THE CITY OF A HUNDRED SPIRES AND CONSTANT RAIN

know that Tibetan monks often set themselves on fire to protest the Chinese occupation and the policies that are imposed on the people of Tibet?"

"I can't imagine setting myself on fire. Why do they do it?"

"It creates a powerful image that can be seen around the world. When you feel that you have no chance of relieving the hardship your people endure, I guess the best you can do is create a scene that is impossible to ignore. Mind you, the Chinese government censors the internet and downplays the unrest in Tibet."

"On that cheery note, shall we head back to our hotel?"

During our long walk back to our accommodation, we stumbled across the unexpected sight of Sigmund Freud dangling from a pole over Husova Street in the Old Town. This would have been a far more interesting tale if I were referring to the man himself, especially as he died in 1939; alas, my anecdote simply features a seven-feet-tall statue of the father of psychoanalysis.

"Did you think that was a real man at first? I had to do a double take to be sure," Carol commented.

"I didn't know what to think. It would have been strange if he was real, as people were taking photographs rather than trying to help him! Also, he appears to be rather blasé about it all, casually hanging from the pole with one hand whilst the other is in his pocket!"

In fact, David Černý's *The Man Hanging Out* has resulted in numerous people calling the emergency services since it was installed in 1996. The artist's work is generally considered to be provocative, as evidenced by his other creations. *Shark* showcases an image of Saddam Hussein in a tank of the chemical compound formaldehyde, whilst *Piss* features sculptures of two men urinating. People can even instruct the men to write messages with their 'urine' by sending a text message to a phone number linked to the installation. Černý is perhaps best known for *Babies*, a group of ten sculptures depicting babies climbing up and down Prague's Žižkov Television Tower.

Rather than taking in a performance at the Prague State Opera or attending a traditional Czech puppet show, we spent most of the evening watching the 2013 UEFA Champions League Final in another smoky pub near our hotel. The match between Bayern Munich and Borussia Dortmund was taking place at Wembley Stadium in our home nation. Carol was obviously thrilled by this romantic choice of evening entertainment! Incidentally, one of the Czech Republic's most successful footballers, Karol Poborský, won titles with Slavia Prague and Sparta Prague. He also made an impact in England, winning the Premier League with Manchester United and scoring an iconic lob during his national side's march towards the final of Euro '96, which was held at the old Wembley Stadium.

We both ordered *goulash* and beer. Feeling rather hungry, I tried to ask the waiter for some chips in addition to the bread dumplings that accompanied the dish, but he mistakenly thought that I wanted chips *instead* of the dumplings. He replied by saying: "OK, goulash with chips, this is something new" whilst rolling his eyes to indicate that I was yet another idiotic English tourist. I let him walk away, dithered for a minute, then summoned the courage to inform him that I wanted the dumplings *and* the chips. He nodded his head whilst wearing an expression that said, "Better, but you are still stupid."

The paprika-infused beef and vegetable dish was tasty, especially the dumplings that I had nearly missed out on. After watching Bayern's 2-1 victory, we returned to our accommodation. Norman wished us goodnight before making his way down to the basement.

* * *

After one final walk in the rain, we checked out of our hotel and said goodbye to Norman. For all of our uneasiness around him, he was a kind host. He had offered advice about tourist attractions and always displayed a friendly attitude. I would still not dare venture into his nightclub in the basement though!

The metro journey was an uncomfortable one. My stomach began to churn immediately upon boarding, and I felt an urgent need to go to the toilet. There was a small building containing public bathrooms near the airport bus departure point, but I did not like the look of it. Although I was sure that it would seem like a palace in comparison to the horrific toilets that I had been confronted with during the China trek, I convinced myself that it would be best to wait until we reached the airport. To my dismay, the bus was not due for over forty-five minutes.

"Are you OK?" Carol asked.

"Yeah, I am fine," I said whilst grimacing.

"Why don't you just go to the toilet now?"

"I'll be OK. I'll wait."

Forty minutes later, I could no longer resist the call of nature. I dashed to the toilet and entered the only open cubicle. It would not lock, so I had to hold the door in place whilst I relieved myself. The feeling of euphoria was short-lived, as I realised why this was the only unlocked cubicle. Each unit required a token to unlock it, which must have been available to rent from the woman who was sat in the side room that I had scampered past. The lock on my cubicle was broken, meaning that it was clear to everyone apart from me that this was not to be used. I washed my hands before putting on a brave face for the inevitable awkward encounter with the toilet attendant. She gave me a look of disgust, as if she were looking at the filthiest human being on the planet. Unsure of the amount I was required to pay, I handed over enough Czech koruna to cover ten visits to the toilet and ensure that I could exit the scene without having to hang around a second longer than required.

"You've just missed the bus," Carol informed me upon my return.

"Sorry. At least there is another one in half an hour. I have just had a really embarrassing episode. And I've caused us to miss the bus that we had spent so long waiting for."

Carol found my toilet anecdote hilarious: "That could only happen to you! Do you feel OK though?"

"Yeah, I'll be fine."

I was not. I had foolishly decided to indulge in more goulash at a restaurant in the airport, which resulted in leaving Carol by herself at the table whilst I made another dash for the toilet. I decided not to purchase any Imodium because I had vague recollections of reading a story about the potential harm of taking medicine that stops your body from flushing out any harmful toxins. Besides, I find that Imodium often takes so long to kick in that it fails to solve the initial issue, and then when this is no longer a concern, makes it almost impossible to go to the toilet for days on end.

I must have felt better by the time we approached Manchester Airport, as the horrifying sight of a parked plane that was ablaze did not cause any involuntary bowel movements. Aside from noticing anything untoward with our aircraft, this was just about the last thing we would have wanted to see during our descent. After a few worrying seconds, we realised that it was just an emergency drill. The firefighters were putting out the flames on a mock aircraft, presumably part of a training exercise. I just wish someone had warned us!

"What did you think of Prague?" I asked Carol.

"I enjoyed the trip, but the weather did not allow us to appreciate the beauty of the city."

"Yeah, I have heard that it is a wonderful city. All I can think of is the rain though. I guess it shows that the weather can have a big influence on one's experience. Maybe we will truly witness the splendour of Prague one day."

One thing was clear though: the spirit of the China trek was now firmly in the past, and I had started to accept the prospect of going on holidays rather than a more adventurous form of travel. I just hoped that this would be enough to satisfy my wanderlust.

BEYOND THE WALL

9: *TWERK OR TREAT?*
TALLINN, ESTONIA
AUGUST 2013

"Do you think I've been spoilt by the amount of travelling I've recently undertaken?" I asked Mum whilst we waited to board our flight at Manchester Airport.

"I'm not sure. Why do you think that?"

"There were some moments during recent trips when I was not as enthusiastic about the experience as I should have been. Maybe it was because of bad weather or just a lull in the proceedings that led to a moment of boredom. Is it inevitable that visiting European cities will not be as exhilarating as trekking along the Great Wall of China? I just wonder whether I have become blasé about it all."

"Are you excited about visiting Tallinn?"

"Yes. It looks like a lovely city, and I can't wait to explore it. I've never been to any of the Baltic countries."

"Well, it sounds like you still enjoy travelling. I would suggest that you are just extremely fortunate."

If there was ever a moment that unexpectedly restored my gratitude about being able to travel, it was when boarding began and we all had to fight for our seats. As it would be another few months before Ryanair introduced allocated seating on all their routes, we found ourselves in a free-for-all with our fellow passengers. I was not particularly bothered about where we sat, I just wanted to ensure that Mum would not have to spend a few hours next to a couple of strangers. Not for the first time in my life, I received a blow to the head from someone's hand luggage as they attempted to place it in the overhead lockers amidst the chaos. Thankfully, Mum and I were able to relax after we secured a couple of adjacent seats.

"Having to fight for a seat on the plane has helped dispel any notion of being spoilt! Thanks Ryanair!" I whispered to Mum.

Recent events in Afghanistan highlight just how lucky I have been throughout my life. Afghans were desperate to secure a place on an outbound flight due to a genuine fear for their lives, whilst the worst that would have happened to me was being sat apart from my mother for a couple of hours.

The last few people to board the aircraft showed no concern about sitting together. They were a group of heavily-intoxicated men in their twenties, seemingly on a stag weekend. It was clear that although they would not be sat together, they would create a substantial racket by shouting to each other across the plane. Tallinn has become a popular destination for stag and hen weekends due to its reputation for being an inexpensive city to spend a few nights in. Cheap beer was obviously the biggest selling point.

The bus from Tallinn Airport to the city centre only cost a couple of euros, which provided an indication of the low prices we would encounter during our stay in the Estonian capital. Interestingly, free public transport was introduced for the residents of Tallinn a few months before our visit, and in 2018 the national government permitted other regions of the country to follow suit. I do not envisage a similar scheme being launched in the United Kingdom, where prices seem to shoot up year upon year.

Upon alighting the vehicle, the glorious blue sky and warm temperature was an indication of the favourable weather conditions that lay ahead. It made a mockery of how British people often say, 'It's Baltic out there,' when referring to cold weather. In contrast with the medieval image of the city, the boulevards were wide, and the buildings were modern. Mind you, we were staying about a kilometre away from the Old Town.

I had booked an apartment that was listed online for the enticing price of just ninety euros for three nights. I had provided the owner with my estimated time of arrival but there was no sign of her when we reached the building. Upon calling the phone number that had been supplied with the booking confirmation, I was greeted with a bit of a telling off. Given that we were only twenty minutes late after flying from Manchester and taking a bus from the airport, this seemed a little harsh. Nevertheless, our host turned up a few minutes later and seemed friendlier than our phone conversation had indicated. She appeared to be in her thirties or forties, and like many of the Estonians that we would see over the next few days, she was tall, with blonde hair and pale skin. Our host provided us with a set of old-fashioned keys and led us up the large Soviet-era steps to our apartment on the second floor. I had always said that I was not fussy about accommodation as long as it was clean, reasonably priced and fairly close to places of interest, but this apartment was testing my boundaries of acceptability. It was old, dusty and in poor condition. Most worryingly of all, the electrical sockets were almost hanging off the wall. At least they worked and did not electrocute me at any point during our stay. I guess that the price of the apartment was reflected by its condition.

"I'm not sure about this apartment," Mum said, after our host had left.

"It will do for three nights. We only need somewhere to sleep, and it's close enough to walk to the Old Town."

"I think you should have chosen somewhere better. I know it was cheap, but sometimes it's best to pay a little more for something important."

"I guess you're right. There's not much we can do about it now though. We will make the most of it."

Before commencing our sightseeing, we had lunch in a restaurant close to our apartment. It seemed to be popular with office workers who were presumably after a quick and relatively cheap bite to eat during their lunchbreak. I had previously shown little sense of adventure when dining overseas, but I decided to start being more daring with my food choices. I opted for a dish that featured sprats, which are a small, oily fish similar to sardines. My *kiluvõileib* consisted of rye bread topped with smoked sprats, onions, herbs and a boiled egg. Granted, they are not the most daring ingredients one may encounter, but it was not something that I would have ordered in Manchester. Mum chose one of the pork and potato stews that seem so popular in Estonia.

The restaurant staff all spoke perfect English, once again highlighting how people in the countries I have visited tend to be able to communicate in different languages, whereas lazy tourists like me barely make an effort to get to grips with the local dialect. This is a habit that I frequently vow to amend but invariably fail to act upon. As expected, my meal had a smoky, salty flavour. It was not the nicest food I had ever tried, but it was not unpleasant. I was certainly glad that I had at least sampled some local produce. Mum seemed to enjoy her stew, so our first dining experience in Estonia was a positive one.

Resisting the temptation to dive straight into Tallinn's famous Old Town, we instead decided to save that for the following day. We began our sightseeing by visiting the National Library of Estonia. The current building was completed in the early 1990s, after the country had regained its independence from the Soviet Union. Given that the Soviets had previously cut ties with foreign collections and had ensured that the library was predominantly stocked with Russian publications, it now has significant symbolic value. This is underscored by its stated goal of collecting and preserving documents relating to the nation or those published in the Estonian language.

Although the building opened in 1993, much of the construction took place during the final years of Soviet rule. This is reflected in the design of the eight-storey structure, which has plenty of right-angles but not many decorative features. I quite liked the clean-cut appearance of the limestone building though; it suited its purpose as a library. Perhaps Soviet architecture, so often derided, can occasionally be pleasing on the eye. There is a statue of one of the most celebrated Estonian poets, Marie Under, in front of the library. Born in Tallinn, when it was known as Reval, she was nominated eight times for the Nobel Prize in Literature. The location of the statue is quite fitting, considering that Under and her family fled Estonia following the Soviet re-occupation in 1944. Her family spent a year in a refugee camp before moving to a suburb of Stockholm. Her story is an example of a refugee overcoming adversity and going on to achieve great things. This would not have been possible, however, if her family had not been taken in by another country.

As one must be a member of the library to enter, Mum and I settled for a quick walk through the quiet Tuvi Park instead. It was a pleasant stroll in the sun but there was not much of interest. The nearby Tõnismägi water tower was more noteworthy, with its appearance in keeping with the city walls and the medieval Old Town. The cylindrical structure was just one of the hundreds of abandoned water towers in Estonia. Once a vital source of water, albeit of dubious quality, the towers became redundant once water treatment plants were introduced in the early-twentieth century. Some have been converted into art galleries or unusual holiday rentals – it seems as though just about any type of building is available to rent on Airbnb these days.

Our next port of call was at Kaarli Kirik, a Lutheran church commissioned by and named after King Charles XI during the period of Swedish rule from the mid-sixteenth to the early-eighteenth century. Lutheranism is a branch of Protestantism prevalent in many northern European countries, including Estonia. It is based on the teachings of Martin Luther, who was a German priest and a professor of theology.

He caused anger within the Roman Catholic Church by rejecting some of its teachings, but he was a key figure of the Reformation whose translation of the Bible helped make Christianity more accessible to

Germans. I find childish delight in the fact that his excommunication came as a result of the Diet of Worms in 1521. When first reading about this, my mind conjured up an image of a man being punished for his habit of only eating earthworms, but the reality was not so humorous. Diet refers to a formal deliberative assembly, whilst Worms is one of the oldest cities in Germany. What a shame!

Something that was far from amusing was Luther's call for the burning of synagogues and the deaths of Jewish people. His violent anti-Jewish rhetoric, particularly in the latter part of his life, may have contributed to the development of antisemitism in Germany. This would, of course, be exploited by the Nazis in the 1930s.

The original wooden church was destroyed in 1710 during the Great Northern War, but it was not reconstructed until the late-nineteenth century. The current limestone Romanesque Revival building follows the tradition of western European Cathedrals, with two towers flanking a rose window. It was closed to visitors at the time of our visit, but it is apparently home to the country's largest church organ and Johann Köler's fresco *Come to Me*.

We encountered an unusual building at some point during the trip. I am unsure of when or where this was, but I recall seeing what I assumed were offices resting upon what looked like trees made of paper straws. Although this unusual architecture may not have been as wacky as Prague's Dancing House, it was still an unusual sight. Despite its traditional image, it was clear that the country had a modern edge to it; after all, a group of Estonians helped to create Skype. Around forty-four per cent of employees of the telecommunication app, which was reportedly used by 100 million people during the early months of the COVID-19 pandemic, are based in the cities of Tallinn and Tartu. Estonia was also the first nation to utilise an online voting system. Introduced in 2005, this has been used in several local, general, parliamentary and European Parliament elections. Just don't tell Donald Trump!

Whilst Estonia may be a forward-thinking country in terms of technology, it also remains committed to remembering its troubled past. Mum and I were soon stood in a place that symbolises key events in the nation's history. Freedom Square is home to the War of Independence Victory Column, which was erected in 2009 as a memorial to the thousands of lives that were lost between 1918 and 1920 during the Estonian War of Independence. The conflict ended with the Treaty of Tartu, which included Soviet recognition of Estonian independence. With a huge cross resting on a 23.5-metre-high pillar, it was a simple but effective design.

This represents only one chapter of Estonia's tragic past. When measured as a proportion of its population, the nation suffered one of the worst death rates of the Second World War, with some estimates placing this at around twenty-five per cent. Despite declaring its neutrality, it was occupied by the Soviet Union in 1940 before being invaded by Nazi Germany. The Soviets then re-occupied the country in 1944. Over 80,000 people are thought to have lost their lives either in combat, due to political persecution, as part of the Holocaust or following Soviet deportations.

It was renamed Victory Square during Soviet rule – it seems fitting that the Soviets were the ones to eliminate freedom. Full of skateboarders and tourists when we visited, the square was once used for parades that honoured key Soviet events such as the October Revolution. The name of Freedom Square was re-adopted in 1989. Estonia's turbulent history, along with its significant ethnic Russian population, has resulted in people adopting differing views on the role of the Soviet Union during the Second World War. The Bronze Soldier of Tallinn, which we did not visit, is an example of a war memorial that has caused controversy. Originally named 'Monument to the Liberators of Tallinn,' it was later changed to 'Monument to the Fallen in the Second World War.' I had encountered something similar in Budapest, where a monument had been renamed due to the rejection of the view that the Soviets 'liberated' its citizens. In 2007, the Bronze Soldier and the remains of some Soviet combatants were relocated to the Defence Forces Cemetery of Tallinn, prompting riots in the city and the besieging of the Estonian embassy in Moscow.

Rather than debating the actions of the Soviet Union, Mum and I decided to have a drink in the terrace belonging to one of the bars bordering the square. Savouring a glass of orange juice in the sun whilst watching carefree youths skate around the vast public space provided me with a positive feeling after we had spent the previous moments contemplating a tragic period of Estonian history. We were also able to regard St. John's Church, which stands on the opposite side of the square to the Victory Column. The unassuming Neo-Gothic building was another Lutheran church constructed in the mid-nineteenth century.

"Tallinn seems a pleasant city," Mum declared.

"I like it so far, and we haven't even seen any of the Old Town. It helps that we have been blessed with beautiful weather. It's nice to relax in the sun whilst taking in views of a historic square."

"Even though you are drinking orange juice with your mum?"

"I like orange juice and I'm rather fond of my mum!"

"Most men your age would not want to go on holiday with their mother. Thank you."

"Don't be silly. We make a good team, and I am enjoying the trip."

We briefly inspected the impressive façade of the Estonian National Opera building on our way to the port area. The opera house suffered significant damage when it was bombed during Soviet air raids in 1944 but was re-opened three years later. Although a wide range of operas, musicals and ballets are showcased here throughout the year, we had no plans to attend a show during our budget weekend in the Estonian capital. The reason we were heading to the port was to collect the ferry tickets that I had purchased online. There are regular services connecting Tallinn to several Baltic cities, including Helsinki, where we were travelling to on Sunday. This seemed a convenient and cost-effective way of visiting two countries during one Bank Holiday weekend.

Our walk took us through the Rotermann Quarter, which was clearly an industrial area that was being rejuvenated. Old warehouses served as a reminder of the importance of the port and highlighted the city's industrial heritage. This seems to have continued in the following years, with more restaurants and offices popping up since our visit. We also stumbled upon the tiny wooden Church of St. Simeon and the Prophetess Hanna. Legend states that the foundation required some landfill, which came in the form of the rubble from shipwrecks. The Soviets, sentimental as ever, converted the church into a sports hall. The Orthodox church was restored following the re-establishment of Estonian independence.

I dread any social situation in which I must leave my comfort zone; therefore, collecting pre-ordered tickets from an Estonian ferry company was a growing concern as we approached the port. This type of interaction can be complicated at the best of times, let alone with the language barrier and the fact that I possessed almost no knowledge of Baltic ferries. After nervously surveying the ticket hall, we located what I hoped was the appropriate desk for collecting pre-paid tickets for the company we had booked through, which I think was Tallink Silja.

"Hi, I would like to collect the tickets I ordered online," I informed the bored-looking woman sat behind the counter.

"Of course. Can I please have your booking number?" she asked whilst contemplating why she chose a job that involves speaking to so many tourists who do not bother to learn a single word of the Estonian language.

"Here it is," I nervously responded as my shaking hands passed her the printout of my booking confirmation.

My prayers of a smooth transaction were answered when she promptly printed the tickets and handed them over.

"Hüvasti," she said with a forced smile.

I froze, wearing a blank expression that made it abundantly clear that I had no idea she had just wished me goodbye.

She followed this up by saying, "Goodbye, Sir," which seemed to be the Estonian for, "Go away, you ignorant English moron."

With another awkward conversation in the books, we began walking back to our apartment. The busy port provided an indication of the crucial role it plays in Estonia's tourism industry, which is vital for the economy. The country welcomed 2.3 million foreign tourists in 2019, many of them via ferry or cruise ship, which is a significantly higher number than its population of 1.3 million. The ferries also offer an essential link between the mainland and the 2,222 islands that belong to Estonia. Judging by the numerology that he incorporated into the construction of Prague's most iconic bridge, Charles IV would have been most impressed by the fact that the number of islands formed a basic palindrome.

I am unable to recall where we dined that evening, but at least my meal was a memorable one. I chose pork and apple strudel. I am not referring to a pastry containing pork and apple; rather, this was a pork fillet served alongside apple strudel, complete with a light dusting of sugar, some grapes and a pot of sticky apple sauce. Pork is a staple food of Estonian cuisine, and it is common to serve apple alongside pork in many countries, but I found it rather bizarre that the restaurant had paired a slab of meat with an item normally served as a dessert. Perhaps I need to get out more.

"How is it?" Mum asked.

"You know what? It's really nice. This bizarre combination somehow works!"

"Sometimes you have to be prepared to try unusual things."

"I read that Kalevipoeg, a character depicted in Estonian folklore, was apparently willing to do just that. Part of his legend states that he used planks as weapons and threw stones at his enemies after being advised to do so by a hedgehog. He was able to build towns and walk through deep water."

"See, sometimes you have to be brave and…"

"Yes, but you have to bear in mind that he died after his legs were cut off by his own cursed sword. The gods then sent his legless body on a horse from heaven to the gates of hell, where he was ordered to strike a rock with his fist. This entrapped him, leaving him to forever guard the gates of hell."

"OK, you should try most things, within reason…that is a weird story!"

* * *

The following morning, we headed straight for the Old Town. Our route took us past the Estonian National Opera building again and through Tammsaare Park, where we briefly inspected the statue of the celebrated Estonian writer A.H. Tammsaare before reaching Viru Gate. Built in the fourteenth century, it was once part of the city walls. Much of the gate has been removed, but the delightful twin towers remain in place. The surviving sections of the walls, including this wonderful entrance to the Old Town, certainly add to the appeal of the historic centre.

Tallinn's Old Town, which is a UNESCO World Heritage Site, has the cobbled streets and charming buildings one would expect to find in a preserved historic centre, but with a lower concentration of people than in most European cities. Although it was undoubtedly geared towards attracting tourists, I felt that it managed to showcase its history without coming across as tacky. Much of this area was destroyed during the Second World War, through Nazi Luftwaffe raids and then by Soviet bombings. From what I could see, though, the Old Town had been restored without erasing its original character.

The Town Hall was the obvious place to begin our exploration of the Old Town. Aside from its sixty-four-metre-high tower, the two-storey Gothic building, located on the ancient market square known as Raekoja plats, has a modest appearance. With a history going back to the thirteenth century, it is one of the oldest town halls in northern Europe. People were making the most of the sunny weather by enjoying an early lunch or a drink outside the numerous restaurants housed in the pastel-coloured buildings surrounding the square. Despite the presence of large groups of tourists, the square still felt spacious. This may change as Tallinn becomes more popular with overseas visitors; then again, I imagine that it can get rather crowded when the Christmas markets make their annual appearance. Incidentally, it has been claimed that the world's first Christmas tree was erected here in 1441, although Latvians argue that this occurred in Riga.

It is possible to explore the interior of the Town Hall and climb the tower, but Mum and I were enjoying walking around in the sunshine. We had a quick look at St. Nicholas Church, which was one of many buildings severely damaged by the Soviet air raids. The restored former church, which has a 105-metre-high tower, now houses an art museum and is also used as a concert hall.

We were more interested in the Alexander Nevsky Cathedral on Toompea Hill, which is said to be the grave mound of Kalevipoeg's father, Kalev. Legend states that his grieving widow, Linda, used boulders to build the mound with her own hands and shed enough tears upon his death to form the nearby Lake Ülemiste. I will leave you to make up your own minds whether there is any truth to the story.

I had a long-held desire to visit St. Petersburg and Moscow, so it was inevitable that the Russian-looking Orthodox cathedral would seize my attention. It was built in 1900, when Estonia was part of the Russian Empire, on the spot where a statue of Martin Luther once stood. It appears that the Empire was keen to assert its religious dominance over the local Lutherans.

The cathedral is dedicated to the man largely responsible for military victories over German and Swedish invaders, which were significant events in Russian history. Having also served as a politician, Nevsky was canonised as a Saint of the Russian Orthodox Church in 1547. He remains an immensely popular figure within Russia, demonstrated in 2008 by a couple of public polls that saw him declared the greatest Russian and the most appreciated hero of the nation's history. Many Estonians, however, did not appreciate the presence of an imposing building that represented a period of Russification. There was talk of demolishing it in the 1920s, but this did not come to fruition.

As is so often the case when I visit a historic site in another country, I was left disappointed by restoration work being carried out. This included scaffolding and some green netting under the central onion dome.

"Argh! Of all the buildings in Tallinn to have scaffolding, it had to be the one I was most looking forward to seeing!" I moaned.

"It's not so bad. The cathedral still looks lovely. You just have to appreciate what you can see."

"You're right. It still looks great. My problem is that I sometimes get an image of a photograph I want to take before I even get there, which inevitably leads to disappointment. At least this is nowhere near as bad as when I visited the National Mall in Washington D.C and the Lincoln Memorial Reflecting Pool had been dredged!"

"You have never gotten over that!"

Even with the presence of scaffolding, the opulent cathedral looked splendid under the beautiful blue sky. There were four other domes on each corner, all topped with a gilded iron cross. The richly-decorated exterior was mostly white, with some sections light brown or red. The interior was just as extravagant, with stained glass windows, three ornate altars and numerous iconostases. We were not allowed to take photographs inside, so you will either have to arrange a visit yourself or take my word for it. I am sure that you are all thrilled to learn that the heaviest of the eleven church bells weighs fifteen tonnes, which is more than the other ten combined.

Mum and I then moved on to the nearby Toompea Castle. The original wooden fortress may have been built as far back as the tenth century, with a stone building erected three hundred years later. Various invaders took over the castle at some point, including Danish and Swedish forces, German Knights of the Sword, the Teutonic Order and the Russian Empire. The outer walls and remaining towers had the typical look of a medieval castle, with the Estonian flag on display above the 45.6-metre-high Tall Hermann, which is its most celebrated tower. The flag is raised as the national anthem is played at sunrise each day. It is lowered at sunset to the song "Mu isamaa on minu arm," which apparently translates to "My Fatherland is My Love." The castle is clearly a key site of national identity.

The Russians added a Baroque wing when they transformed the castle into a palace. As this was the most visually impressive and unique section of the castle, it was typical that, like the Alexander Nevsky Cathedral, it had scaffolding attached to it. The pastel-pink façade of the building that now houses the Riigikogu, the Estonian Parliament, was pleasant, even if the presence of scaffolding was slightly frustrating.

St. Mary's Cathedral is the oldest church in mainland Estonia and it was the only building in Toompea to survive a seventeenth-century fire. Originally established as a Roman Catholic cathedral by the Danes in the thirteenth century, it was converted to a Lutheran church thee hundred years later. Having already seen so many churches and read about its history, I had assumed that Estonia must be a devout nation; however, it is now regarded as one of the least religious countries in the world.

Possibly due to the Soviet policy of state atheism, the Estonian populace became increasingly irreligious from the 1940s onwards, with only around fourteen per cent of its inhabitants now deeming religion to be an important part of their lives. I had discovered something similar in Prague, where there are plenty of churches but a mostly non-religious population, at least in comparison to other nations. In a similar vein, my interest in churches was diminishing with each one that I encountered. Although most were visually impressive, I was no longer enthusiastic about exploring their interiors. We gave the building and bell tower little more than a cursory glance before moving on to Patkuli viewing platform.

Kohtuotsa viewpoint is favoured by social media influencers because of a wall on the viewing platform that has the phrase 'The times we had' written on it. I had read that the view from Patkuli is just as wonderful but does not have the irritating sight of tourists queueing up to pose next to the sign. The view was as beautiful as I had hoped for, with church spires, castle towers and terracotta rooftops providing a picturesque image of the medieval Old Town. On our other side, we could see the expansive Toompark and Snelli Pond. The climb up Toompea Hill had been well worth it, as we were able to admire a beautiful Orthodox cathedral, a historic castle and the best view in town.

From our vantage point, we could plot our next move like a chess player, which is fitting given that Estonia has a strong association with the sport. Although he fell agonisingly short of winning a world title on multiple occasions, Paul Keres is regarded as the nation's greatest ever player and a legend of the sport. Such was his standing in Estonia, around 100,000 mourners attended his funeral in 1975. That was close to ten per cent of the entire population!

Whilst walking through the cobbled streets of the Old Town, we passed a restaurant where the waitresses were dressed as 'medieval wenches,' seemingly tasked with posing for photographs with tourists and enticing them to dine there. We soon reached St. Catherine's Dominican Monastery, which is one of the oldest buildings in Tallinn, with a history going back to the thirteenth century. Only fragments of the original monastery remain, as it was all but destroyed in 1524 during the Reformation. It is still possible to visit a monks' dormitory, a library and a refectory though. The ruins of the complex have been used in a variety of ways over the years, including a car repair shop, a warehouse and a granary. Due to its acoustics, St. Catherine's Church often serves as an intimate concert hall and theatre venue.

The complex can be accessed via St. Catherine's Passage, which is almost hidden from sight. With its unusual arches, this charming medieval passageway has become a tourist attraction in its own right. The winding passage connects Vene Street with Müürivahe Street, where there are several handicraft workshops and galleries. There were some small restaurants operating in the passageway, but not enough to ruin this historic area. One could easily picture this place in a bygone era when religion played a more important role in Estonian society and Skype was hundreds of years from being created.

Any illusion of being transported back to medieval times was shattered by a reunion with the stag party that had been on our flight from Manchester. Clearly intoxicated, they were chasing pigeons in the Old Town. I am unsure of their ultimate goal, but they seemed to find it hilarious watching each other flail around trying to capture a pigeon with their hands. At least the birds they were chasing were not women, as men often refer to them. By the looks of it, Tallinn had fulfilled their criteria of being a cheap place to drink lots of beer and act foolishly. Another potential reason for spending the weekend in the city was the fact that Estonia has one of the lowest male-to-female ratios of any country in the world. At the time of our visit, the national figure stood at 0.84 – this was even lower in Tallinn, where there were 230,514 women and just 185,990 men. Judging by the look of disgust on female passers-by watching these drunk Englishmen chasing pigeons, however, the ratio did not seem to help the stag party attract anyone from the opposite sex. I doubt that any Estonian men found this childish display endearing either.

Mum and I spent the rest of the afternoon aimlessly wandering through the Old Town. We saw the Three Sisters, which is comprised of a trio of tall and narrow fourteenth-century pastel-coloured Hanseatic houses. A boutique hotel now operates from the premises that shares a name with a nature reserve in my hometown of Wigan and a rock formation that I had visited in Australia's Blue Mountains in 2011. There seems to be something about trios that leads people to refer to them as sisters.

We also stumbled upon yet another religious building, in the form of St. Olaf's Church. Completed no later than the thirteenth century, and once one of the tallest buildings in Europe, it has reportedly been struck by lightning on ten occasions and burned down three times. Initially Roman Catholic, it became Lutheran before converting to a Baptist church in 1950. In typical Soviet fashion, the KGB used the 123.8-metre-high spire as a radio tower and surveillance point.

I felt brave enough to opt for a portion of *verivorst* for my evening meal. This is a blood sausage, consisting of barley, marjoram, onions, allspice and pig's blood, regarded as the national dish of Estonia. Although usually eaten during the winter, particularly around Christmas time, I was keen to sample another local dish, even if it was out of season. With a similar taste to black pudding, it was served alongside roast pork and potatoes. I had an accompanying pint of Saku beer, taking my grand total of alcoholic beverages consumed that weekend to exactly one. I am certain that the stag party would have scarcely believed that someone of a similar age to them on the same flight from Manchester only had one alcoholic drink and spent the entire weekend with his mother!

Thank goodness that we did not bump into them again that evening, as Mum was wearing a T-shirt with the phrase 'Twerk or Treat?' written on it.

"Do you know what twerking is?" I asked her.

"I have no idea."

"It is a type of dance that involves ferociously shaking your buttocks!"

"Oh well, I only bought it because it cost two pounds."

"Will you stop wearing it after tonight then?" I pleaded.

"No, I'm not bothered. I bought it so I may as well wear it."

I had visions of a group of youths taunting her, so I again suggested that it may be wise to part company with the T-shirt. Much to my horror, however, she indicated that she would keep it. I am not ashamed to admit that upon our return to Manchester, I stole the item of clothing from her and donated it to a charity shop!

TWERK OR TREAT?

135

BEYOND THE WALL

10: A STING IN THE TALE
HELSINKI, FINLAND
AUGUST 2013

Having arrived at the ferry terminal much earlier than required, I spent a considerable amount of time worrying that our tickets would be invalid or that we would somehow end up on a ferry to one of Estonia's remote islands. Reassuringly, when the boarding process finally began, the large sign that read 'Helsinki' indicated that the vessel was heading to the correct destination. Mum and I were used to politely queueing in Britain, but there did not seem to be any organised system in place here. The wide walkways were full of people jostling for position and shuffling closer to the front. Just like with our Ryanair flight, we did not have allocated seating, which caused me to fret about the prospect of standing up on a rocky boat for the duration of our journey. It was some relief, therefore, to see that there were plenty of available seats.

I kept myself occupied during the two-hour journey, and probably bored Mum senseless, by reading about the country we were travelling to.

"Did you know that wife-carrying contests originated in Finland?" I asked Mum.

"What on earth is that?!"

"It says here that male competitors have to carry a woman – who does not actually have to be his wife – along the full length of the 253.5-metre track. Known as *eukonkanto* in Finnish, it is regarded as a serious sport by those involved. The Wife Carrying World Championships have been held annually in Finland since 1992, with the winner receiving their wife's weight in beer! This must be a minimum of forty-nine kilograms."

"Are you making this up?!"

"No, it's true," I assured Mum whilst showing her an image of a determined-looking man carrying a woman as if their lives depended on it. "It says that this man is using the Estonian technique of carrying the wife upside-down on his back with her legs over his neck and shoulders. It seems as though we will have visited two countries famed for their wife carrying this weekend!"

"That sounds like a weird sport!"

"Disturbingly, it says that its origins may be traced back to the nineteenth century when groups of young men would abduct women from neighbouring villages by carrying them on their backs. The more palatable tale involves an outlaw named Rosvo-Ronkainen training his gang of thieves by making them carry heavy sacks on their backs."

"I think I prefer the second story. It's less scary, anyway."

"Finns seem to love their unusual contests. The country also hosts The Annual Air Guitar World Championships and the Mobile Phone Throwing World Championships."

"You must be making these ones up! What is air guitar?"

"I'm not making it up. People pretend to play a guitar…"

"So, they just stand their holding a guitar?"

"They do not even hold a guitar. They mimic playing a guitar in thin air whilst a song plays, and the judges decide who gave the best performance."

"That sounds silly to me!"

"You will probably think the same about the mobile phone throwing then! Wait a minute…the world championships took place in Finland yesterday! We just missed out on seeing this prestigious sport! Apparently, the top three places in the men's contest were claimed by Finns. The longest throw was 97.7 metres! The world record is 102.68 metres though."

For what it is worth, a new record of 110.42 metres was set by the Belgian Dries Feremans the following year. More importantly, recycling centres and organisations have often partnered the events to ensure that the phones are recycled. At the time of the first championships, it was thought that there were phones lying in thousands of lakes and landfills in Finland. Phone batteries can become toxic waste, so this bizarre contest may spur people to help the environment by recycling their old devices.

Upon disembarkation, we followed our fellow passengers, who all seemed to be heading towards the area where most of the historic sites are located. As our return ferry was scheduled to depart in a few hours, we were keen to commence the sightseeing as soon as possible. Bearing in mind we were in a capital city, the sloping streets seemed remarkably quiet. Then again, it was a Sunday and Finland is one of the most sparsely populated countries in Europe. There are estimated to be 42 people per square mile in Finland, whilst the comparative figure for the United Kingdom is 725. Unsurprisingly, the tiny principality of Monaco is the most densely populated sovereign state in Europe, with just over 49,000 people per square mile.

Despite all of this, I would have expected Helsinki, which is home to more than a quarter of the 5.5 million people in Finland, to be much busier than it was. The beautiful summer weather was surely enough reason to venture outside. Perhaps the residents of Helsinki had used the weekend break to temporarily escape the city and visit the spectacular scenery that Finland is known for. After all, around three-quarters of the country is forested and there are 188,000 lakes. The phrase *Jokamiehen Oikeudet* demonstrates how Finns cherish their natural landscape. This translates to 'Everyman's Right,' and refers to the notion that all residents and visitors should have the freedom to roam the land. The public have the right to access most areas for recreational use and to enjoy the countryside, as long as they are respectful of the environment and its wildlife.

We were soon walking through a park and admiring its colourful flowers and trees. Although crafted by human beings rather than nature, Esplanadi was an indication of the importance of green spaces to the people of Finland. There was not a cloud in the vibrant-blue sky and the temperature was thoroughly agreeable; this was a pleasant introduction to the heart of the city. We were encountering more people now, but nowhere near as many as one would usually find in a European capital.

Perhaps they were paying homage to Johan Ludvig Runeberg, whose statue stands in the centre of the park. Regarded as a national poet of Finland, he penned the original Swedish lyrics to "Maamme", which has been adopted as the unofficial national anthem of Finland. There is no Finnish law regarding an official national anthem, but "Maame", which translates to "Our Land," has been established by convention over the years. The same melody is used for the Estonian national anthem, whilst the lyrics are similar to those used in the anthems of Norway and Sweden. Riveting stuff, I know.

More likely reasons for the increasing number of humans included the weather, the possibility that people were starting to emerge from their Sunday church service, or that they were on the lookout for somewhere to have lunch. Kappeli, which has had a prime location in the park for over 150 years, seemed to be a fashionable and expensive-looking place to dine in. The terrace provides a picturesque setting for a meal, although I expect that the prices would have been beyond our budget. There were plenty of people enjoying a cup of coffee, which did not come as a surprise, given that Finland has the highest per capita coffee consumption of any country in the world. On average, each person consumes over ten kilograms per year. It is unclear whether the long, cold, dark winters contribute to its popularity, but drinking coffee has become an important part of Finnish culture. This is done with most meals, in addition to several other times each day. There is even a law stating that workers must be given two daily coffee breaks in addition to a thirty-minute lunchbreak.

Almost immediately upon exiting the park, we were stood in front of Helsinki City Hall. Overlooking the waterfront and Market Square, the elegant pastel-blue building had the look of a posh hotel, which is what it originally served as. Completed in 1833, it was converted into an administrative building in the early-twentieth century before it was redesigned and given a more modern appearance in the late-1960s. We watched a tram, which belonged to one of the world's oldest electrified tram networks, glide past before we headed towards the nearby Presidential Palace.

The former Russian Imperial Palace was used as a hospital during the First World War, but the nineteenth-century pastel-yellow building is now one of three official residences of the President of Finland. Renovation work was taking place, of course, so the presence of cranes and scaffolding rather diminished its appearance.

Our whistle-stop tour of Helsinki continued as we crossed Katajanokka Canal in order to visit Uspenski Cathedral. From its position upon a hillside, the largest Orthodox church in western Europe looms large over the surrounding area. Emperor Alexander II was the sovereign of the Grand Duchy of Finland during the cathedral's construction in the 1860s. The golden copulas of the red-brick building were a clear sign of the Russian impact on Finnish history.

The *Clash of Clans* and *Angry Birds* franchises, which have spawned countless video games that have been downloaded to mobile phones all over the world, were created in Finland, but it was an angry wasp that I was about to clash with. Whilst we were admiring the imposing building in front of us, I heard an ominous buzzing sound by my ear before I felt something land on my neck.

"There is a wasp on you – stay still and I'll try to shoo it away," Mum instructed.

Unfortunately, her efforts only guided the vicious beast down the back of my Johan Cruyff T-shirt. Trapped between my skin and the fabric of my clothing, it lashed out by sinking its venomous stinger into my upper back. Having spent my life terrified by the prospect of being stung, to the extent that I would freeze whenever a wasp was within ten metres of me, it was finally time to experience the agony that can be inflicted by these flying devils. I felt a sharp pain as if someone had stuck a drawing pin in my back. This soon turned into a burning sensation.

"It's starting to swell," Mum informed me.

Although she looked dismayed that she had inadvertently played her part in the sequence of events leading to my horrific assault, Mum came to the rescue. Whatever crisis occurs, she invariably has some obscure item to remedy it. Not only that, but she often carries supplies that can be used in a potentially tricky situation when out and about. Mum is probably one of the few people on this planet who would have taken an antihistamine cream with her on a long weekend in Estonia and Finland, on the off chance that someone would get stung by a wasp. After rummaging through her handbag, and sorting through other unusual but theoretically useful items, she produced the cream.

"See, this is why I carry these things with me!" she declared.

"Although I'm grateful that you have it, I always find it strange that you carry these items around with you!"

"That's what mums do!"

After she applied the cream to the affected area, we walked to the city's other famous cathedral. Located on the edge of Senate Square, Helsinki Cathedral is arguably the symbol of the city. Constructed in the Neo-Classical style, it is one of several buildings designed by Carl Ludvig Engel surrounding the square. The immaculate white structure, complete with five green domes, has a colonnade and a pediment on each of its four façades, in addition to rooftop statues of the Twelve Apostles watching over the city. The cathedral was inaugurated in 1852, twelve years after Engel's death.

After a passer-by kindly asked if we would like to have our photograph taken, we posed by the colossal staircase in front of the sixty-two-metre-tall building. Mum was wearing a T-shirt that had several phrases written on it, including 'I Love Disco' and 'Get on the Dancefloor.' At least it was a significant improvement from 'Twerk or Treat?' If Mum had been wearing that garment, I would have feared that the man taking our photograph would have requested one of the options on offer.

We returned to the centre of the square to inspect the statue of Alexander II. The sight of the former Russian Emperor standing in the political and religious heart of Finland once again highlighted how the country's history has been influenced by its giant neighbour. There were calls to remove the statue following the establishment of Finnish independence in 1917, but its enduring presence hints at the close relationship between the respective nations, even if this is largely due to Finland's pragmatic approach to the significant presence across the border.

Facing Helsinki Cathedral, we could see the main building of the University of Helsinki to our left and the Government Palace, which houses the Prime Minister's Office and other governmental departments, on the opposite side of the square. Both are a pastel-yellow colour, which seems to have been in fashion when many of the historic buildings in the city were erected.

"We have already seen the Presidential Palace – so Finland has a Prime Minister and a President?" Mum asked.

"Apparently, the President no longer has much authority over domestic policy but remains a key figure in foreign affairs. From what I can gather, the Prime Minister and government oversee the running of the country and its day-to-day business."

Six years after our visit, the newly-elected Finnish government made headlines across the globe. At thirty-four years of age, Sanna Marin became the world's youngest democratically-elected state leader and the youngest Prime Minister in Finland's history. All five party leaders of her coalition government were female and most were under the age of forty. The appointment of what was regarded as a progressive government has been hailed by many, with the country scoring relatively highly in the EIGE's Gender Equality Index in recent years, although there has been the inevitable criticism from some conservative members of society.

We did not enter the city's places of worship – I am unsure if we would have been allowed to, given that it was a Sunday – nor any of the government buildings, including Parliament House, which is around 1.5 kilometres from Senate Square. Aware of our time constraints, I led us to a nearby area where a cluster of significant buildings are located. The Ateneum, which is one of three museums that form the Finnish National Gallery, houses one of the largest collections of classical art in the country. It is a grand nineteenth-century building that has decorative features of celebrated artists, including Raphael, Phidias and Bramante.

Helsinki Central Station is not only the city's main transport hub but also a wonderful piece of architecture. Designed by Eliel Saarinen and opened in 1919, the Art Nouveau granite building is best known for its 48.5-metre-high clock tower and the statues holding spherical lamps either side of the main entrance. Considered ahead of its time, there is a huge arched window above the entrance that has similarities to many of the Art Deco train stations that later became popular in America.

The Finnish National Theatre stands adjacent to Central Station. Completed in 1902, the National Romantic building is symbolic of the importance of the arts. At the time of its construction, there was a growing movement to preserve the cultural identity of the country, which eventually contributed to the establishment of independence from the Russian Empire in 1917. It has been claimed that there are numerous spirits who haunt the theatre, including the ghost of the actor Urho Somersalmi, who had worked in the National Theatre and within the film industry. Previously awarded the Pro Finlandia Medal of the Order of the Lion of Finland, he was presented with an axe by the Finnish Actors' Union. In 1952, he used this to kill his wife, Aili, before hanging himself. Although I am rather dubious as to whether any murderous ghosts haunt the theatre, there is definitely a statue of the celebrated writer Aleksis Kivi in front of the building.

Feeling hungry, and aware that it would be wise to have lunch well before our ferry was scheduled to depart, we began looking for a suitable restaurant to dine in. Many establishments were closed because it was a Sunday, and the ones that were open all had astronomical prices. This did not come as a huge surprise, given that we were in the capital city of one of the most expensive countries in Europe. Unwilling to pay up to eighty euros for a bite to eat, we returned to the harbourside. Entering the nineteenth-century Old Market Hall was an option, but we noticed that there were lots of food stalls in Market Square. For ten euros, Mum and I both had a mixed plate of fish that are popular in Finland, including salmon, trout, perch and herring, which was accompanied by a mountain of vegetables.

The only negative was that I once again revealed my tendency to rely on other people speaking English rather than attempting to learn some basic phrases in the local language. Ordering food from the stall was the first time that we had been forced to speak to anyone Finnish. Embarrassingly, I mumbled something about fish and pointed towards the board that was advertising the mixed plate. The woman serving us spoke fluent English and wore what appeared to be a genuine smile. A lack of confidence, in addition to a good dollop of laziness, has contributed to my hesitancy to learn many of the languages belonging to the countries I have visited. In my defence, the Finnish language has a reputation for being tricky to get to grips with. For example, there are twenty-nine letters in their alphabet and they use many compound words. This includes one of the world's longest words, *lentokonesuihkuturbiinimoottoriapumekaanikkoaliupseerioppilas*, which apparently means 'aeroplane jet turbine engine auxiliary mechanic non-commissioned officer student.' Thank goodness that I did not have to say that to anyone in Helsinki! Not that I can think of any scenario in which I would need to utter that rather ridiculous word.

I had been wary of having food from a market stall, but it was delicious. The lively atmosphere of the market, the warm weather and the multitude of boats meant that the harbourside provided a pleasant setting for our meal. Even the potential eyesore of pirate ships catering for tourists failed to diminish the aesthetics.

It was soon time to head back to the ferry departure point. If we'd had more time at our disposal, we could have visited some of the other popular attractions. Kamppi Chapel is an unusual structure that provides a quiet place for reflection within the busiest city in Finland, whilst Temppeliaukio Church is another unique religious building, as it has been hewn from bedrock. We did not get to see the well-known monument dedicated to the composer Jean Sibelius nor the remaining wooden house districts that were built for the 'working class' in the early-twentieth century. More adventurous tourists may wish to visit Linnanmäki, which is an amusement park that was built in 1950.

I relayed some more Finland-related information to Mum on the ferry back to Tallinn.

"Do you know that Finland is regarded as one of the world's happiest countries? They have conducted some polls in recent years and Finland ranked near the top."

"People seemed happy enough, although we didn't really speak to anyone!" Mum replied.

"Maybe that's because we are not as happy as Finnish people!"

Finland has rocketed up the charts since our visit, claiming top spot on the United Nations' World Happiness Report for three consecutive years from 2018 to 2020.

"It is also regarded as one of the safest countries in the world," I continued. "There have been experiments in which researchers left wallets in public places so that they could observe how people reacted. Apparently, most of the wallets were handed in or returned, further enhancing the country's image."

"It felt like a safe and friendly place."

"I did get stung by a wasp though!"

I rattled off some more regurgitated information: "There are more saunas per capita here than anywhere else, the Northern Lights can be seen from much of Finland, and it is the home of Santa Claus!"

"Santa lives here? Really?"

"Lapland has long been associated with Father Christmas, which has provided a boost to the Finnish economy."

"So, there is a lot we didn't see."

The return journey, first to Tallinn, then on to Manchester the following day, went smoothly. The trip had been a roaring success, with two delightful cities visited in one long weekend. If it was ever in doubt, my enthusiasm for travelling had been restored.

BEYOND THE WALL

11: *SUN, SEA AND BLOODSHED*
BENALMÁDENA, TORREMOLINOS AND SEVILLE, SPAIN
SEPTEMBER 2013

"I am looking forward to showing you around Benalmádena. Me and my family have created so many memories there," Carol stated whilst we were midway through our flight to the south of Spain.

"What's it like? I've always imagined it's full of generic holiday resorts and British ex-pats. It's funny that we call them ex-pats rather than migrants – I guess people view things differently when the shoe is on the other foot."

"It's lovely. Yes, there are lots of Brits, but there are authentic Spanish places too. I know you will like it."

The region clearly meant a lot to her. Her parents, Bert and Dorothy, used to holiday there every year. Since her mother sadly passed away, Carol and her sister, Michelle, take Bert back to Benalmádena every Autumn. The family have made friends there over the past couple of decades, so this was more than just a holiday destination to them. However, I had a pre-conceived idea of what the Costa del Sol was like: boozy Brits, tacky resorts and a distinct lack of Spanish culture. I wanted to see historic sites and learn about the region, but I feared that the next ten days would be akin to spending the time in Blackpool during a heatwave.

"It feels strange to say it, but we are heading towards somewhere that was created by a dictator. In fact, holidaymakers flooded the area whilst his authoritarian regime instilled fear into its population," I mused.

"Are you talking about Franco?"

"Yes, the Spanish tourism industry took off under his rule. Foreign visitors enjoyed luxurious breaks in the sun, either unaware of or unmoved by the terrible things occurring there."

Carol and I were indeed following in the footsteps of millions by heading to a holiday resort created by a fascist dictatorship. The Costa del Sol may have become one of the world's most popular tourist destinations, and synonymous with package holidays, but it was not so long ago that this stretch of coastline was home to small fishing villages rather than scores of enormous hotels full of international visitors. There had been attempts to entice tourists to the province of Málaga during the early part of the twentieth century, but the Spanish Civil War soon put a halt to that.

Often regarded as a pre-cursor to the Second World War, the fighting took place between 1936 and 1939. Led by General Francisco Franco, various right-wing factions formed a Nationalist alliance that would eventually overthrow the Republican government. The opponents of the Nationalists did not show the same level of unity, and were undermined by internal conflict between Communists, Anarchists, Socialists and those seeking independence for Catalonia and the Basque Country.

In December 1936, George Orwell travelled to Barcelona to join the Republican battle against the Nationalists. Having sustained a gunshot wound to the throat, he returned to England the following summer, where he wrote *Homage to Catalonia*. In a section of the book, he recalls his dismay at encountering fighting between what should have been left-wing allies. His experience of the war, and the subsequent establishment of a totalitarian state, is thought to have partly inspired the dark themes of his novels *Animal Farm* and *Nineteen Eighty-Four*.

Both sides inflicted atrocities on a scale rarely seen before, with a frightening prevalence of those willing to eradicate their ideological opponents. Franco's forces carried out purges of areas they had captured, with bodies often left in mass graves. For this reason, and because the statistics and the narrative were re-imagined by Franco's victorious regime, the volume of death incurred at the hands of the Nationalists during and after the war is difficult to determine. Most common estimates place the total figure of lives lost in the conflict in the 250,000 to 500,000 range. In addition to this, many Republican women were raped by Nationalist forces, and hundreds of thousands of people were sent to concentration camps or conscripted to fight in Franco's army. There have recently been efforts to exhume bodies from suspected mass graves in the hope of identifying as many of the 100,000-plus people who disappeared, presumed dead, during or after the war.

Many of the major world powers had signed a non-intervention agreement, but the fascist regimes of Adolf Hitler and Benito Mussolini soon aided the Nationalist cause, whilst Stalin's Soviet Union subsequently supplied some old weapons to the Communists and an amount of manpower small enough not to raise too many eyebrows. The United Kingdom and the United States stuck to the agreement, most likely due to a fear of entering a war that had the potential to escalate into a global conflict, and because appetite for intervention had been diminished due to the fact that thousands of Catholics were executed by Republican supporters.

Franco's totalitarian dictatorship continued to punish and silence its opponents in the post-war years. It remained largely isolated from the international community until the 1950s, when a shift in the regime's economic policy to one that required engagement with the wider world, together with the Americans seeking anti-Communist allies during the Cold War era, resulted in the normalisation of relations with many countries. It was at this point that Spain rekindled the idea of building up its tourism industry. Luxurious resorts were built in Marbella and on the southern coast, which was branded the 'Costa del Sol,' or the 'Coast of the Sun.' Despite the ongoing oppression of the Spanish population, the likes of Grace Kelly and Marlon Brando jetted in for glamorous holidays. This helped cultivate a fashionable image that attracted holidaymakers from across Europe and further afield.

Málaga Airport, which Carol and I were flying to, was expanded in the 1960s to accommodate the increasing number of visitors. Tourism played a huge part in the resurgent Spanish economy, which saw growth in this period second only to Japan. Franco's dictatorship had started to become more open and liberal by the time that he stepped down as Prime Minister in 1973, at which point he had already chosen Juan Carlos I as his successor as head of state. After Franco's death two years later, Juan Carlos became the King of Spain and subsequently guided the country along the path to democracy.

The history of Spain raises an issue for travellers: is it suitable for tourists to visit a country, or region, that is being ruled by a regime that brutally oppresses its population? The Costa del Sol was once full of holidaymakers who were unintentionally putting money into the coffers of a dictatorship and legitimising the ruling powers. Some people will say that tourists should refrain from visiting such places, whereas others will point to the probability that Spain's economic boom hastened the country's transition to democracy. I am not going to attempt to provide a definitive solution to that dilemma, but I have travelled to many countries that have a dubious human rights record. I have discussed some of the areas of concern regarding China in previous chapters, but I have also been to the likes of the United Arab Emirates, where people who fall foul of the authorities are subjected to arbitrary arrest and ill-treatment. Migrant workers are vulnerable to abuse and exploitation, whilst criticism of the government can lead to imprisonment. However, the country is more liberal than many others in the region, most likely due to its desire to maintain a respectable global image and attract Western tourists. It can be debated whether visiting the country helps or hinders the situation.

My trip to Cuba in 2017 further highlighted this issue. Although the Cuban government provides its citizens with education, healthcare, housing and some basic amenities free of charge, it is known for political repression. The picture is complicated by the economic squeeze caused by the United States' embargo, which the United Nations General Assembly has consistently condemned. Overall, I left the island with a feeling that at least some of the Cuban population were benefitting from the increase in international visitors – that is the impression I gained from the people we chatted to. This has aided the economy, particularly for those fortunate enough to work within the tourism industry, and it has coincided with the ruling Communist Party softening its stance on certain issues. Perhaps it is possible to support the tourism industry, and the local people it benefits, whilst also applying pressure on the current regime. Perhaps it is not.

At the time of our trip, the United States and Cuba had taken tentative steps to re-establish diplomatic relations and the Caribbean island nation seemed to be inching towards becoming a slightly more open and liberal state. Unfortunately, the relationship between the two countries has subsequently deteriorated and there has been a recent wave of protests against the government. Such gains are fragile, it would seem.

One thing I can be certain of is the fact that I would not feel comfortable holidaying in a region where the most horrendous crimes against humanity are currently taking place. For example, taking selfies in Xinjiang, where Uighurs are being subjected to genocide and other atrocities, seems highly inappropriate at this time.

Back on the plane heading towards Málaga, some of our fellow passengers were discussing more light-hearted affairs: "I can't wait to get on the golf course. Then we'll head over to Gibraltar, which is great because it's just like Britain in the sun. Lots of cheap drinks and golf – happy days!"

This did little to alleviate my concerns about spending ten days in a place that I feared would be like a sunnier version of Skegness.

After touching down at Málaga Airport, we encountered the most chaotic baggage carousel that either of us had ever seen. Following a long delay, luggage finally descended onto the conveyor belt in a haphazard manner. Suitcases were being dropped at breakneck speed, inevitably leading to items landing on top of others. Some did not pass through the opening in the wall back to the loading area, causing a pile-up. This soon turned into an almighty mess, with dozens of cases either falling off the carousel or jamming against the stationary items blocking the route. We all waited for a member of staff to resolve the issue, but no one came to the rescue and suitcases continued to be dropped onto the conveyor belt. More assertive passengers eventually lost patience and jumped onto the carousel to remove the clogged items or retrieve their own luggage. Fortunately, I did not have to do so, as our cases glided past once the backlog had been cleared. "Ridiculous! What a shambles!" muttered one disgruntled passenger. Hopefully, this was not an indication of what lay ahead.

We took a taxi to our hotel, which had a Torremolinos address but was just yards away from Benalmádena Marina. I could see glimpses of Málaga through the window, but we would not explore the city for another couple of years. Miley Cyrus's "Wrecking Ball" was booming out from the radio, which did not provide the traditional Spanish musical welcome that I had been hoping for. Strangely, this song seemed to be aired more than any other during our trip.

Carol and I were staying in a private apartment in what was then known as Sol Aloha Puerto – the hotel had been rebranded Sol House Mixed by Ibiza Rocks and had shifted its target audience to twenty-something partygoers by the time of our most recent visit. As we collected the key that had been left behind reception, we were afforded an enticing view of the sea at the end of the open-plan lobby. Carol had previously stayed there several times, so she led us to our room without hesitation.

"The key is not working," Carol informed me as she struggled to open the door with the old-fashioned key we had been given.

"I'll have a go," I offered, sensing an opportunity to impress her with my manliness. This failed, definitively proving that I possess no such characteristics.

"It's clearly the correct key, but it just won't turn. I'll have to phone Marijke," Carol declared, referring to her friend who owned the apartment.

Fortunately, Marijke informed us that she was in the area and could come to the hotel to sort out any issues with the key. As we would have to wait forty-five minutes, we headed to a bar that Carol was familiar with. Mirage was owned and operated by a couple from Preston, Mick and Debbie, who had become friends of Carol's family. They once helped Carol's parents when their passports and all of their money had been stolen by a thief on a motorbike. Mick and Debbie lent them some cash to see them through to the end of their holiday, which they promptly repaid upon their return to England.

"Starting our holiday with a shandy and a chip barm in Mirage has become a family tradition. I prefer Spanish food and culture, but I don't mind going there, as they have been good to my parents over the years," Carol explained to me.

"I can cope with a shandy and a chip barm!"

We made our way over to Mirage, more or less across the road from our hotel, where we were given a friendly greeting from a man with an accent that was unquestionably from the north of England: "Where's Bertie boy?! Mind you, you guys usually come in October."

"Hi Mick, Dad's not joining us on this trip. As usual, I will be coming back here with Dad and Sis next month to coincide with Mum and Dad's anniversary. This is an extra trip with my boyfriend, David," Carol enlightened him.

Mick shook my hand and introduced me to Debbie, before reeling off a series of playful remarks that I could not understand. I am unsure whether this was due to his accent or the 'northern banter' he was attempting. Either way, I smiled and pretended that I knew what he was talking about. As I had anticipated, it was a most British start to our Spanish holiday.

Having gleefully consumed our food and drink whilst soaking up the sun in the terrace, we returned to the hotel to meet Marijke, who performed a series of complicated manoeuvres that eventually unlocked the door.

"It's a bit temperamental. You just have to turn the key forty-three degrees to the left, then twenty-nine degrees to the right, complete seven revolutions, and achieve world peace. It will open every time if you do that," she advised us. Well, something to that effect.

We thanked her and entered the apartment, knowing that it would be a struggle each time we had to unlock the door. The apartment was as old-fashioned as the key, but it had a certain charm to it. The wooden décor provided a more homely feel than the clinical appearance of the hotel rooms we had peered into whilst walking down the corridors. The price was much more agreeable too!

I soon ran into trouble whilst unpacking my suitcase.

"I may need some help!" I shouted to Carol.

She ran into the bedroom, where she was presented with the bizarre sight of me struggling to keep my balance whilst holding aloft the mirrored door of the wardrobe that I had inadvertently removed. Carol helped me slide the door back into place before asking the inevitable question: "How on earth did you end up in that situation?!"

"It just came off when I tried to open it! It must be an old wardrobe."

Although the furniture may have seen better days, the view from our balcony was stunning. The sight of golden sand, a tranquil sea and a glorious blue sky was a reminder of why these resorts are so popular. We switched off the radio, which was once again playing "Wrecking Ball," and headed out to explore the surrounding area.

"We can walk along the promenade in either direction," Carol explained. "Benalmádena Marina is to our right, and if we turn the other way, a thirty-minute walk along La Carihuela will take us to the centre of Torremolinos. Shall we start by having a look around the marina?"

"Yeah, that sounds good."

"You're not wearing that bum bag though!"

"What's wrong with it?"

"It looks ridiculous. It's something my dad would wear. Actually, he would be too embarrassed to put that on!"

Ignoring my girlfriend's desperate pleas to ditch the bum bag, Carol and I began walking towards the marina. Although I was not hungry, the smell of smoked seafood coming from the *chiringuitos*, which is what the beachside food and drink establishments are known as, was intoxicating and appealing. There was a steady stream of tourists walking in either direction, which meant that the promenade was the ideal location for 'independent vendors.' Lots of people had set up shop there, with all their goods, mostly counterfeit clothing or generic souvenirs, laid out on cotton sheets.

"If the police enter the area, they quickly lift the sheet, making a sack, and run away. They will return ten minutes later and start selling again," Carol explained.

"It's a bit of a game then? It sounds as though the police will give them a nudge to move them along but make no serious effort to apprehend them. I guess the police need to make it look like they are doing something but don't want to spend all their time and resources on something they regard as trivial. Is that what it's like?"

"Yeah, that's pretty much it. No one gets hurt and no one really cares. Maybe I will buy you a fake Liverpool shirt!"

"No, thanks."

Part of me was glad that the vendors were effectively allowed to sell their knock-off goods. Most of them appeared to be people of African origin trying to make a living; taking away their goods would leave them with no means of earning money.

The owners of the expensive-looking apartments in Benalmádena

Marina clearly had no such problem. Located across the water from the shops we were perusing, the apartments matched the white-coloured buildings of the marina. There were plenty of boats in view, which was not surprising, given that there are over a thousand moorings. Clearly a source of local pride, it has been awarded the title of 'Best Marina in the World' on several occasions.

I will try not to bore you with too many details, but over the course of the next ten days, we purchased a couple of souvenirs and several ice creams whilst strolling through the marina. Nothing quite represents a summer holiday like desperately trying to eat an ice cream before it melts under the intense heat! We also took the three-kilometre walk to Torremolinos, where we bought a belt and a purse from one of the numerous leather stalls.

We were not on our feet for the entire duration though; plenty of time was spent perpendicular on the beach. Over the years, Carol and her family had become acquainted with Luis, the man responsible for the all-important commodity of sunbeds. He always stopped by for a friendly chat and made sure we found a favourable spot. Unfortunately, he could not prevent me from following another holiday tradition: getting sunburnt. Despite applying plenty of sunblock, a few blisters soon formed on my arms and chest. Mercifully, my sunburn was not too severe, and the blisters were most likely due to sweat rather than the degree of the burn.

We enjoyed meals in our favourite chiringuito, Larry's, and several restaurants that were being run by familiar faces. This included El Trillo, where Toni and another Luis served us with delicious food and the strongest Rioja I have ever tasted. Wherever we dined, each evening concluded with a visit to Champi. This small bar was our favourite establishment in the area, as well as a place where a few of our friends worked. Julio was co-owner with a Brit called Colin, whilst a British couple called Mark and Jenny both worked there. We felt at ease sat by the bar, chatting to staff all night whilst nibbling on tapas and drinking sangria. Although located in another country, it was the closest we had come to finding somewhere as welcoming as the famous bar featured in *Cheers*. It goes without saying, but everybody knew our name. Actually, that is a lie because no one had a clue what our names were apart from our friends behind the bar! Sadly, Julio and Colin recently sold Champi, and Mark and Jenny sought work elsewhere. Many happy times were spent in that bar.

Despite my reservations, I thoroughly enjoyed a relaxing break on the Costa del Sol. There were enough Spanish establishments to provide us with an authentic taste of Spain, and we also had British friends who always guaranteed a warm welcome.

Carol and I have returned to Torremolinos and Benalmádena several times but are yet to visit Castillo de Colomares, which is a huge monument dedicated to Christopher Columbus. I always feel a little uneasy when I see how Europeans celebrate the famous explorer; after all, the common narrative may be that he 'discovered' much of the Americas, but there were indigenous people there before his voyages. Not only were Native Americans robbed of their land, but the Taíno were all but eradicated from the Caribbean. Despite my reservations about paying homage to Columbus, it looks interesting enough to warrant a visit. Given that it was built between 1987 and 1994, it is hardly a site of historical significance, but it houses what some say is the smallest church in the world. Occupying just 1.96 square metres, it surely has a strong claim!

Torremolinos provides a solid base for exploring the south of Spain. Strong transport links and an abundance of tour operators mean that a multitude of other cities and regions can easily be reached. This is one of the reasons why I have been happy to return on numerous occasions. We had arranged a trip to Tangier for the penultimate day of our holiday, but first we were off to Seville.

* * *

"It will only take a couple of hours to reach Seville, so we will be there by lunchtime," I declared.

"That's quick!"

"Yeah, they have good trains here."

By the time of our visit, Spain had created an extensive network of high-speed rail. Whilst Britain's railways had almost been left to rot, the Spanish population were provided with services that covered long distances in the blink of an eye. This has been expanded in recent years, creating Europe's longest high-speed network, with a total length of over 3,000 kilometres. However, this is still dwarfed by the comparative figure for China.

We had taken a taxi from our hotel to Málaga-Maria Zambrano, which is a major transport hub with excellent links to many Spanish cities. Passengers are required to undergo a security check, consisting of a metal detector and an airport-style baggage scanner, when travelling on the high-speed rail network. Although some may consider this a nuisance, it made me wonder why such checks are not carried out for British train services. It is rather frightening to put yourself in the shoes of a terrorist and consider how easy it would be to bring a bomb onto a crowded train back in Britain.

The train was spacious and modern. We placed our luggage on the available racking, and without realising that there was allocated seating, settled down for the journey ahead. Moments later, a British couple informed us that we were sat in the wrong seats. Aside from the accent, I could tell that they were British because of the way they informed us of our error. Despite being fully aware that their place had been stolen, they politely said: "Excuse me, but I think you may be sat in our seats. I could be wrong, of course. I am really sorry for the inconvenience."

There is an endearing quality to the unnecessarily genteel way that many British people handle such situations, often going as far as apologising for pointing out someone else's mistake. After relocating to our allocated seats, we enjoyed a smooth and scenic journey through the mountainous terrain.

We were travelling between two cities that had atrocities inflicted upon them during the Spanish Civil War. In 1937, as Nationalist forces closed in on the Republican stronghold of Málaga, over 100,000 citizens fled towards Almería. As they made the arduous 200-kilometre journey, which took two weeks to complete, they were left exposed to aerial attacks. Thousands were slaughtered, many of them children, by the time that the 'Caravan of the Dead' reached Almería. Those who opted to stay in Málaga were rounded up then raped or killed, with their bodies dumped in mass graves.

Seville, which the Nationalists had established as a key base during the early stages of the war, had already experienced similar horrors. Republican supporters were executed en masse, with approximately three thousand people killed in the weeks that followed the 1936 military uprising. It is also thought that many political prisoners from nearby towns were sent to Seville for execution. Considering tourists can now travel in comfort to a city where people were once transported for such an evil purpose, this makes one appreciate the good fortune that they have been blessed with.

It was a short walk from Sevilla-Santa Justa railway station to our accommodation for the next couple of nights. I had booked a room at Hotel Patio de las Cruces for just ninety euros. Locating this small establishment whilst dragging our cases in the unrelenting heat was no easy task. The sight of what appeared to be a small section of the remnants of the ancient city walls provided some fleeting interest, but we were focused on locating our hotel. Like a true hero, I eventually guided us to our destination.

"Hola! English? Please can I see your passports?" asked the elderly man behind the counter.

"We've not brought them. I never thought to pack them, as we were only travelling within Spain," I whispered to Carol, dreading the prospect of having to abandon the trip and take the next train back to Málaga.

I attempted to look innocent and trustworthy as I informed the hotel proprietor of the situation.

"It is OK. Do you have any other documentation?" he asked.

We showed him our booking confirmation and Carol's driving licence. After a worrisome pause, he indicated that he would accept this, most likely because the tiny hotel could not afford to lose custom.

Hotel Patio de las Cruces was delightful. There were plants hanging down from the balconies above the charming courtyard, which had an open feel to it. Our room on the second floor was basic but good enough to serve as a place to recharge our batteries in between our explorations of the city.

We were soon roaming around the narrow streets of the historic city centre. It was a hive of activity, with a multitude of shops, bars and restaurants in operation. The sight of people stood next to barrels that served as tables only big enough to accommodate one plate and a couple of glasses fitted in with our pre-conceived image of the bustling *bodegas* of this part of Spain. Sightseeing was the first item on the menu though.

The sixteenth-century Catedral de Santa María de la Sede is the world's largest Gothic church. It took over a hundred years to build the cathedral on the site where the city's mosque once stood. Occupying an area of around 11,500 square metres, Carol and I were blown away by the sheer size of it. La Giralda is perhaps its most well-known feature. The 105-metre-high bell tower was converted from the minaret of the mosque that was present during Moorish rule.

Indeed, many of the historic sites of Andalucía reflect the period between the eighth and the late-fifteenth centuries when the Moors, specifically the Almohads from North Africa, controlled much of the Iberian Peninsula. The regime introduced Muslim culture, traditions and architecture to this part of Europe. Cities such as Córdoba, Granada and Sevilla, known as Seville in the English language, gained a reputation for impressive art, scientific advancement and philosophical teaching. The whitewashed buildings that are commonplace in countryside villages, known as *pueblos blancos*, were established by the Moors. As with European empires, though, the bloodshed and despair caused by the invading forces should not be overlooked in favour of any supposed cultural advancement.

Built to demonstrate the region's wealth, the cathedral is now the symbol of the city. Carol and I admired the intricate detail of the façades before we paid a handful of euros to enter the building. As expected, there was a huge altar, extravagant statues and a multitude of artwork on display. Despite the stained-glass windows allowing some daylight to enter, the interior was as dark as one expects within a Gothic church.

"Christopher Columbus is buried here," I informed Carol.

His presence highlighted how he played a key role in establishing Spain as a global power. Although his voyages may have caused misery in the Americas, they marked the dawn of the 'Golden Age' of the Spanish Empire.

"Shall we find him or climb the bell tower?" I asked.

"Can we just move on to the palace? I don't know if I can face climbing the tower when it is thirty-six degrees outside!"

"I was hoping you would say that! Let's go to the palace."

The cathedral may have links to the Moors, but the scene outside was very much Spanish – a huge Roman Catholic church, rows of orange trees and the presence of numerous people offering horse-drawn carriage rides through the city.

"I feel sorry for the horses," Carol stated.

"It's so hot, and they are just stood about waiting to transport the next set of tourists."

"You can see loads of flies irritating them. Poor things."

The Alcázar of Seville is a royal palace built on the site of a former Moorish fortress near the cathedral. With a history going back to the tenth century, it is said to be the oldest European royal palace still in use. As the queue was not as lengthy as we had feared, we paid an admission fee of around ten euros to enter the lavish complex.

A young couple asked if I could take their photograph. I always dread receiving such requests – not because I am unwilling to help but due to the pressure of capturing the perfect image.

"Your finger is covering the lens," one of them informed me.

Not the best of starts. Thankfully, I held it together long enough to take a nice photograph and return the phone without dropping it on the floor, causing it to shatter into a thousand pieces.

The main gate, Puerta del León, looked like it belonged to a European medieval castle, but the rest of the complex had a completely different appearance. A series of beautiful courtyards, exotic gardens and wonderful *majolica* and *arista* tiles gave it a distinctly Moorish vibe. The Garden of the Pond and the small statue of Mercury were delightful, but the Patio de las Doncellas was the area that sticks in my mind most vividly. An elongated, rectangular reflecting pool was flanked by sunken gardens and surrounded by a gallery with serrated arches. The patio was used in Ridley Scott's film *Kingdom of Heaven*. The Salon de Embajadores, otherwise known as the Ambassadors Hall, was another stunning section of the palace. The colourful tiles of the ancient throne room, particularly those on the ceiling, were nothing short of spectacular.

Upon leaving the Alcázar, we wandered through the narrow, cobbled streets of the Santa Cruz neighbourhood, or *barrio* as it is known in Spanish. When Ferdinand III of Castille captured Seville from the Almohads in 1248, he confined the Jewish population to this part of the city. The labyrinth of quaint streets developed a distinctly separate culture from the rest of Seville until the joint Catholic Monarchs of Spain, King Ferdinand II of Aragon and Queen Isabella I of Castille, established the Spanish Inquisition in 1478. With practicing Jews and Muslims facing the threat of violence or expulsion, around two-thirds of the 300,000 Jewish people in Spain were forced to convert to Catholicism. It has been estimated that 150,000 people were prosecuted and up to 5,000 executed before the Inquisition was abolished in 1834.

"I can see why the neighbourhood is now one of Seville's most popular tourist attractions," I stated.

"The streets are so narrow that neighbours can almost shake hands from their respective balconies."

"Apparently, there is a balcony that inspired Shakespeare's *Romeo and Juliet*. Shall we check it out?"

"Yeah, that sounds nice."

We walked towards Plaza Alfaro, where we encountered a group of tourists taking photographs of an ordinary-looking balcony.

"This must be it. What do you think?" I asked.

"It's quite nice but doesn't look anything special."

"I think the *Romeo and Juliet* claims are rather dubious, but they were enough to bring us here!"

There were plenty of restaurants, bars and bodegas competing for our lunchtime custom. We avoided the crowded premises in Santa Cruz, opting to temporarily leave the historic quarter in order to scour the streets for a suitable place in which to dine. Most of the restaurants seemed to be spraying a cooling mist onto their outdoor dining areas. After making the most of the mist whilst dawdling in front of a sign advertising a wide range of *tapas*, we felt obliged to enter one such establishment. The wooden décor and the rows of pigs' legs hanging above the bar gave it an unmistakably Spanish vibe. We ordered a couple of glasses of Rioja and several tapas. Aside from *chorizo* and *jamón Ibérico*, I am unable to recall what dishes we opted for, but some of Seville's most famous offerings include pork loin served with whisky sauce, spinach and chickpeas, snails, and fried dog fish. Whatever we ate, I seem to remember it being delicious.

I have always appreciated small-plate food, not just for the variety of dishes one can consume in one sitting, but also the culture of accompanying a drink with a small bite to eat, perhaps just one *tapa*. Incidentally, the word *tapas* originates from *tapar*, which means 'to cover.' It is thought that taverns in Andalucía began covering glasses of sherry with thin slices of meat or bread to prevent fruit flies from plunging into customer's drinks between each sip. Salty food made customers thirstier, which was obviously favourable for the owner of the establishment. This practice eventually expanded so that the accompanying food became an important part of the drinking experience. Although Carol and I are not major consumers of alcohol, we love nothing more than a tapas crawl around the bars of a Spanish city.

The Torre del Oro, or 'Tower of Gold,' was the highlight of our late-afternoon sightseeing. Situated by the Guadalquivir River, its name reputedly derives from the golden shine it projects onto the river. The dodecagonal military watchtower was constructed by the Almohads in the thirteenth century, with lime and pressed hay amongst the building materials used. As much as I would like to tell you that I am referring to the citrus fruit, the lime in question is the calcium-containing mineral. Not quite as interesting as sticky rice or eggs.

Reaching a height of thirty-six metres, the tower is comprised of three sections, with the first level significantly taller and wider than the others. Its position by the Guadalquivir made it a key component of the city's defensive fortifications. The tower now houses a naval museum and a panoramic terrace, but we opted to cross one of the historic bridges, most likely the Puente de San Telmo, before embarking on an enjoyable slow-paced walk along the opposite riverbank. We also wandered through the streets of Los Remedios and Triana, districts that are said to have developed their own subcultures. The walk through this less crowded area was pleasant, although in truth, I am unable to recall much of what we encountered; however, we did see the small but impressive Capilla del Carmen, which is a colourful Moorish Revival chapel.

On our way back to our hotel, we passed the sixteenth-century Archivo de Indias building, which documents the 'Golden Age of the Spanish Empire.' We then spent a ludicrous amount of time lost in the maze of narrow streets of the historic centre. To the undoubted amusement of anyone who noticed, we must have passed through one section half-a-dozen times. Our hotel was agonisingly close, but we just could not make sense of the map. At least we were lost on the prettiest streets in Europe. We unexpectedly came across some spice stalls – I am referring to the spice that one may use in cooking rather than the 'zombie drug' that so many people have become addicted to in recent years.

I vaguely recall having some pork shoulder for dinner, but I may be mistaken.

Carol is a huge fan of dance and Latin culture, so she would have loved to have rounded off the night by watching a flamenco show. Unfortunately, I was aware of our dwindling cash reserves. We had left some money in our safe in Benalmádena, reasoning that it would be risky to keep all of our cash on our persons. The Flamenco shows can be expensive, especially those targeting tourists, so I made the case that we could watch a show the next time we were in the region. Part of me also feared somehow being dragged onto stage and made to dance in front of a raucous crowd. Carol was disappointed, but given our financial situation, she agreed that it was sensible to give the show a miss. I regret this decision; it is not often one has the opportunity to take in a dance show in the home of the performing art in question. It was akin to turning down the chance to watch a tango show in Buenos Aires!

Upon returning to our hotel room, it was Carol's turn to make a lamentable decision. She sounded a note of caution as I walked over to the air-conditioning unit: "I'm not sure we should use the air-con. It looks old and you hear stories about people dying from Legionnaires' disease after being exposed to dodgy air-con units. What do you think?"

"The chances of contracting Legionnaires' disease are miniscule, but you've planted the seed of doubt! I can't really say that we should use the air-con, as I will be the one that causes our death! It's so hot though, and the humidity is unbearable."

"We'll just have to cope. Sorry, I shouldn't have said anything."

"If it was on your mind, you did the right thing, I guess. I just hope we don't melt in the night."

* * *

After an uncomfortable night's sleep in a room that felt like a sauna, and a basic breakfast consisting of toast, tomato, ham and orange juice, it was time for more sightseeing. It felt even hotter outside than it had the previous day. I began to perspire from the instant we stepped out onto the street.

"We'll have to drink lots of water," Carol advised.

"Definitely. I've sweated out half my body weight since we've been here. There was an occasional breeze when we were by the coast in Benalmádena, but it's so humid here. It's like being in the tropics."

Plaza de España and the bullring were the most significant tourist attractions left on our itinerary. Our route to the former took us past Palacio de San Telmo. I felt that this grand building, constructed in the late-seventeenth century using the Baroque style, bore a greater resemblance to a European royal palace than the Alcázar we had visited the previous day. Originally serving as the Universidad de Mareantes, a school to educate children and train them as sailors, it was later used by the Railway Society and the Literary University, before being acquired by the Duke of Montpensier, who had been exiled from France following the Revolution of 1848. It was willed to the city of Seville, and then ceded to the Andalusian Autonomous Government in 1989. The huge building had a red and dark-yellow façade and an ornate portal reminiscent of the splendid marble of the Duomo di Milano. There were columns on either side of the main entrance, a balcony and a series of statues depicting figures from the world of art and science, and several esteemed Sevillians. Bizarrely, it looked like a section of a cathedral had been affixed to a royal palace.

The nearby Parque de María Luisa was once part of the grounds belonging to the Palacio de San Telmo. It is now a one-hundred-acre public park that is home to a variety of native and tropical plants, parakeets, swans and, most notably, a significant population of doves. Carol and I enjoyed this dedicated green space but were too hot to delve into the history of the numerous statues and fountains in the park. Apparently, one of the monuments is dedicated to Miguel de Cervantes, the celebrated Spanish writer best known for his novel *Don Quixote*. Although this is often regarded as the first modern novel, he spent most of his life in poverty and obscurity. In a familiar tale for writers, his fame and adulation largely came after his death in 1616. There is still hope for my literary success then!

"I'm so thirsty! We've already finished one water bottle; I'll have to buy a soft drink and save the rest of our water for later. Do you want one?" I asked Carol.

"Yes, please. I can't believe how hot and humid it is."

"It's like there's no air! The sun is unrelenting. At least you have a straw hat to offer some protection."

"I'm just glad I found a hat that fits me. I have a pea head, so most hats are usually too big. This was from the children's section!"

We also bought a couple of ice creams, but after just a second in the sun, they were more or less reduced to liquid form. One of the electronic information boards indicated that it was now thirty-eight degrees. It felt much hotter.

Occupying over 50,000 square metres, Plaza de España was built within the grounds of the park for the Ibero-American Exposition of 1929. The design of the plaza's huge semi-circular building borrowed from a mixture of different architectural styles, with a tower at each end. In front of it, there are four bridges representing the four kingdoms of

Spain, which span the 500-metre-canal that follows the curve of the building. There were no boats available to rent on the day of our visit, but they have become popular with tourists in recent years. Carol and I took it in turns to pose for photographs by the beautiful ceramic features on one of the bridges. Movie buffs are probably aware that the plaza featured in *Star Wars: Episode II – Attack of the Clones*.

There are forty-eight alcoves surrounding the building – one for each province of Spain, complete with the relevant tableau and map displayed on colourful ceramic tiles. Spanish tourists enjoy posing for photographs next to their respective province's display; Malaga was as close to a home as we had in Spain, so we took our photos in that alcove. Although we did not enter the buildings, which are now used as offices for government agencies and museums, it was hard not be impressed by the grand architecture, the dazzling ceramic tiles, the picturesque canal and the vast expanse of the plaza.

After a hearty lunch that included bull's tail, we made our way over to one of the city's most popular attractions. Considering what we had just eaten, perhaps it was fitting that we visited the bullring. Officially known as Plaza de Toros de la Real Maestranza de Caballería de Sevilla, it is one of the world's most historic bullfighting arenas. The 14,000-capacity bullring, complete with Baroque façade, hosts a series of events from Spring until early-Autumn, with the bullfights of the Feria de Abril considered the most prestigious. Carol and I are not fans of the gruesome spectacle, but we felt that a visit to this famous arena was a way of gaining an understanding of the city's history and culture. Although many younger citizens are appalled by bullfighting, its popularity endures amongst older generations. Despite our disapproval, we paid a small fee for a tour of the bullring.

We were informed that construction began in the mid-eighteenth century and that the electric atmosphere created by the crowd was legendary. Our tour took us through a small museum that displayed bulls' heads, *matadores*' extravagant outfits, weapons and memorabilia from bullfights from across the centuries. Our guide described how bullfighting was originally seen as a sport for the rich, and that being spotted at one of these events carried a sense of prestige. A prolific matador would be revered and earn the celebrity status that is now afforded to football players. We were shown the stalls where the bulls, which can weigh up to 600 kilograms, are kept and the chapel where fighters pray before entering the bullring. Apparently, around twenty per cent of bullfighters, otherwise known as *toreros*, end up requiring emergency treatment – the bulls are not so fortunate.

Whilst it was interesting to learn about the history of bullfighting, it was impossible to avoid thinking about the cruelty of parading the animals in front of large crowds, then taunting them for a prolonged period that is split into three distinct stages before the inevitable slaughter. After wounding the bull using a variety of weapons and methods, aggravating the animal in the process, the matador will attempt to pierce the heart or cause other fatal injuries. If this does not result in death, the bullfighter will then use a dagger to sever the spinal column.

Bulls are not the only animals killed during a bullfight. Men on horseback, known as *picadors*, jab the bull with lances at one stage of the proceedings, often resulting in the bull charging the horses. On top of the tens of thousands of bulls killed each year, scores of horses also perish. It says something about the brutality of it all that Heinrich Himmler, a man who was one of the main architects of the Holocaust, was reportedly so disgusted by what he witnessed at a bullfight in Madrid that he left early.

"I'm glad we visited, but I wouldn't want to watch a bullfight," Carol declared.

"It was informative, but I am still abhorred by the thought of bulls being subjected to such cruelty. Many areas of Spain have banned the sport – I wonder if that will ever happen here?"

The bullring was, of course, where the titular character of *Carmen* met her grisly demise. She was killed by a human rather than a bull.

Our final evening in Seville consisted of more tapas, wine and another unbearably hot night in our tiny hotel room. Half-way through the night, I could not bear it any longer, so I turned on the air-conditioning. We did not contract Legionnaires' disease.

It had been a marvellous trip to a vibrant city with its own distinctive culture. We may not have had time to visit any of the museums or the recently-built Metropol Parasol, which is one of the world's largest wooden structures, but our brief stay had exceeded expectations. After a pleasant train journey back to Málaga, and then a taxi ride to Benalmádena, we had a day to recharge our batteries before a quick jaunt to Tangier.

SUN, SEA AND BLOODSHED

12: *CONTINENT HOPPING*
TANGIER, MOROCCO
SEPTEMBER 2013

"I hope this is worth it," Carol remarked whilst holding back a yawn.

The tour operator was due to pick us up outside our hotel at six in the morning before driving us to Tarifa, the southernmost end of the Iberian Peninsula, where we would take the ferry to Tangier. After a whistle-stop tour of the Moroccan city, we would complete the gruelling return journey. A fourteen-hour round trip that required us to wake up at the crack of dawn and spend a considerable chunk of the day either on a coach or a ferry – I could understand Carol's concerns but the opportunity to visit a country, and a continent, that I had never previously stepped foot in was just too good to turn down.

"It will be an adventure. How often do you get the chance to travel to Africa and back in a day? We're continent hopping!" I enthused.

The usual concerns were present as our coach pulled up in front of the hotel. Would the tour operator have any record of our booking? Would we be informed that there was a change of plan because all ferries were cancelled due to adverse weather conditions? More realistically, would the only remaining seats be situated at opposite ends of the coach? Thankfully, no such problems materialised. Our guide, Paco, simply explained that we would all have to fill out arrival cards and keep these with our passports.

"I feel travelsick. Can you fill my card in for me?" Carol asked me. This was not the best start to what was likely to be a long and tiring day.

After picking up more guests in Fuengirola and Marbella, we tried to get some much-needed sleep. Unfortunately, we were dressed for a day spent in sweltering Morocco rather than sitting in an air-conditioned coach.

"I feel sick. It's cold, I'm tired and feeling queasy," a weary-looking Carol stated.

"Will you be OK? Do you think you will be sick?"

"No, I don't think so. I've taken some travelsick tablets. I'm sure I'll feel better soon."

Following a long and uncomfortable journey to Tarifa, it was time to catch the ferry across the Strait of Gibraltar.

"The ferry will take between an hour-and-a-half to two hours," Paco explained. "Please stay together as a group whilst we prepare to board."

The queue for the ferry was disorganised and slightly chaotic, with some passengers trying to push their way to the front. We are used to seeing images of refugees and migrants, often from Africa, desperately trying to reach Europe, but here there were crowds of people in a hurry to make the opposite journey. We were not fleeing genocide or abject poverty though; we were just popping over to North Africa for a day of sightseeing. Once again, I realised how privileged my life was.

"I feel much better now. The tablets must have worked," Carol declared midway through our journey.

"That's good but my stomach is churning now. I'm going to have to find a toilet."

I sincerely hoped that my stomach would settle. The prospect of frequently dashing to the toilet whilst roaming around Morocco, knowing that we would not be back at our hotel for over ten hours, was more than a touch concerning.

Upon arrival on Moroccan shores, Paco informed our group of twenty that a local guide would show us the sights of Tangier before returning us to his care. We said our goodbyes before boarding another coach.

"Hello, my name is Abdullah and I will be your guide. Welcome to Tangier. Have any of you been here before?"

There were a few mumbled responses indicating that none of us had previously visited the city before Abdullah provided some information about Tangier: "People used to call it the 'Door of Africa,' due to its position at the northern tip of the continent. The main languages here are a type of Arabic known as *Darija* and a standardised form of the Berber dialects. Fortunately for you, me and my fellow guide, Mustafa, speak English!"

The collective tiredness of the group translated into a somewhat unenthusiastic audience. We would only become livelier and more receptive to the information we were being given once we disembarked the coach and began exploring the city.

Undeterred by the sterile atmosphere, Abdullah continued to provide further insight into the region as our coach made the short journey from the port to the historic centre: "Tangier has a history going back to the tenth century BC. It became part of the Carthaginian Empire before being occupied by a series of ruling powers. The Ancient Greeks, the Romans and the Almohads all seized control of Tangier at some point. From the fifteenth century, European empires fought over the land, with it changing hands between the likes of the Portuguese and the Spanish. It was even given to King Charles II as a wedding present from the Portuguese! In 1923, it was declared an international zone under the control of France, Britain and Spain. Finally, the Kingdom of Morocco gained independence in 1956. Tangier's history has resulted in a melting pot of cultures and religions – Muslims, Jews, Christians, Africans, Arabs, Europeans. You will find it interesting!"

It was difficult to absorb what seemed like the entire history of Tangier whilst trying to ward off tiredness. Nevertheless, it was interesting to listen to a summary of the city's complicated past. Abdullah had not even mentioned the fact that Tangier was seized by the Spanish on the same day that the Nazis took Paris. Meanwhile, the titular city of the 1942 film *Casablanca* was under Vichy French control until it was captured by American forces during the allied invasion of North Africa just a few weeks before the iconic movie was released.

We had recently visited a Spanish city that had previously been occupied by invading forces from North Africa; now we had arrived in a North African city that had once been ruled by numerous European powers, including the Spanish. The land on either side of the Strait of Gibraltar has always been attractive due to its proximity to another continent and the strategic importance of being able to exert a level of authority over the passage between the Atlantic Ocean and the Mediterranean Sea. One only has to consider the fact that Gibraltar is a British Overseas Territory despite being affixed to mainland Spain, and Cueta is a Spanish enclave within Morocco.

Television news reports of African migrants being apprehended and turned away at the border in Cueta highlights the European absurdity regarding colonialism and migration. We are happy to cling on to land that we stole from other parts of the world, but when people from that region attempt to access that land, and therefore a better life, they are treated with disdain.

Meanwhile, Morocco has occupied most of the Western Sahara since 1975, when the Spanish relinquished control. The Sahrawi people, who have lived there for centuries, oppose the occupation, with accounts of mistreatment becoming increasingly common. There are countless examples of countries controlling lands that would logically belong to another nation, usually because of their strategic importance. The Russian annexation of Crimea in 2014 is often attributed to the fact that Russia does not have another warm water port – it rented its naval base in Sevastopol from Ukraine but now has direct access to this.

As the coach slowly moved through the traffic of Tangier, Abdullah pointed out some of the landmarks: "That is the minaret of Mosque Mohammed V. There are many mosques in the city. We will not enter any, but you will have the opportunity to take photographs of their exteriors. We passed through the Grand Socco earlier. It is the most famous marketplace in the city and has become a popular meeting point. As you saw, there are market stalls, heavy traffic and beautiful gardens."

Upon arriving at the Medina, which is the old quarter of Tangier, Abdullah advised us that although the dirham is the official currency of Morocco, euros are widely accepted. We disembarked in a rather unattractive car park but encountered a vibrant and intriguing place on the other side of the gate marking the entrance to the Medina. The whitewashed buildings, narrow alleyways and colourful markets were a visual delight, but I was most captivated by the different doors belonging to the houses. Some were wooden, others were forbidding iron structures, but each had unique decorative features and individual character.

Abdullah explained how each told its own story: "The doors inform us about the property. More elaborate designs and certain colours, such as green, indicate that the owner is wealthy and that the building may have importance to the city. There are sometimes other decorative clues as to what occupation the resident has or the what the purpose of the building is. Some even have separate knockers for the different residents, or different ones for men, women or children. Have a look around – there are all sorts of unique designs."

Although the architecture, culture and climate of Morocco has some similarities with Andalucía, the atmosphere was noticeably different. The maze of narrow streets we encountered was as vibrant as what we had seen in Seville, but there was a rawness here. The area was not as polished or as visibly accommodating for tourists, indicating that less money flowed through this city and that living conditions were not as favourable. Whilst I could see why relocating to southern Spain was generally a more attractive proposition for Europeans, North Africa offered something that is at the heart of what travellers are constantly seeking: a glimpse into a life that is totally different to theirs.

"Look over there," Abdullah instructed. "Café Baba is a legendary place where lots of famous people have visited. The Rolling Stones, Kofi Annan, Jimi Hendrix, the King of Spain and many more. I won't comment on who was more likely to have ordered mint tea and who indulged in the hashish that the café is renowned for, but there is a photograph of Keith Richards lighting up a pipe here!"

The café, and Tangier in general, was once a popular hangout for European and American artists and celebrities who were interested in hippie culture. This was a place where you could drink tea or coffee and smoke whatever you wanted. It did not look like a significant establishment; the stairs leading up to the entrance were in poor condition, whilst the white and pale-blue building was crying out for a lick of paint. We did not have time to enter the premises, but I suspect that it has retained its authenticity rather than pandering to tourists and becoming a sanitised version of what once existed.

"Look up at the rooftops – you may recognise them from Hollywood movies. Tangier has been a popular location for spies, both real and fictional. You may have seen James Bond or Jason Bourne jumping across the rooftops or running through the narrow streets," Abdullah said with a hint of pride. The films he had alluded to were *The Living Daylights* and *The Bourne Ultimatum*, both of which had scenes that were indeed set and filmed in Tangier.

Our tour through the Medina took us past the Tomb of Ibn Battuta, which is purportedly the final resting place of the Muslim scholar, judge and legendary explorer. He travelled through Central Asia, Southeast Asia, South Asia and the Iberian Peninsula, covering a cumulative distance greater than Marco Polo and Zheng He combined. As the tomb was locked, all we had to inspect was a small plaque on an otherwise nondescript street corner.

The Grand Mosque of Tangier was the next point of interest we were shown. Built on the site of a former Roman church, the historic mosque hosts Friday noon prayers and is a vital institution within the local community. It is situated by a small but notorious square known as Petit Socco, or Souq Dakhli. In addition to having a reputation for excellent mint tea, this was another area of Tangier that was popular with writers and artists. Although we were only afforded a limited view from our position on Rue de la Marine, we could still appreciate some of the mosque's architecture. The rectangular minaret was mostly white and green, with some multi-coloured tile mosaics adding to its splendour. Given the mosque's importance, it was not surprising to see a rather impressive entranceway. What I assumed was an iron gate was surrounded by a decorative green and white arch adorned with geometric motifs beneath a wooden canopy. The doors of Tangier rarely fail to impress.

Whilst traipsing through the streets of the Medina, and frequently wiping our brows due to the increasing level of sweat brought about by the searing heat, a few street vendors tried to sell their goods to various members of the group, with little success. One of them shouted "Bruce Lee!" whilst pointing at my T-shirt that displayed a large image of the legendary martial artist and film star. I desperately hoped that this did not indicate that I would be an easy target for opportunistic hawkers throughout the day. In any case, I ignored his sales pitch.

We were unable to dismiss such efforts at the next scheduled stop on our tour. After being led into a traditional chemist, the group had to listen to the owner talk profusely about the virtues of his products for over thirty minutes.

"Ladies and gentlemen, if there is one thing you purchase in Morocco it should be argan oil! Shampoo, face cream, soap – the most important ingredient is argan oil! This is extracted from the kernels of the argan tree, which is only found in Morocco and Algeria," he enthused.

Carol and I chuckle whenever we see an advert for a shampoo or cream containing argan oil. We are instantly transported back to the chemist in Tangier and can almost hear the man roll his Rs as he extolls the virtues of this seemingly magical ingredient. This highlights how travelling to other parts of the world can broaden one's knowledge and provide unusual memories that can be shared for eternity.

As the chemist provided vivid descriptions of the healing powers of numerous products, I discreetly glanced at the countless jars of seeds, oils, plants and herbs. It reminded me of an old sweet shop back in England, although I imagine that the contents of the jars were not as tasty. This type of prolonged sales talk comes with the territory when you book an organised tour. It may be unwanted and boring, but you must accept the fact that most tours will include at least one stop at a venue where there is a longstanding agreement with a merchant of some description. It is best to use this time to recharge your batteries before the next leg of the trip. A handful of people bought some products in the hope of alleviating their various health issues, so it was clearly a profitable arrangement.

We were all given a small piece of bread that we were instructed to dip in argan oil before eating. This traditional and popular Moroccan food item was reasonably tasty; it just felt bizarre to be consuming it having spent the last half-hour listening to the chemist tell us about how it is used in cosmetic and medicinal products!

We were soon being treated to a more substantial meal in the form of a lunch that was included in the price of the tour. There was another arrangement in place, with the eatery happy to provide block bookings for large groups of visitors, presumably at a discounted price. The restaurant was adorned with the type of intricate carpets and cushions one associates with North Africa. This was to be the first significant test for my stomach since I had felt unwell on the ferry. Carol enjoyed some lamb, but I stuck to the less adventurous options such as vegetables, *houmous* and *couscous*. The food was delicious, and more importantly, my stomach suffered no ill effects. Carol had a glass of tangerine juice with her meal – as the name suggests, tangerines originate from Tangier and the surrounding region – whereas I went for the safer bet of Moroccan mint tea. This immensely popular drink had a much sweeter taste than I had expected. It took a while to get used to the unusual flavour, but by the time I had consumed the contents of my cup, I gave it my approval.

Having been well fed, the group was led to the *kasbah*, or citadel, that presides over the Medina. Built after the Moroccans had reclaimed the city in 1684, the defences had to be restored due to the English blowing up the existing fortifications upon their departure. A self-contained fortified district was created, where government, military and judicial buildings were erected. Dar al-Makhzen, the Sultanate Palace, is the kasbah's crowning glory. Situated on one of the highest points of the city, it now serves as a museum and tourist attraction. In keeping with the rather rushed nature of our tour, we were not permitted to enter the palace. It is apparently as grand and luxurious as one expects from a former royal residence, but we had to settle for a brief examination of the splendour of its exterior.

The minaret of the Kasbah Mosque is more extravagant than those belonging to Mosque Mohammed V and the Grand Mosque. Unlike the traditional rectangular-shaped minarets we had previously seen, this was octagonal. Once again, there were multi-coloured tiles and geometric motifs, but they were part of a more aesthetically-pleasing structure. The charm of Tangier, even in the kasbah, was that such grandeur could be found amongst fading buildings and rundown streets.

Abdullah and Mustafa guided us to an open area by the walls of the kasbah where a trio of men wearing traditional beige robes – which I believe were the unisex, loose-fitting, short-sleeved *gandora* – were waiting for us. We were told that we would be treated to a performance from a snake charmer. This was another cosy arrangement between the tour operator that benefitted local people trying to make a living and tourists hoping to see a custom associated with Morocco. It soon became apparent that two of the men were the supporting cast, with their roles primarily involving tapping on a type of wooden-framed drum known as the *bendir*. The leader of the group, the snake charmer, placed a cloth bag on the floor and began playing some form of flute. The crowd collectively held its breath as what appeared to be a cobra emerged. It stood upright as if it was ready to attack. In reality, the snake most likely felt threatened.

Although snake charming has a long history in North Africa and Asia, it is increasingly seen as a cruel form of entertainment. The Indian authorities have taken steps to prohibit the practice in recent decades, but this has largely gone unchecked in Morocco. Most performing snakes have their fangs removed or their mouths sewn shut, with just enough of a gap left for the forked tongue to appear and trick tourists into thinking that the snake poses a danger to the charmer. This was almost certainly the case with the reptile we were watching, as the charmer picked it up and held it close to his face. He manoeuvred the snake in a multitude of directions whilst the audience gasped, buying into the illusion that he was risking his life. The sad truth is that the snake probably posed no threat to him and would soon die as a result of the enforced modifications to its mouth.

Whilst I disapprove of this practice, it must be noted that it is easier for me to take this position from my life of comfort and prosperity. Snake charmers are typically from poor backgrounds, often learning their trade from their parents in the hope of earning enough money to survive in the world. Animal cruelty is something I have encountered during my travels, but this frequently occurs out of desperation. Although bullfighting has historically provided a significant source of income, numerous regions in Spain have been able to ban it because they have alternative means of generating money. This is much harder for the average snake charmer in North Africa, as they may have no other qualifications or skills that would enable them to forge a living. For many, it is a stark choice between being cruel to an animal or not having the means to support themselves. Perhaps the best course of action is to avoid these tourist traps and decrease the demand for such events.

After the performance had concluded, we were taken into a large shop. The ground floor was filled with ceramics, furniture, pottery and decorative light fittings. It all looked delightful but most of the items were too big and delicate to transport back to Europe. At least not without paying extortionate shipping charges. We were then led upstairs, where hundreds of colourful and elaborate rugs were hung from the walls. A series of benches lined the room, a clear signal that we were about to be told to sit down whilst the shop owner bored us with a talk about the fabrics on display. Carol and I listened politely, feigning interest and willing the seconds away. Carpets and rugs are an important part of Berber and Moroccan culture, but a twenty-minute monologue extinguished any enthusiasm I had for them. They all seemed outlandishly expensive, so there was no prospect of us buying a rug anyway.

We were then taken back downstairs, where we were encouraged to find items that we were interested in purchasing. With shop attendants hovering, I decided that the best tactic was to move around the store to demonstrate a polite curiosity without lingering in any given section long enough for someone to pounce and subject us to a sales pitch. Having navigated our way through the shop without drawing unwanted attention, Abdullah informed us that we had thirty minutes to peruse the souq before reconvening. Already feeling apprehensive about persistent attempts to sell us all manner of useless trinkets, this was just about the last thing we wanted to hear.

"Mustafa! Please can I have a photo with you?" Carol asked.

I could sense the desperation in her voice, as if his presence would somehow ward off the advances of any street vendors. He politely posed for a photograph then left us to our own devices.

"Well, that killed about thirty seconds! We just have another twenty-nine-and-a-half minutes to go!" I muttered.

It did not take long before we were approached: "Bruce Lee! Would you like to buy a traditional Moroccan drum?"

"No, thanks. I don't want any instruments," I politely responded.

"They are very good quality. We can arrange a good price," he pleaded.

"Sorry, I do not need any drums. Maybe someone else in our group will buy them."

I had no intention of bartering for a set of drums that I would have no use for, but I did not want to seem rude or offensive. I looked around the souq and noticed an increasing number of people approaching tourists. When one man opened his wallet to pay for a souvenir, several hawkers descended upon him. I made a note not to make the same mistake. We eventually sought refuge in a shop. I was soon feeling confused when the owner called us over and placed a large photobook on the counter.

"Muhammad Ali, Mike Tyson, Franck Ribéry," he said whilst pointing to the photographs displayed on the open pages of the book.

I paused for a moment before realising that he was showing us a collection of celebrities who had converted to Islam. We now had the choice of returning to the chaos of the souq and the unwanted attention of street vendors or staying in the shop where a stranger would potentially try to convert us into Muslims. Deciding that the latter made us feel the most uncomfortable, we trudged back out into the souq. Thirty minutes seemed to last a lifetime, but we survived without purchasing anything we did not want or causing undue offense. As the group walked back to the coach, the man with the drums approached me again.

"I can sell them for ten euros. To be honest, I do not have much money, so this would be a big help for me."

As I pondered whether to buy the drums off him and then give them away, several other people gathered around trying to sell various items. I felt bad for the guy with the drums, as he seemed friendly and polite, but the presence of the growing crowd had discouraged me from reaching for my wallet. Upon boarding the coach, a young boy appeared and asked if we would like to buy some chewing gum. It was at this point that I realised that, as the man with the drums had alluded to, they were selling cheap items of little use as a more respectable alternative to asking for handouts. The boy with the chewing gum had underscored this reality. The coach drove away and I felt awful about how dismissive I had been. I had regarded the attempts to sell useless souvenirs as a nuisance, but I could easily have provided some financial assistance to someone without them having to feel embarrassed about asking for money.

A short coach journey took us to Cape Spartel, where we were given a few minutes to take photographs of the splendid views on offer. We could look out across the Strait of Gibraltar or admire the vast Atlantic Ocean. It was clear that this was an important area that provided a crucial link to the Mediterranean. Indeed, a key naval battle of the Spanish Civil War took place here in 1936. The Battle of Cape Espartel resulted in the Nationalists breaking the Republican blockade of the Strait of Gibraltar, securing a vital naval supply route during the early stages of the war. Carol's biggest concern, however, was the coastal wind making a mess of her hair whilst posing for photographs.

The nearby Caves of Hercules, as the name suggests, is a cave complex where, according to Roman legend, Hercules stayed prior to completing his eleventh labour. Conflicting stories state that Hercules either separated the land to create the Strait of Gibraltar or narrowed the strait to stop monsters entering the Mediterranean Sea. More realistically, the Phoenicians are said to have shaped the stunning caves, whilst the grooves in the walls are a legacy of the Berbers who quarried millstones. Abdullah informed us that we had a few minutes to inspect the interior of the complex and take photographs. Carol and I took a selfie that painted me in a most unflattering light. My proximity to the camera meant that my face was lit up by the flash, resulting in an image that made me look approximately ninety-five years old – Carol still laughs at this photograph. Thankfully, Mustafa offered to take another photo of us.

Upon exiting the caves, we had the option of paying a small fee for a camel ride. After a long day in the sun, we lacked the energy to take up this offer. Perhaps it was for the best, as I did not fancy being sprayed with camel spit. I imagine that this would be particularly unpleasant, considering that when they feel threatened they bring up the contents of their stomach and project this along with their saliva. Besides, the camels did not look thrilled at the prospect of carrying the weight of tourists on their backs. The sad sight of a camel shackled to the ground with a rope tied around its face was rather off-putting. I feel that camels highlight humans' complicated relationship with animals. They proved essential to the survival of desert dwellers such as the Berbers. Their ability to transport people and goods across difficult terrain, and survive long periods without food and water, meant that human life was possible in such places – although the experience may not have been so pleasant for the camels. Regardless, it just did not seem right to be exploiting them for entertainment purposes.

As I mentioned earlier, it is easier for me to say this coming from a life of relative luxury in Europe. The broader issue of how humans view animals can be a curious one – it is deemed acceptable to ride certain animals but not others; it is seen as normal to have selected animals as pets but strange to keep different species; and people regularly eat some animals, and their eggs, but are appalled at the prospect of consuming what they are not familiar with. I am not saying that there should be a clear-cut rule for any of the above, other than whether any obvious ill-treatment is occurring and whether there is a threat of extinction, but it can seem strange how people view different species.

The unexpected sight of Achakkar and Sidi Kacem beaches was a pleasant surprise. We did not have time to join the smattering of people indulging in a spot of sunbathing, but it looked as enticing as any Spanish stretch of sand. For some reason, I had not associated Morocco with beaches. Perhaps this was because in the West our image of Morocco consists of camels, deserts, bazaars and the Fez. In recent times, the Moroccan authorities have made substantial efforts to renovate coastal areas to attract more overseas tourists, with immaculate promenades installed, particularly in an area by the marina known as the Corniche.

Our tour of Tangier was more or less over. We just had to return to the port and take the ferry back to Spain. Our brief visit to Morocco had provided a glimpse of life in this fascinating North African country. We may not have had time for an in-depth exploration, but we had seen enough to at least gain a basic understanding of some aspects of Moroccan culture and history, even if we had barely scratched the surface. The places of interest that we had not visited gave an indication of some of the additional layers of Tangier's past. Plaza de Toros, the city's bullring, and Gran Teatro Cervantes, the theatre built in 1913, demonstrate the cultural legacy that the Spanish left behind. The Anglican Church of St. Andrew is a reminder of the significant English community that once existed here, whilst the American Legation was the first overseas property acquired by the United States government. More daring travellers can visit the Atlas Mountains or take the train to Marrakesh and experience the magical type of journey that inspired the Crosby, Stills and Nash song "Marrakesh Express."

Upon arrival at the port, we expressed our gratitude to Abdullah and Mustafa, verbally and financially, before following Paco onto our return ferry. I wonder how he occupied himself in Tangier for several hours. Taking a moment to admire the shimmering sea and the backdrop of the numerous minarets of Tangier was a fitting way to conclude our time in North Africa. The ferry and coach journey went smoothly, and with the aid of intermittent napping, did not seem to take as long as expected. By the time we were all being dropped off at our hotels, it was clear that some people were feeling agitated after a long and exhausting day.

"We are at the Riu Hotel," Paco announced to the group. "If you are staying here, it is time to get off the coach."

No one responded.

"OK, we will move onto the next hotel."

As the coach drove off, a stocky forty-something couple realised that they had just missed their stop.

"Hey! That is our hotel! You have gone past it!" the female half of the duo bellowed.

"I did announce that we were outside the Riu," Paco replied.

"We are staying at the Nautilus! You should have told us!"

"The hotel is called the Riu Nautilus. We were parked outside it for a minute, and I announced to the group that we were there."

"The Nautilus, you pig!" she shrieked.

"You will have to get off at the next stop. It is only a couple of hundred yards down the road," Paco informed them.

Our hotel was the next designated stop, of course. This led to an awkward situation when we got off the coach, because the couple were still berating Paco as I waited to tip him. I am always nervous when trying to discreetly tip someone, but with the angry couple in attendance, I felt even greater pressure to subtly hand over the cash. The words of Alan Partridge were rattling around in my mind: "Oh, you combined the card with the handshake. I used to do that but kept getting it wrong. Gave a papercut to a man from Nestlé."

Against all the odds, I heroically performed this task without inflicting any physical damage to Paco or prompting the angry couple to turn on us for rewarding their newfound nemesis. Carol and I still laugh about this angry confrontation. Completely out of the blue, I will occasionally say to Carol, "The Nautilus, you pig!"

We headed straight to Champi for some tapas and a nightcap. Mark and Jenny were working behind the bar, so we chatted to them about the trip.

"What did you think of Tangier?" Jenny asked.

"It was a good but long day," Carol replied.

"We went to Tangier a few years ago," Mark stated. "Jenny and I made the mistake of booking the overnight trip. We felt uncomfortable, as if everyone was eyeing us up. Interesting though. Glad we did it for the experience but wouldn't go back."

"It certainly takes you out of your comfort zone, but it was a fascinating day," I concurred. "Everyone we encountered seemed friendly enough. I'm just amazed that it's possible to travel to Africa and back in a day!"

An organised trip with fellow holidaymakers staying on the Costa del Sol may not have been a patch on the Great Wall of China trek, but it was special in its own way. It demonstrated Africa's proximity to Europe and provided some insight into the historical and cultural links between the two continents. The novelty of travelling to North Africa and back in a matter of hours gave me a different type of exhilaration than what I had felt in China. I guess it shows that even if your stay is brief and constrained by the nature of an organised tour, this does not mean that it is without merit. There are all sorts of travel experiences, each magnificent in their own way.

BEYOND THE WALL

13: A CHANGE OF COURSE
BARCELONA, SPAIN
OCTOBER 2013

I was excited about visiting Egypt – the Pyramids of Giza, Luxor, the Red Sea and an incalculable amount of history awaited us. That was until a military coup put a halt to that. In July 2013, the democratically-elected president, Mohamed Morsi, was removed from power after just one year in office. Several hundred people, perhaps even thousands, were killed during the ensuing protests. In the following years, the military crackdown on dissent has seen journalists imprisoned and caused concern amongst the international community. Morsi's short-lived presidency, and the subsequent coup d'état, took place not long after mass protests resulted in Hosni Mubarak resigning from office in 2011, bringing an end to his twenty-nine-year reign.

This was part of a wider movement commonly referred to as the Arab Spring. The ongoing instability in Syria, Yemen and Libya demonstrates how a country's troubles can remain, and possibly worsen, after an authoritarian regime is removed from power, or attempts are made to do so. It can also scupper the holiday plans of a privileged European hoping to take his mother on yet another overseas trip.

With Jet2 refusing to refund our flights, we were forced to switch to another destination that the airline serviced. After considering the average October weather patterns of the available options and bearing in mind that we would have to pay any additional costs if the flights were more expensive than our original ones, we decided to try something completely different: we booked a Mediterranean cruise that departed from Barcelona. I had always dismissed the notion of going on a cruise, as I had regarded them the exclusive domain of geriatrics. There had been a shift in consumer habits in recent years, however, with cruises becoming increasingly popular with younger people. I had also held the belief that you had to be extremely wealthy to afford a week-long jaunt around the Mediterranean. I was pleasantly surprised, therefore, to discover that our cruise cost approximately three-hundred pounds per person, which seemed good value considering it covered our accommodation, food and entertainment.

Less than a year after harbouring grand ambitions to join expeditions in remote corners of the planet, I had booked what is often regarded as one of the least worthwhile forms of travel. It was clear that any illusions of becoming an intrepid explorer were being pushed to one side whilst I juggled a nine-to-five job with my desire to visit as many countries as possible, no matter how briefly. Before the cruise, however, there was an opportunity to explore Barcelona for a second time.

* * *

I had previously visited Barcelona in 2011 with my friend Paul. He was more interested in football than culture, so I knew that the upcoming trip with my mother would certainly have a different dynamic to it. Our flights from Manchester to Barcelona were booked independently from the cruise, which caused me to worry about the possibility of our luggage being lost en route and the cruise company simply not caring. There was a considerable amount of relief, therefore, when both of our suitcases arrived intact at Josep Tarradellas Barcelona-El Prat Airport.

The Aeurobus to the city centre was cheap and efficient, dropping us off at Plaça de Catalunya around thirty minutes after departure. The public square marks the heart of the city, where several prominent streets converge. Large numbers of Catalan pro-independence protesters have gathered here in recent years, most notably on the National Day of Catalonia on the 11th of September. It is difficult to gauge how much of the Catalan population truly seeks independence from Spain, as many would prefer, or settle for, a greater level of autonomy and what they would regard as a fairer allocation of funds from central government. In any case, the long-standing argument had become more prominent by the time of our trip, with a pro-independence majority established in the Catalan Parliament for the first time in 2012. An independence referendum was held five years later, without the authorisation of the government in Madrid. Although over ninety per cent voted for independence, the low turnout of just forty-three per cent and the failure to meet international standards for elections meant that the result was declared null and void. Several Catalan separatist leaders were jailed for their part in the referendum, leading to significant protests on the streets of Barcelona.

Although there were no protestors, we had to negotiate our way through a sea of humanity, statues and fountains before locating La Rambla. It is one of the most celebrated pedestrian streets in Europe and is constantly buzzing with activity. Tourists seem to be drawn here, whether to eat in the countless restaurants, take photographs of the surrounding architecture or observe the army of street performers competing for visitors' currency. We had not even made it to our hotel before being lured here, suitcases still in hand.

Walking across various coloured-stone mosaics, we witnessed clowns on stilts, artists providing rapid-fire caricatures and mimes offering humorous entertainment to the throngs of passers-by. Some simply opted to dress up as robots or furry animals, which looked particularly unwise due to the sweltering mid-day heat. Their routine may have only involved standing completely still for hours on end, but I would have found it unbearable in temperatures hovering above twenty-five degrees. It was bad enough wearing jeans and a T-shirt. Fortunately, there were not any mischievous idiots knocking about. I have seen some YouTube videos of people taking things too far when trying to distract the stationary performers by touching their face and generally being unpleasant. I find myself almost punching the air in delight when one of these videos culminates in the performer lashing out at the troublemaker. I must stress that it is not often that I celebrate an act of grievous bodily harm!

The route to our hotel took us past the Font de Canaletes, which is the ornate drinking fountain where fans of Futbol Club Barcelona celebrate victories, the bustling market known as Mercat de la Boqueria and the nineteenth-century Gran Teatre del Liceu before we temporarily left this famous tree-lined street. It soon became apparent that we had made a good decision to book a couple of nights at the bizarre-sounding Hotel Best Autohogar. Our pleasant accommodation, situated on Avinguda del Paral·lel, was a short walk from the port area and some of the tourist attractions. With around forty-eight hours until embarkation, Mum and I deposited our luggage in our room and began our sightseeing by heading back to La Rambla.

Somehow resisting the urge to take my mother to the self-explanatory Museu de l'Erotica, I guided us along one of the streets leading to the Gothic Quarter, which is known as Barrio Gótico in Spanish and Barri Gótic in Catalan. As I had discovered during my previous visit to

Barcelona, this is where the city's cathedral is located. Many people incorrectly assume that Sagrada Família holds this distinction, but it is in fact a basilica. The Cathedral of the Holy Cross and Saint Eulàlia, understandably referred to as Barcelona Cathedral, is the most notable landmark of the surrounding area.

Legend states that Eulàlia, the co-patron saint of the city, was martyred when she was just thirteen. Having confronted the Roman governor Dacian due to his persecution of Christians, she was stripped naked and tortured. Unwilling to renounce her beliefs, she prayed that God would take her to heaven. It is said that a dove flew from her mouth upon her death and a snowstorm covered her exposed body. There are alternative versions to the story, including one stating that the Romans placed her in a barrel with knives stuck in it, before rolling her down a street that is now known as Baixada de Santa Eulàlia.

The thirteenth-century cathedral is exactly what you would expect a magnificent Gothic building to look like: dark and brooding yet ornate, with a multitude of gargoyles present on the roof, which reaches a height of over fifty metres. The staircase leading up to the cathedral is a popular meeting place for residents of the city. The interior is impressive but not particularly distinguishable from other Gothic cathedrals in Europe, where tall ceilings, grand altars and an almost gloomy atmosphere are the norm. I was unaware of some of the more unusual traditions though. Apparently, there are thirteen geese kept in its cloister, presumably representing each year of Eulàlia's life. A quirky tradition involving a dancing egg takes place at the cathedral each May or June for the Feast of Corpus Christi. A hollowed egg is placed over a water jet from a fountain, causing it to turn without falling. I imagine that the 'dance' is probably not as exciting as the name suggests.

The Gothic Quarter has other tourist attractions such as the Museum of the History of Barcelona and numerous public squares such as Plaça Reial, but I feel that the greatest joy comes from simply walking through the labyrinth of narrow, characteristic streets. The charming balconies overlooking the hustle and bustle below are my favourite feature. Not even the multitude of restaurants and bars can detract from the splendour of the oldest part of the city.

After re-joining La Rambla, Mum and I walked towards the opposite end of the street. I should point out that although I have been referring to La Rambla as one street, it is in fact a series of smaller streets that are often referred to as Las Ramblas, or Les Rambles in Catalan. Either way, the poet Federico Garcia Lorca declared that it was "the only street in the world which I wish would never end." I could understand why he was fond of it, but after seemingly traipsing up and down the 1.2 kilometre-length of La Rambla since we arrived in the city, I would not necessarily have agreed with his sentiment!

"Remember to look out for pickpockets," Mum cautioned for the umpteenth time.

"Don't worry, I keep a close eye on my belongings wherever I am."

Barcelona, and La Rambla in particular, has garnered a reputation as a place where opportunistic thieves frequently target tourists. I have not noticed anything untoward during any of my visits to the city, and I imagine that the odds of being robbed in the Catalan capital are similar to what they are in major cities like London and New York. Mind you, the nature of pickpocketing means that one would not notice this unless some of their valuables go missing.

"What is at the end of the street?" Mum asked.

"There is a huge monument dedicated to Christopher Columbus and that is where the port area is."

It was not long before we were facing the Columbus Monument. At sixty-metres tall, we could hardly miss it. The Catholic Monarchs Queen Isabella I and King Ferdinand V sponsored his voyage to the 'New World' in 1492, and the monument commemorates his return to Barcelona after his initial expedition. It is another reminder of how much the man born in Genoa – now part of Italy – has been revered in many European countries despite some of the dire consequences of his voyages.

"Apparently, there is a shuttle bus that regularly transports people between the cruise terminal and somewhere near the monument. I'm not sure exactly where that is though," I stated.

After aimlessly walking around for ten minutes, Mum began asking passers-by if they knew where it was. At the age of twenty-eight, I still needed my mother to ask people for help! We were eventually directed to one of the appropriate bus stops.

"At least it should be straightforward on embarkation day," I declared.

"Yes. I am glad you are thinking ahead. I always try to prepare for future journeys. You are becoming just like your mum!"

Maybe she was correct in her assertion that I was developing some of her traits. Either way, I was aware that I was old before my time. I preferred a quiet night in rather than a drunken night out, I did not swear, and I regularly went on holiday with my parents as opposed to 'going away with the lads.' Perhaps that just makes me a bit of a sad case rather than old!

We rounded off our day's sightseeing by heading to a couple of attractions that I had not had the pleasure of visiting during my last trip to Barcelona. A twenty-minute walk past the outskirts of the Gothic Quarter took us to the Arc de Triomf. Built for the 1888 Barcelona Universal Exposition, it had a different appearance to the triumphal arches that I had previously seen in Paris and Brussels. The red-brick arch was designed in a style of Moorish Revival architecture known as Neo-Mudéjar. It was adorned with elaborate sculptures, with the artwork on the front frieze titled *Barcelona rep les nacions*, which is Catalan for 'Barcelona welcomes the nations.'

Before entering the nearby Parc de la Ciutadella, I took far too much enjoyment from photographing a large map of the city that was displayed on the floor a hundred yards or so from the arch. Like the Arc de Triomf, the park owes its existence, at least in its current form, to the exposition of 1888. With the world's eyes on Barcelona, the local authorities wanted to create a more impressive green space where the citadel once stood. In the subsequent years, the seventy-acre park has become a popular place to temporarily escape city life and, due to the location of the Parliament of Catalonia within the grounds, a flashpoint regarding independence.

I did not pay much attention to the bandstand we passed, as my focus was understandably drawn to the grand nineteenth-century fountain and monument known as *Cascada del Parc de la Ciutadella*. It turns out that in the year of our visit, the bandstand was re-dedicated to the memory of Sonia Rescalvo, a trans woman who was murdered there by a group of neo-Nazis in 1991. It is a rare memorial for someone persecuted for their gender identity.

Like so much of the celebrated architecture in Barcelona, Antoni Gaudí played a role in the creation of the *Cascada*. He was a little-known architecture student at the time, assisting Josep Fontsére during the project. Inspired by Rome's Trevi Fountain, the spectacular two-tiered monument features crab pincers that serve as stairs, numerous waterspouts, and statues depicting figures from Roman mythology, including one of Venus stood on an open clam. Topped by a golden quadriga of the goddess Aurora, and set behind a sizeable pond amongst verdant foliage, it certainly made for spectacular photographs.

It is fair to say, however, that the children in the park seemed to prefer the mammoth near the lake. Norbert Font y Sagué's *Mamut* has lived within the park for over a century. Kids in school uniforms were gleefully climbing on the trunk and tusks of the three-metre-tall sculpture, whilst others sought refuge from the sun under its colossal body. Mum and I did not have the time nor energy to explore all of the attractions within the impressive park, choosing to skip a visit to the zoo and cast little more than an admiring glance at the parliament building and the *Als Voluntaris Catalans* monument. The latter was created in honour of the Catalan volunteers who fought alongside the French during the First World War. The inauguration was delayed for many years, with any art deemed to promote Catalan self-determination forbidden, and it had an uneasy relationship with the ruling powers. Josep Clarà's statue, which depicts a naked man with both arms raised and a bayonet and laurel branch in one hand, is now dedicated to the Catalans who died in defence of freedom in both world wars. The parliament building was converted into barracks after the city fell to the Nationalists during the Spanish Civil War but was restored to its original purpose in 1980.

We paid a little more attention to the Castle of the Three Dragons, partly due to its proximity to the park's entrance. Constructed as a café-restaurant for the 1888 exposition, the castle-shaped brick and sheet-iron building later hosted the Zoology Museum of Barcelona until 2010. There were three metallic sculptures in front of the building, but I thought that they resembled small lizards rather than dragons.

"Why do people call it the Castle of the Three Dragons?" Mum asked.

"I'm not sure, but it seems an extravagant setting for a café! Anyway, shall we go back to the hotel, freshen up and get some dinner?"

Having had a quick shower and some much-needed relaxation, we headed back out for some food. Despite knowing that La Rambla was a tourist trap full of overpriced, generic restaurants, we once again gravitated towards the most crowded street, or streets, in the city. It really does seem to cast a spell over tourists. Or at least the ill-prepared ones. After declining to enter numerous restaurants, we settled for a surprisingly cheap tapas establishment. For ten euros each, we could select three tapas and either a pizza or *paella*. To at least kid ourselves that we were being treated to authentic Spanish food, we both opted for paella. This was the tourist version that included *chorizo* rather than the original rabbit, chicken and green beans dish that originated in Valencia. I am unable to recall which tapas we ordered, but there is a good chance that we enjoyed some *patatas bravas*, *abóngidas* and *tortilla española*.

"Barcelona is a great city, isn't it?" I asked Mum.

"Yes, it is lovely. Interesting architecture and it seems like a vibrant place."

"We still have plenty to see, as we've spent most of the day avoiding pickpockets whilst walking up and down La Rambla!" I joked. "You will like the Gaudí buildings we visit tomorrow, especially Sagrada Familia."

"Seriously though, we need to look out for pickpockets!"

Most diners chatted about what alcohol to order and which nightclubs to frequent, whereas I was spending the first evening of the holiday discussing architecture and pickpockets with my mother. I would not have wanted it any other way.

* * *

Our second day of sightseeing commenced with a visit to the magnificent Park Güell. Having purchased day passes for the Barcelona Metro, Mum and I braved public transport for the first time since our arrival in the city centre the previous day. I had experienced a severely crowded Metro system after attending a football match at Camp Nou during my last visit to Catalonia, so the semi-congested journey to Lesseps seemed rather pleasant by comparison.

Count Eusebi Güell, who came from a family that made a fortune from the industrial revolution, was inspired by the English garden city movement and wanted to create a housing estate for wealthy members of society; therefore, the official name contains the English word 'park' instead of 'parc.' Güell, who moved into Larrard House within the grounds, enlisted the services of celebrated Catalan architect Antoni Gaudí.

In a commercial sense, the project, which began in 1900, was a dismal failure. Only two houses were built, with one of them purchased by Gaudí. From an artistic perspective, however, the park has been warmly received since it was officially opened to the public in 1926 – the same year that Gaudí died after being hit by a streetcar. His shabby appearance and the lack of any formal identification reportedly led to people refusing to transport him to hospital, as they believed that he was a vagrant. If true, this surely provides a telling message about how we tend to judge people by their appearance and often fail to aid those who we suspect may be homeless. Since I began working for a charity that deals with people who are experiencing homelessness, poverty and debt crisis, this is an issue I have been faced with on a regular basis.

Appreciation of Gaudí's work has increased in recent decades, especially since the end of the Franco dictatorship, with the park being declared a UNESCO World Heritage Site in 1984.

The entrance was flanked by a couple of buildings that reminded me of the famous house made of gingerbread and other sweet treats featured in the "Hansel and Gretel" fairy tale. The roofs of these structures resembled icing on a cake. Perhaps I was just hungry. One of them is known as Casa del Guarda, as it was where the park's guard lived. The small house has a basic interior, which now serves as a museum. I believe that the other building currently operates as a shop, but we did not give it much attention. There was already a large number of tourists milling about, so we decided to move on. Once again wearing jeans and a T-shirt, I realised that I had made the foolish mistake of not packing any shorts for our Mediterranean holiday. The heat was steadily building, and it was only mid-morning. At least Mum had been sensible enough to wear a hat that offered some protection from the unforgiving sun.

The park seemed as big as I remembered from my previous visit. Rather than attempting to cover every inch of its seventeen hectares, we focused on the more noteworthy sections. Mum and I did not have to wait long to encounter the next attraction, as visitors are almost immediately greeted by the Monumental Staircase. This series of stairs, sculptures and benches is extremely popular. The 2.4-metre-long salamander statue halfway up the staircase has not only become one of the most iconic installations of the park, but also one of the symbols of the city. *El Drac*, as it is commonly known, is covered in colourful broken-tile mosaics that belong to the *trencadís* technique favoured by Gaudí. Or so I am told.

"The salamander has a surprisingly friendly face, and the pale-blue, turquoise and orange colours of some of the tiles seem to have been incorporated into past F.C. Barcelona away kits," I mused.

"If you say so," Mum replied whilst wearing an expression that made it clear that she had absolutely no idea what I was talking about.

The Hypostyle Room, or Sala Hipostila, is located at the top of the staircase. Originally designed as a marketplace for the housing estate, it has eighty-six imposing six-metre-high columns. The slightly inclined columns and the vault were constructed in a manner that ensured rainwater is recovered in cisterns under the marketplace, providing a steady supply for the fountains and an ecological watering system for the gardens. The mosaics on the ceiling represent the four seasons and the lunar cycles.

The most popular place to pose for photographs rests on top of the Hypostyle Room. The Nature Square is home to the Serpentine Bench, which is a favoured location for Instagram users taking selfies. The winding bench may be 110 metres long, but we had to wait a few minutes before we were able to snare one of the coveted spots overlooking Casa del Guarda. Sitting on the bench was a comfortable experience, perhaps lending credence to the legend that states Gaudí's ergonomic design was the result of him asking a workman to drop his trousers and sit in soft plaster to record the correct anatomical curve.

"Shall I take off my jeans to test the ergonomics next time we purchase a sofa?" I joked.

"What are you talking about," Mum replied with a look of bemusement.

Perhaps it would have been better to relay the story about the workman before making that comment. Whether the tale is true or not, it was a nice bench to rest on whilst observing the surrounding splendour. Covered in multi-coloured ceramic tiles, it was a beautiful creation. Wavy lines and serpentines feature heavily in Gaudí's designs, as he was fascinated by the natural world and its lack of straight edges. Many observers also think that the architect's work reflects his religious and political beliefs, including Catalan independence. Feeling the intense glare of people waiting for us to free up our spot, we quickly took some photographs then made our way to the next point of interest.

The Laundry Room Portico, constructed at a heavily-slanted angle, is one of the best examples of Gaudí's creations blending in with their natural environment. The textured rock walls and pillars would not look out of place within a network of caves. The view along the portico was delightful, although the throngs of tourists somewhat diminished the quality of my photographs. Bloody tourists!

The Austria Gardens, you will not be surprised to learn, owes its title to the donation of Austrian trees in the 1970s. The area was originally intended to be a key component of the housing estate, with sixty villas planned, but the failure of the project meant that it became a plant nursery instead. This is where one can find Gaudí's house, which now serves as a museum. We were aware of spending too much time in the park when we had numerous other tourist attractions to visit, so we merely had a brief look at the exterior of the house then left. I think it was pink, but I am unable to offer any meaningful description.

Continuing the day's Gaudí theme, we took the Metro to Passeig de Gràcia, a tree-lined avenue that reminded me somewhat of the Champs-Élysées in Paris. It is home to many of the city's upmarket shops, as well as two of the architect's most famous buildings. Casa Milà is often referred to as *La Pedrera*, or 'The Stone Quarry,' due to its rugged appearance. This was initially a derisory term used by critics, but it eventually became one of endearment as the city showed its appreciation for the building. Its official name derives from the man who ordered its construction, Pere Milà. He had the house built for his wife, Roser Segimón, who was the widow of Josep Guardiola. I am obviously not talking about the legendary former player and manager of F.C. Barcelona; I am referring to the colonist who made his fortune from a coffee plantation in Guatemala.

As with other Gaudí creations, the lack of straight lines is noticeable. Part of the *Modernista* movement, he adopted an organic style influenced by the natural world and believed that the absence of perfectly straight lines in nature should be applied to architecture.

Occupying 1,620 square metres on the corner of Passeig de Gràcia and Carrer de Provença, it is hard to miss Casa Milà. The wavy stone façade and wrought-iron balconies, together with the numerous Catholic statues, give it a distinctive look, but we did not have the time to explore the interior or its most celebrated section: the roof. Although we caught a glimpse of the elaborate chimneys and some of the decorative features of the rolling rooftop terrace from street level, it was a shame that we were not able to join the people we could see walking along the top of the building and examining the stunning architecture at close quarters. If we had not already filled our itinerary, we could have explored the vast interior, known for its lack of supporting walls and the presence of eye-catching paintings.

"The owners apparently clashed with Gaudí over a number of design features, even going to court on one occasion. Apparently, Segimón got rid of a lot of the furniture and re-decorated much of the building in a different style after Gaudí's death," I informed Mum.

"I guess it was harder for him to take them to court once he was dead!"

After walking a few hundred metres further along Passeig de Gràcia, we were standing in front of another Gaudí masterpiece. I found Casa Batlló to be more aesthetically pleasing than Casa Milà. The multi-coloured ceramic and glass façade was dazzling, with the undulating lines of the balconies and the oval windows leaving me in no doubt who was responsible for the design. Partly due to the skeletal-like pillars by the entrance and the first-floor windows, the building is often referred to as *Casa dels Ossos*, meaning 'House of Bones.' The building had a less noteworthy appearance prior to Gaudí's involvement, which came about due to Josep Batlló's desire to transform his previously unremarkable house.

There was a large queue of people waiting their turn to be granted entry, so we once again elected to skip a self-guided tour of the interior. As with Casa Milà, the roof terrace is one of its most celebrated features. Arching our necks back whilst stood on the opposite side of the street, we gained some understanding of the symbolism relating to the patron saint of Catalonia. The colourful ceramic tiles resemble a dragon's back, which is of course linked to the legend of Saint George. The large cross is said to represent the sword with which he killed the dragon.

Like England, Catalonia celebrates St. George's Day on the 23rd of April. Local tradition involves men giving a rose to their love interest, whereas women provide a book in return. Nowadays, people give flowers or books to family, friends and work colleagues, regardless of gender. Personally, I prefer this tradition to the flag-waving nationalism associated with this day in England. In any case, I am sure my wife prefers to receive a red rose rather than a St. George's flag!

"Which of the two buildings do you prefer?" I asked Mum.

"Probably this one, as it is more colourful."

"It would have been nice to have gone inside them both. Maybe next time, hey?"

I returned to Barcelona in 2018 but again failed to make time for a tour of the interior of either building. I guess that is the problem of having so much to see and do in the city. Another football match at Camp Nou and a day trip to Andorra took up much of the itinerary on that occasion.

"We've already seen three of Gaudí's most famous creations today. Shall we visit his most celebrated building now?" I asked Mum.

"Is that Sagrada Família? I am excited to see that."

"Yeah, that's the one. Another Metro journey and more Gaudí architecture. That's been the theme of the day."

We were soon staring in astonishment at his unfinished masterpiece. Construction of the Roman Catholic basilica began in 1882, with Gaudí taking over as chief architect the following year. By the time of his death in 1926, only a quarter of the project had been completed. The Spanish Civil War did not help matters, with some of his plans and models destroyed when the crypt was set alight by anarchists. The building suffered another arson attack in 2011, the same year as my previous visit. Just to clarify, I was not the perpetrator!

It is truly one of the world's most breathtaking buildings. The spires already seem to touch the sky but once the final work is completed – there will eventually be eighteen spires – the highest point will increase. Reaching a height of 170 metres, the central tower will make it the tallest religious building in Europe. This will apparently represent Jesus, with the other spires symbolising the Twelve Apostles, the Virgin Mary and the Four Evangelists. It is the level of detail rather than the size that makes Sagrada Família so special though. Nearly every inch of the basilica is ornately decorated with religious symbolism. Countless statues, carvings and other intricate details seem to give the ever-changing structure an organic quality. The presence of several huge cranes has become commonplace here, although surprisingly they do not diminish the building's beauty. In fact, it will probably seem strange once they are no longer there. The constant progression of this unique building, with its distinctive characteristics and decorative features, gives legitimacy to claims that Sagrada Família resembles a living organism.

There were huge crowds and queues that indicated it would take over an hour to gain access to the interior, so we declined the opportunity to purchase admission tickets. I had stood inside the beautiful basilica on my previous visit. The pillars of the central nave resembled trees rising to the incredibly tall ceiling, and an impressive amount of natural light shone through the large windows of this vast building. Paul and I took the elevator up one of the towers, where we were able to admire some of the external artistry from close quarters. As with Casa Milà and Casa Batlló, Sagrada Família is a UNESCO World Heritage Site. Fittingly, Gaudí is buried in the crypt.

"I love this building!" Mum declared.

"It's amazing to think that they started this building in 1882. That was seventeen years before the city's most famous football club was founded, with Planes and modern cars yet to be introduced to the world. There have been two World Wars and the Spanish Civil War since then; several countries did not even exist at that point!"

"A lot has changed since construction began then."

"They expect to complete the project by the centenary of Gaudí's death in 2026. It has taken much longer to build than the Great Pyramid of Giza, which we could have been staring at right now if it were not for the military coup and ensuing violence, but not as long as it took to construct the Great Wall of China."

The semi-pedestrianised Avinguda de Gaudí cuts diagonally across the grid layout of the Eixample district. We walked along this pleasant street, occasionally turning around to take in the splendid view of Sagrada Família, until we reached Hospital de la Santa Creu i Sant Pau. The Hospital of the Holy Cross and Saint Paul, as it is known in English, may no longer be in operation but the Art Nouveau complex still attracts plenty of visitors. This is comprised of numerous buildings, with some of the older ones now housing museums since the opening of the new hospital. After approximately one-third of Barcelona's population died of the Black Death, the need for a more comprehensive hospital was apparent. Built in the early-twentieth century, it replaced the original one erected in the Raval district five hundred years earlier. Mum and I skirted around the perimeter of the complex, casting admiring glances at the Gothic architecture.

After a whirlwind day of Gaudí-themed sightseeing, we took a moment to recharge our batteries – those belonging to our bodies rather than our mobile phones – before making our way to the Montjuïc area. Alighting the Metro at Plaça d'Espanya, where heavy traffic was circling, we had a brief look at the square's fountain and the former bullring on the other side of the road. From there we walked along Avinguda de la Reina Maria Cristina, passing the forty-seven-metre-high red-brick Venetian Towers that were modelled on the Campanile of St. Mark's Basilica in Venice, until we reached the Magic Fountain of

Montjuïc. On my previous visit, I had missed out on watching the popular light and water show that is held every thirty minutes each evening from Thursday through to Saturday.

As there was still a couple of hours before the first show of the evening commenced, we made our way up the steps to the gigantic Neo-Baroque Palau Nacional. This houses the Museu Nacional d'Art de Catalunya, which contains extensive collections of Catalan, Spanish and European art. With over 5,000 pieces stored within 32,000 square metres, one is best setting aside a few hours for a visit. We were too late to enter the museum or explore the hill known as Montjuïc, which is the highest point in the city. This did not bother me too much, as I was not in the mood for an art museum and I had already spent an exhausting afternoon ascending the hill during my previous trip. The botanical gardens, the 1992 Olympic stadium and the fort at the top of the hill were interesting the first time around but I had little appetite to return anytime soon.

We were happy to simply admire the view from the terrace in front of the museum. With the sun starting to come down, the city and the surrounding hills looked magnificent beyond the four recently-restored Ionic columns. Originally erected in 1919, the twenty-metre-high columns symbolised the four red stripes of the Catalan flag; thus, they were regarded as a source of pride for the local community. For this reason, Primo de Rivera's dictatorship had them removed prior to the 1929 Universal Exposition. With the eyes of the world on Barcelona, any artwork hinting at Catalan identity was replaced by something more in line with Spanish nationalism. Under this regime, a certain Francisco Franco became the youngest person in Europe promoted to the rank of general.

Mum and I enjoyed our evening meal as we waited for the light show. The *fideuà*, a noodle-based alternative to paella, and the cod fritters known as *buñuelos de bacalao* were delicious. Even the basic bread and tomato dish, *pa amb tomàquet*, was tasty. Our food was so nice that we did not complain when a couple of bombs were placed on our table! *La bomba* is a deep-fried potato ball filled with meat, similar to a croquette, served with a spicy sauce and *allioli*. The name of the dish was, apparently, an attempt to make light of the frequent bombing by anarchists during the Spanish Civil War. We rounded off our meals with the traditional choice of dessert in this region, the *crema catalana*. Almost identical to *crème brûlée,* it is a custard made from egg yolks, milk, citrus zest, cinnamon and a burnt caramel crust. Given that I am not particularly fond of the aforementioned French dessert, it was no surprise that this was my least favourite dish of the evening.

The Magic Fountain show was delightful. Water shot up from the fountain in a ferocious yet controlled manner, with the lighting periodically changing colour. Fluorescent shades of orange, blue, yellow and red took it in turns to light up this wonderful fountain against the pitch-black sky. The crowd in front of us became silhouettes against the dazzling display, with enchanting music and lasers projected from the art museum completing this impressive scene. Having missed out on witnessing such a performance in 2011, it was well worth the wait.

Back in our hotel room, I asked Mum what she thought of our second day in the city.

"I had a great day. Gaudí's buildings are amazing and the Magic Fountain show was lovely," she replied.

"More importantly, we've survived two days in Barcelona without being pickpocketed!"

"You make fun of me, but it's good to be careful."

"It's been a great couple of days, and we still have the cruise to come."

"I'll be sad to leave Barcelona but I'm excited for what lies ahead. And I get to experience it all with my darling son."

"In the absence of a darling son, I guess you'll have to make do with me!"

* * *

We had a final task to complete before heading to the cruise terminal. I had seen photographs of a giant cat sculpture when searching the internet for points of interest in Barcelona. A little bit of research informed me that we could find the bronze feline on Rambla del Raval, a short walk from our hotel. Fernando Botero's *Cat* initially led a nomadic lifestyle following his birth in 1987, appearing in various locations such as Parc de la Ciutadella and outside the Olympic Stadium on Montjuïc. It was only in 2003 that he found permanent residence on the street we were heading to. As it had rained earlier in the morning and the clouds above looked ominous, I hoped that we would not be subjected to horrendous weather for our week-long cruise.

We soon caught sight of *El Gato de Botero*, as it is commonly referred to, halfway along the street. He was chubbier than I had expected, and several times larger than me, although I doubt that this was because the locals had been over-feeding him. Exaggerated and chunky bodies are seemingly a hallmark of the Colombian artist's work. Apparently, there is a similar sculpture of a bulbous horse in Terminal 2 of Barcelona-El Prat Airport. With all the delicious food in the city, I would probably have ended up with a similar body if we had stayed any longer! After taking the obligatory photographs of the giant cat, we returned to our hotel and checked out. A quick journey on the shuttle bus took us to the cruise terminal, where our next adventure awaited.

A CHANGE OF COURSE

BEYOND THE WALL

14: ALL ABOARD!
MARSEILLE AND AVIGNON, FRANCE
OCTOBER 2013

Barcelona Cruise Terminal was a hive of activity; small vehicles were transporting luggage, excited passengers were alighting shuttle services like the one we had just used, and an army of employees were directing the traffic and trying their best to keep this huge operation running smoothly. It was clear that this was not a case of just hopping onto a boat and setting sail. Our ship, *MSC Preziosa*, could accommodate over 4,800 people, including the crew. There were three other similar-sized vessels docked next to it. Mum and I had checked in online a few days beforehand and printed our luggage labels. Before entering the relevant hall of the terminal, we handed them over and hoped they would not be lost amongst the thousands of others. We were assured that they would be brought to our cabin, but I instinctively feared the worst. Would I have to wear the same set of clothes for the entire week?

    We waited within what resembled a small airport departure lounge as passengers were called forward in groups. It took around an hour before we were summoned to the check-in desk. Although we had already submitted our details online, we had to fill in a health questionnaire and confirm some further information. The suntanned Spanish man behind the counter perused the answers we had provided on our forms before asking: "So you are both feeling well today, with no signs of illness within the last few days?"

    "We feel fine," I answered.

    "OK, we hope you enjoy your cruise."

Ticking a box on a form and verbally confirming our good health was all that was required to secure entry; I imagine that things will be markedly different as cruises resume in a world scarred by COVID-19.

"I just need to take your photographs for your all-important cruise cards," he continued. "They will be your proof of identity for whenever you board or disembark the vessel. Any expenses will be charged to your cruise cards, with your bill settled on the final morning of your stay. It will be the most important thing you have on your person for the next week, so don't lose it!"

We laughed.

"Seriously. Don't lose it. The cards are required for pretty much everything on board."

Fumbling with my documents and hand luggage, I inadvertently left our cards on the check-in desk as we began to walk away.

"Sir!" shouted the man behind the check-in desk. He was holding our cards aloft and displaying a look of incredulity.

"Thanks. Is that the quickest anyone has lost their cruise cards?" I asked.

"I think you have set a new record. Take care of the cards…and yourself. You look like the type who could lose your mother in one of the countries you visit this week, so please be careful." I made the last bit up, but I am sure that is what he was thinking.

Moments later, we were having our photograph taken again. This was the first of many attempts to entice us into needlessly racking up expenses on our cruise cards. All passengers were encouraged, almost forced, to pose for photos in front of a green screen, which would no doubt be replaced with a tacky image of a cruise ship or a captain's wheel. We would have the option of purchasing the doctored photograph during our time on board; the company just hoped that enough people would get carried away by the exuberance of being on holiday that they would pay a small fortune for a ridiculous-looking image despite taking hundreds of real pictures of the ship over the course of the week.

The scale of *MSC Preziosa* became apparent as we walked across the skybridge towards the Italian cruise liner. With a length surpassing 333 metres and a height of over 66 metres, it was no wonder why people refer to them as floating cities. Some view them as grotesque eyesores, whereas others adore them. One thing was clear though: it was impossible to ignore a ship with a gross tonnage of more than 139,000. Cruise ships have continued to increase in size, with some vessels transporting over 6,000 guests around the Mediterranean or the Caribbean every week. MSC Cruises derived from the shipping line Mediterranean Shipping Company – I guess that it has become increasingly clear that holidaymakers are amongst the most profitable cargo!

With exhaust fumes billowing from the funnel, the environmental impact of these humongous ships is hard to ignore. A passenger's carbon footprint is said to treble once stepping foot on board. It has been claimed that the particle emissions of a large cruise liner are equivalent to those from over a million cars. The level of pollution is said to result in air quality similar to that found in the world's most polluted cities. Perhaps the smog of Beijing would seem mild in comparison! Following numerous instances of ships caught dumping rubbish, sewage and fuel into the sea, there has been a push for cruise companies to clean up their act in recent years. Cleaner fuel systems and more sustainable practices have been introduced, but there is no escaping the impact they have on the environment.

A beaming woman of Southeast Asian appearance was the first to greet us: "Welcome on board, we hope you enjoy a pleasant stay."

It was immediately noticeable that most of the staff, at least those in the service sector, were from Asia. Free from the 'burden' of many of the workers' rights in place on land, cruise companies are able to pay relatively low wages to entry-level staff and implement gruelling schedules that can see employees go weeks without taking a day off. For this reason, they look to countries such as the Philippines, Indonesia and India for much of their workforce. Whilst the pay would be considered low in most of Europe and North America, many from the aforementioned countries jump at the chance to secure six-month contracts on wages that are much higher than what is on offer on land. The free food and accommodation is a further incentive.

There are plenty of Europeans and Americans working in the bars and theatres, but not many are prepared to spend fifteen hours a day turning over people's beds and cleaning bathrooms for less than the minimum wage in their home country. In recent years, there has been increasing pressure on cruise companies to offer higher wages and better working conditions. Things may have marginally improved, but a true appetite for significant change is unlikely when there is such a large pool of potential employees who are keen to sign up. Many of the workers stay with the companies for years, indicating that they are willing to put up with the gruelling schedule because they can earn significantly more than would be possible on land. Many crew members I have met have told me that they send their wages to their family back in their homeland, often going months without seeing them.

The crew were smartly dressed in their whites as they lined up to welcome us on board. Their immaculate appearance against the backdrop of the stunning atrium, which included Swarovski crystal staircases, provided an impression of grandeur that I had associated with the golden age of ocean liners. Speaking of which, I recall a colleague offering bizarre parting words on my last day of work before the trip. In an awkward attempt at humour rather than a malicious comment, he said: "Enjoy your cruise. By the way, have you seen *Titanic*?"

I added to the strange atmosphere by reminding him that the *Costa Concordia* sank in 2012. Fatal accidents involving cruise ships are, in fact, incredibly rare. It was crew failings that led to the *Concordia* striking some underwater rocks whilst deviating from the planned course to attempt a sail-past salute near Isola del Giglio. Several people received prison sentences, with the captain jailed for manslaughter. Not only did his errors contribute to the disaster that claimed thirty-two lives, but he also prematurely abandoned ship. I tried to push such thoughts firmly to the back of my mind. At least he could not possibly be the captain of our ship.

The illusion that we would not charge much to our cruise cards over the course of the following week was soon shattered by an encounter with a couple of departments who preyed on naïve passengers like ourselves. Given that Mum hardly ever drank alcohol and I only had the odd tipple here and there, we managed to resist any of the alcoholic beverage packages on offer but eventually succumbed to the water package. Although I am sure that the staff were hoping for a bigger sale than the twenty euros we spent on bottled water, MSC had managed to entice us into adding the first item to our bill.

The excursion team managed to fare much better. I had done some research into independently visiting places of interest in the various ports of call, but a crew member highlighting some of the apparent difficulties of finding our own way to those places rattled me enough that I purchased excursions for all but one of the destinations *MSC Preziosa* would call at. My intention of exploring each city at our leisure, without the added cost of an organised excursion, had been scuppered by a moment of panic in the face of a well-oiled sales machine. We had added hundreds of euros to our bill before we had even made it to our cabin!

Finding our home for the next week proved to be more challenging than I had anticipated. There are over 1,500 cabins and 13 passenger decks, so locating the correct one can be an overwhelming experience. We walked up the stairs to Deck 9 and tried to make sense of the signs breaking down the layout of the ship. Odd-numbered cabins were on one side, with even numbers on the other. The front of the ship is the bow, the rear is the stern, the left side is port, and the right is starboard. I would love to tell you that we used the correct terminology throughout the trip, but front, back, left and right was the extent of our maritime knowledge! Every corridor looked the same, with the seemingly endless number of cabins and unexpected side-corridors almost causing us to lose all hope of stumbling across our lodging. After a few twists and turns, we eventually completed our mission.

"You realise we will have to find our cabin several times a day. Hopefully, it becomes a little easier each time!" I commented.

"We will be OK with you guiding us."

"I think that may be the problem!"

Our luggage had not yet been brought to our cabin, which once again caused me to worry that we would have no change of clothing for the week ahead. Daniel, one of the cabin attendants who was responsible for our section of the ship, assured us that it usually takes an hour or two for luggage to arrive. Our suitcases were still working their way through the system, but it was time to have a look at our living quarters. We had booked an inside cabin, which was the cheapest available option, so I was braced for the worst. A problem presented itself immediately upon opening the door. It was not the fact that the room was barely bigger than a double bed; rather, the issue was that there was just one bed. As much as I love my mum, sharing a bed with her for a week was not all that appealing. Besides, what would Daniel think? Would he assume that I was Mum's toy boy, in a relationship that would be at home in the television show *The Love Boat*? Right on cue, he knocked on our door and asked if everything was OK.

"Sorry to be a pain, but we require two single beds. Please can that be arranged?" I asked, desperately hoping that my request could be met.

"Of course, Sir," he politely replied. "I will separate the beds when you are having dinner this evening."

"Do you like working on the ship, Daniel?" Mum enquired.

"Yes madam. It is hard work, but I make a nice amount of money to send back to my wife and children."

"How many kids do you have? You must miss them."

"Yes, I miss them dearly, but I am working hard to provide for them. I have been on the ship for six months and hope to earn another contract."

"Where are you from?"

"The Philippines. How about you guys?"

"I am from Hong Kong and my son David was born in England."

Just as I thought we had established some common ground with our Asian origins, Daniel's response highlighted the different economic backgrounds of the two locations: "I have friends and family members who went to Hong Kong as domestic workers. I have never been though."

"I've never been to the Philippines either, although I hope to go one day." I replied.

"I'm sure you will love my country," he proudly declared. "Anyway, I will leave you in peace now. If you need anything, do not hesitate to ask. I wish you a pleasant stay."

The conversations we had with Daniel and the rest of the crew throughout the following week highlighted the importance of leaving a decent tip. Although the ship took a service charge that would supposedly be divided between crew members, we were sceptical about how much of this the likes of Daniel would receive. Upon leaving the vessel, we left an additional tip and a note wishing him good luck for his future endeavours. It was disappointing to overhear another passenger boast about how he had saved himself a bit of money by cancelling the ship's opt-out service charge. The crew members are away from their families for months at a time, working long hours and often going weeks without a day off; the very least they deserve is a decent tip from a relatively wealthy tourist.

Aside from the bed situation, the cabin exceeded our expectations. I was used to budget hotels, so the lack of space was nothing out of the ordinary. It was basically a more upmarket version of a Travelodge. The small living quarters and cramped bathroom were sufficient to meet our needs. Some people would be perturbed by the lack of daylight due to the absence of any windows, but we only needed somewhere to sleep at night and get changed when required. A view of the Mediterranean Sea would have been nice, but cabins with a balcony can cost twice as much as what we paid for ours.

Mum and I travelled down another set of stairs, realising that our legs would get a robust workout over the course of the week, and began exploring the vessel. The 1,600-capacity theatre, the main evening restaurants, several bars, the reception desk and a small shopping gallery were located on Decks 5 and 6, which seemed to be the fulcrum of the ship. The atrium was beautiful and most reminiscent of the sophisticated image I had associated with *Titanic*. People were sipping glasses of gin and tonic in the bar in front of reception whilst others posed for photographs on the Swarovski crystal staircases.

We walked up some more stairs to Deck 15, where many of the outdoor festivities take place. The ship's interior resembled an elegant Italian restaurant, but the top section of the vessel had the feel of an all-inclusive holiday resort. There were hundreds of sun loungers surrounding the outdoor pool and an army of bar staff transporting an array of cocktails to the guests who had already made themselves at home. It did not matter whether they had received their luggage yet, there was drinking to be done! Mind you, if I had paid for an all-inclusive drinks package, I may have been tempted to get my money's worth too. The weather had brightened up since our morning walk through Barcelona, providing a clear view of the city. Or at least of the port area. My asthma-affected lungs did not report any obvious issues with the quality of air on deck, but this was not likely to be something that was immediately noticeable. Perhaps it would become more apparent once the engines were operating at full capacity.

I was relieved to see our luggage outside the cabin. Before we had time to unpack, there was an announcement on the public-address system informing all passengers that they had to go to their designated muster station for the compulsory safety drill. Our lifejackets were stored in the wardrobe and the location of our muster station was displayed on the book of our door.

"Remember not to put on your lifejackets until you gather at your station," was the final instruction before the emergency alarm sounded. This consisted of six short blasts of the ship's horn followed by a prolonged one. We exited our cabin and joined a stream of passengers heading towards their respective muster stations, many of whom were bumping into others because they were already wearing their life jackets. It was rather chaotic, which briefly caused me to worry about the crowd of people turning into a stampede. God help us if there were a genuine emergency.

Our route involved descending a couple of flights of stairs and travelling towards the mid-section of the ship. Thankfully, there was a group of helpful crew members pointing us in the right direction. Our cruise cards were scanned in order to prove our attendance and we were instructed to stand in lines underneath the lifeboats. Mum and I patiently watched a demonstration of how to work our lifejackets and what to do in the unlikely event that we had to abandon ship. This may have been a tedious affair that seemed to drag on forever, but it was information that could potentially save thousands of lives.

Due to the safe arrival of our suitcases, I was able to make myself somewhat presentable for dinner. After a quick shower and change into shirt and trousers, I was ready to head down to the restaurant. Each cabin was allocated a dining time, which was either the first sitting at 6:30 pm – we were assigned this slot – or the later one at 8:30 pm, and a specific table for the duration of the cruise. As I had no experience of formal dinner parties and rarely felt comfortable in the presence of strangers, I was feeling uneasy about sitting with six unfamiliar faces for the next seven evenings. We joined the queue for The Golden Lobster and hoped that our dining companions would be pleasant. Or at least not a group of cannibals with a preference for Chinese flesh.

Smartly-dressed restaurant staff guided us to our table, where we met our fellow diners for the first time. After an awkward silence, someone suggested that we all formally introduce ourselves. Geoffrey and Margaret were a retired couple from the south of England who had enjoyed numerous river cruises but had never previously taken to the seas. Peter and Helen were fellow northerners who seemed more down to earth than Geoffrey and Margaret. Mark and Kayleigh were from Atlanta in the United States of America. I have made up most of their names as I am unable to remember what they were actually called.

After the initial introductions, Mark decided to break the ice: "The *Preziosa* was originally going to be built for Gaddafi's son, who wanted to launch a luxury cruise company, but the contract was cancelled due to the Libyan Civil War. MSC stepped in and purchased it, requesting an identical copy of *Divina*. It shows how much money they have that they can buy another cruise ship just like that."

"Wow, that's remarkable! I'm glad we're sailing with MSC rather than the Gaddafi family!" Peter quipped.

Margaret was next to speak up: "We have only ever taken river cruises. This is so much bigger than what we are used to. We just hope that it will be equally enjoyable. We do love our river cruises. We sailed along the Duoro and the Moselle last year."

When I find myself in this type of social situation, I tell myself that I can remain quiet for most of the proceedings if I occasionally provide a comment of some description. Therefore, I decided to briefly enter the conversation: "I am sure you will enjoy it. This is our first cruise of any type and we have been blown away by it all."

Hopefully, that would allow me to relax for a few minutes.

Traditional Italian menus consist of several courses. The meal begins with an *aperitivo*, which is usually a drink such as prosecco or wine, accompanied by something small like olives or nuts. The starter is known as *antipasti*, with cured meats, cheese and bruschetta popular options. The first course, or the *primi*, will often include pasta, risotto, gnocchi or a broth of some sort. Meat or seafood is commonly the primary component of the *secondi*, which is often accompanied by a vegetable-based *contorni* dish. Cheese and fruit, or *formaggi e frutta*, is sometimes served before the dessert, referred to as *dolce*. This can be followed by coffee, before the meal is concluded with a *digestivo*, such as *limoncello* or *grappa*.

Keen to sample the full Italian meal experience, and to get my money's worth from the cruise, I selected as many courses as possible.

There may not have been any aperitivo as such, but I foolishly stuffed my face with sourdough rolls and a platter of cured meats. I adored the aubergine, mozzarella and tomato dish known as *parmigiana di melanzane*, although I became concerned about my ability to consume the remaining courses. After devouring some seabass, I sincerely regretted my decision to plump for a selection of cheese before dessert. With a severely bloated stomach, and trousers that were in danger of tearing at the seams, I heroically finished the cheese and a portion of *tiramisu*, before washing it all down with a cappuccino. Feeling ill but triumphant, I said farewell to our dining companions and exited the restaurant, pondering whether my body could cope with another six evenings of heavy-duty eating.

We decided to watch some live entertainment whilst we attempted to digest our dinner. The theatre was grand enough for performances that would not have looked out of place in the West End or on Broadway. We were treated to a slick thirty-minute production featuring spectacular acrobats, can-can dancers and stellar singing tied together by the *Witches of Paris* theme. It was a far cry from the entertainment provided by Butlins or the Jane McDonald-type vocalists I had associated with cruise ships.

At the conclusion of the show, we had a walk around the ship. Every bar was full of men in suits and women in cocktail dresses sipping grown-up drinks; the casino was full of carefree gamblers, and a musician was dazzling all those in the atrium with his piano-playing skills and vocal gymnastics. There were many sections of the vessel that we had not yet seen, some of which we would not pay any attention to throughout the week. The food in the main restaurant was so good that we were not tempted by the exclusive restaurants that came at an additional cost, whilst the 4D cinema and the spa did not appeal to us. Mum and I rounded off our evening with a cup of tea, which did not come at any extra charge, in one of the buffet restaurants on Deck 14. We were surrounded by floor-to-ceiling windows, but it was pitch-black outside. We had set sail at some point during dinner, but it felt so steady that I had forgotten we were moving. The view would be transformed by the time we came back here for breakfast.

Another confusing search for our cabin was concluded slightly quicker than our previous attempts. If we could continue to shave off a few seconds on each occasion, then we would be able to make it back to our quarters in only a mildly embarrassing amount of time by the end of the week! As promised, Daniel had separated the bed into two twins, alleviating any concerns about having to spend my first night in bed with Mum since I was a five-year-old scared of the dark.

"What did you think of our first evening?" I asked Mum.
"It was lovely. Everything is so grand that I felt a bit out of place!"
"Don't be silly – you look beautiful. The star of the show."
With that comment, it was a good job that Daniel was not in earshot, as he may have questioned why we had requested twin beds.
"Goodnight, David."
"Goodnight, Mum. We will be in France tomorrow!"

* * *

The buffet restaurant was completely different in the morning. It had been a tranquil affair when we had stopped by for a cup of tea the previous evening, but it was absolutely heaving now. Although it was not yet seven o'clock, nearly every seat was taken, and people were scurrying past in all directions carrying platefuls of all manner of food. This was primarily because all of the excursions departed before nine.

Even the passengers who were going to independently explore Marseille wanted to disembark as soon as the ship docked. I was a little disappointed with myself for abandoning the idea of strolling around the city at our leisure, especially after looking at the daily newsletter that detailed how to reach the city from the cruise terminal, but part of me was relieved to be free from the responsibility of guiding us through an unfamiliar place and then back to the ship before it departed.

The crew did well to manage the chaos, clearing plates away the instant they were no longer needed and pointing out available tables. We were soon sat down looking out at the port of Marseille. For all my ethical and environmental concerns about the cruise industry, I was thrilled to have woken up overlooking a different city, knowing that we would be transported somewhere else whilst we slept each night. From a selfish point of view, it was an efficient and cost-effective way of visiting several destinations within the same week. Having been in Spain the previous day, we were about to briefly explore a couple of French cities before moving on to Italy in less than twenty-four hours.

I filled our glasses with orange juice and our cups with coffee – a sure sign one is on holiday – before we took it in turns to explore what food was on offer. I tend to be wary of buffets, as I imagine unhygienic guests spreading their germs on the produce and generally showcasing poor behaviour that ruins the experience for everyone in the restaurant. This was a rather upmarket buffet though. There was just about every food known to man available for consumption, and chefs were cooking omelettes in front of queueing passengers. I usually opt for a continental breakfast, as I can rarely stomach any cooked items so soon after emerging from a deep sleep. On this occasion, however, I stacked my plate with a ridiculous amount of hash browns, adding a bit of bacon, toast, eggs and beans for good measure. I will attribute this to the psychology of getting my money's worth from the cruise and being mindful of a long day ahead. This was also the moment that I became addicted to hash browns.

We had been instructed to wait for our excursion in one of the lounges. Highly-organised crew members were taking names on their respective registers and co-ordinating the mammoth operation of guiding each of the twenty groups out of the ship and to their relevant coach whenever it became available and all guests were accounted for. This was reminiscent of a farmer rounding up their cattle and leading them to the cowshed.

Tour groups, especially those from a cruise ship, are often seen as the lowest of the low when it comes to the world of travel. Intrepid explorers view them with disdain, whilst independent travellers pity them for the restrictive nature of their experience. I took a pragmatic approach: sure, organised tours were usually only partially satisfying, but the cruise excursions provided a sample of each destination with minimal stress involved. We could make a note of places of interest and one day return on our own terms.

Although we had booked an excursion that involved visits to Marseille and Avignon, I was aware that in order to see both cities, which are over a hundred kilometres apart, we would be provided with little more than a glimpse of either. Our tour guide introduced herself to the group and gave an outline of what to expect: "Hello, my name is Dominique. Today we will have the pleasure of exploring two wonderful cities. We begin here in Marseille, known for its splendid basilica, before moving on to historic Avignon."

A short coach journey took us through the Vieux Port area, along La Canebière, often referred to as the Champs-Élysées of Marseille, and the outskirts of the old town, known as Le Panier, and past the Romanesque-Byzantine Revival domed towers of the Cathédrale de la Major. It all looked pleasant, but that was as far as our 'exploration' of the city went. I had read that Marseille had largely managed to shake off its reputation as a sleazy port city once associated with drunken sailors, crime and prostitutes, but it was difficult to form any conclusion from the view through our coach window. I was disappointed that we had not been given the opportunity to wander around the characteristic streets, sample its food and admire historic monuments such as Palais Longchamp but at least I could say that I had *seen* some of Marseille.

Our coach momentarily stopped by the Monument to the Deaths of the Armies in the East and in the Distant Lands. Situated on the three-kilometre Corniche du Président John Fitzgerald Kennedy by the seafront, the memorial was built at the conclusion of the First World War. In keeping with other European monuments of this nature, a female figure stands with her arms aloft to symbolise victory beneath the triumphal arch. The arch is flanked by sculptures representing soldiers from different parts of the French Empire. The monument is highly regarded by most of the city's residents, although many have pointed out that, like most colonial memorials, it has a narrative that celebrates European success whilst barely acknowledging the endeavour and suffering of people from lands that were colonised. In any case, the brilliant clear blue sky and the calm Mediterranean Sea served as a beautiful backdrop to the monument.

At least we were given thirty minutes at the basilica to spend however we liked. Notre-Dame de la Garde overlooks the whole city from its position upon the 150-metre-high Garde Hill, which has a long history as an observation post. A fort was erected here in the sixteenth century, with the basilica built on its foundations three hundred years later. It had been an Assumption Day pilgrimage site long before the current basilica become the symbol of the city.

The considerable foundations of the fort were visible as we ascended the stairs leading up to the basilica. From our position on the highest natural point in Marseille, we were treated to a delightful view overlooking the city and the port. The chill of the coastal air did not seem to tally with the cloudless blue sky and the bright sunshine, but it was still early in the morning.

Dominique pointed out to sea and began addressing the group: "If you look over there you will see Île d'If, which was made famous by the Alexandre Dumas novel *The Count of Monte Cristo*. The tiny island is about 1.5 kilometres from the mainland and is home to the sixteenth-century fortress and prison known as Château d'If. The story may be fictional, but many prisoners were once held there. Unlike Edmond Dantès, nobody from the real world managed to escape!"

From what we could see, there was little else on the island other than the fortress. The sight of a prison on an island off the mainland was reminiscent of Alcatraz, which also became a popular setting within the world of fiction. I would certainly not fancy trying to escape from the prison and swim through this potentially hazardous 1.5-kilometre stretch of the sea. Mind you, unless I fall foul of an authoritarian regime in a country I visit, I struggle to fathom a scenario in which I end up imprisoned. The most trouble I have ever found myself in was when I was sent home from school for a week because my hair had been shaved too short. I have never owned a credit card due to the fear of being even one penny in debt, and I feel guilty whenever I leave a shop without buying anything. The life of crime is certainly not for me!

From an aesthetic perspective, the basilica was worthy of its elevated position above the city. If the locals are unable to escape the presence of one building, it may as well be an attractive one. The contrasting colours of the layered stonework catches the eye – white Calissane limestone alternates with green Golfolina sandstone – whilst the undoubted crowning glory is the 41-metre-tall bell tower topped by a bronze statue of the Virgin Mary.

Dominique rattled off more rapid-fire background information: "The basilica, like the chapels that came before it, holds a special place in the hearts of the residents of Marseille. There is a famous custom of sailors leaving ex-votos, often in the form of a votive painting, as a sign of their gratitude for surviving accidents at sea. The re-capture of Notre-Dame de la Garde in 1944 was a hugely symbolic moment of the liberation of Marseille, and indeed France."

Although the multitude of mosaics and the alternating red and white marble columns of the interior were impressive, I much preferred the outer walls. For this reason, Mum and I spent most of our free time taking in the panoramic view and admiring the numerous statues belonging to the basilica. My favourite one depicted a little boy with his finger pressed to his lips. Having charmed me, he featured prominently in the foreground of a photograph I took of the bell tower.

The coach journey to Avignon took just over an hour. Dominique used some of this time to inform the group about the medieval centre that is surrounded by 4.3 kilometres of city walls. In the fourteenth century, seven successive popes resided in Avignon rather than Rome. Many viewed the popes as mere puppets controlled by the French authorities, with the Papal Court stacked with French clerics. This has been disputed by some historians, who have stated that Avignon was an advantageous location for the papacy for many reasons, such as being able to retain an element of independence from the ruling powers in Rome whilst benefitting from the city's communication links with both Italy and France.

Upon our arrival in Avignon, we were ushered off the coach and taken to the Pont Saint-Bénézet. The bridge is regarded as one of the city's most important landmarks and is classified as a UNESCO World Heritage Site, despite there being just four surviving arches and a gatehouse. Perhaps this is why it is so revered. The original twelfth-century bridge was destroyed in 1226 as King Louis VIII orchestrated the besieging of Avignon during the Albigensian Crusade. This important section of the route between France and Spain was rebuilt in the ensuing decades.

I had expected to be told that it was once again destroyed during another war, but Dominique explained why the bridge was in its current state: "The rebuilt bridge was 900 metres in length, with 22 arches. As you can see, not much remains. The bridge collapsed many times when the Rhône flooded, and it was eventually abandoned in the seventeenth century. You may have heard about the Pont Saint-Bénézet from the famous song 'Sur le Pont d'Avignon.' It celebrates the tradition of people dancing on the bridge, although it is thought that people actually used to do this on the islands beneath it. You have five minutes to walk on the bridge, dance or do whatever you please – then we move on."

We resisted the urge to dance on or under the bridge, instead opting for a gentle stroll along the short segment that was still in place. The Chapel of Saint Nicholas is situated at about the halfway mark. One of its sanctuaries is dedicated to Saint Bénézet, who was the driving force behind the bridge's construction. Despite being an uneducated shepherd, his plan was approved by the Bishop of Avignon. Roman engineers had shied away from building a bridge across the Rhône at this point, but Bénézet claimed to have received a divine vision. Eighteen miracles, including the blind having their vision restored and the deaf regaining their hearing, are said to have occurred during the bridge's construction. The bridge once contained Bénézet's body, and subsequently became a pilgrimage site. Divine inspiration did not stop it from repeatedly collapsing though.

The nearby Palais de Papes, home to the popes during the Avignon Papacy, was the next attraction we were taken to. The addition of the Palais Neuf to the Palais Vieux that had been built for Benedict XII created the largest Gothic palace in Europe, occupying an area of 15,000 square metres. After over 350 years of papal control, and a period of deterioration, it was sacked in 1789 during the French Revolution, and became the scene of a notorious massacre a couple of years later. The building had the look of a medieval castle, which is unsurprising given that the Napoleonic French state later used it as a military barracks and prison. After such a volatile and gruesome past, it has been welcoming tourists since the early-twentieth century.

Dominique took us around the huge complex that overlooks Pont Saint-Bénézet, leading us through a series of vast halls and pointing out the intricate frescoes and tapestries that had survived various tumultuous events. We were given a tour of the cloisters, courtyards, chapels and papal bedrooms whilst our friendly guide provided further information to the group: "With Urban VI elected as pope in Rome in the late-fourteenth century, Clement VII of Avignon was regarded as the antipope, signifying the split in the Catholic Church. The Avignon Papacy came to an end in the early-fifteenth century. It was not all about massacres, prisons and power struggles though! The library was one of the largest in Europe and the palais became a centre of enlightenment. Many artists, musicians and scholars spent time here, including Petrarch, who was one of the key figures within humanism."

Following the conclusion of our tour, we admired the exterior of the palace and its ten towers before we were informed that we had an hour to spend as we pleased. The Cathédrale Notre-Dame des Doms d'Avignon is situated next to the palace but it was closed for restoration work. The Romanesque building is best known for its fifteenth-century belltower, which is now topped by a gilded statue of the Virgin Mary.

Mum and I purchased some ice creams from a stall then ate them whilst aimlessly strolling around the historic centre. We passed a carousel and the grand nineteenth-century Opéra d'Avignon, before navigating our way through some of the tiled shopping streets. Eventually, we simply sat on a bench and took in the ambience of this charming city. The streets were lined with colourful flowers and the sky was a brilliant shade of blue. The gentle warmth provided by the sun felt good against my skin. The only thing spoiling this scene was the presence of a large group of noisy schoolchildren who seemed to be on an organised excursion. Given that I was part of a tour group comprised of cruise passengers, I could hardly complain!

I spent the coach journey back to the ship contemplating the merits of such an excursion. Sure, it paled in comparison to the depth of feeling and insight that comes from a week-long trek along the Great Wall of China, but it was still a pleasant day. Just because it was not as awe-inspiring or memorable does not make the whole experience worthless. Besides, I could hardly embark on an expedition across one of the wonders of the world every week.

I often incorporate food into any analogy regarding travel; taking a day trip is like sampling a few items from an international buffet – it allows you to make a note of what you enjoyed and whether you would like to return for a more substantial meal, or trip. Long weekends can be seen as the equivalent of dining at a nice restaurant, whilst more adventurous journeys represent a thorough exploration of a particular cuisine. Each meal involves a varying degree of quality and authenticity, but they can all be appreciated in their own way. Devouring some junk food after a hard day's work can sometimes taste as good as an expensive meal at a reputable restaurant. It is certainly more affordable!

Staying on the subject of food, we were soon back in the ship's buffet restaurant. Croissants, pastries and hash browns had been replaced with an incredible array of food items. The counters were stacked with pizzas, steak, noodles, rice, burgers, casserole and just about every other dish one can imagine. There was so much food on offer that it was almost impossible to resist piling so much on your plate that the possibility of suffering an immediate heart attack became a genuine concern. Although I managed to avoid any catastrophic health consequences, my waistline was stretched to its limit after I consumed every food known to humankind. The fear of missing out meant that I was unable to pass up the opportunity to sample most dishes on offer, regardless of whether it was likely to send me into a food coma. Putting a hungry person in a room full of grub they do not have to pay for invariably leads to this outcome!

I was ill-prepared for the warm Mediterranean weather. For some unbeknown reason, I had not brought any shorts or swimwear. Perhaps I had believed that we would spend all of our time exploring a series of cities and would not have the opportunity to relax in the sun. In any case, I had underestimated the difference in temperature from the United Kingdom. It was October but it felt hotter than the finest of summer days in Manchester. Having a dip in the pool on Deck 14 was out of the question, but it was too crowded for my liking anyway. We were lucky that there were a couple of available loungers, so Mum and I spent the next hour or so basking in the sun. It felt unusual but pleasant to be sunbathing whilst admiring the coastline of Marseille from our vantage point. Hard-working waiters occasionally checked whether we wanted to order any cocktails, but Mum and I stuck to our bottled water. How rock 'n' roll!

It was gala night, so we put on our smartest clothes for dinner. Nowadays, I have my affordable suits tailored to fit my short, stocky build, but this time I had bought one straight off a shop rail. This resulted in me resembling the lead character in the film *Big*, with my sleeves almost reaching my knuckles. There was a queue to meet the captain, and the ship's photographers were capturing images of the endless number of passengers dying to pose on the Swarovski staircases. The photographic theme continued in the restaurant, with a couple of photographers interrupting our meal to snap away with their cameras. Gala nights can be lucrative for cruise lines, as passengers are more likely to purchase photographs of themselves dressed in their finest tuxedos and dresses.

Our fellow diners discussed how they had used their time ashore. Geoffrey and Margaret had taken a city tour of Marseille – the latter remarking how they had already visited Avignon several times – whilst Peter and Helen had been on the same tour as we had, albeit on a different coach.

Mark described how he and Kayleigh had independently explored Marseille: "There were taxis queued up by the port. We just hopped in one of those and arranged a price for him to show us around the city. We had as much time as we liked at each place, and it cost less than an organised tour."

Regretting not being brave enough to stick to my guns and wander around Marseille without the help of a tour guide, I consoled myself with the knowledge that we would not have seen any of the splendour of Avignon without booking the excursion. Having eaten my own bodyweight several times over during the past twenty-four hours, I restrained myself by merely opting for four courses. I wanted to celebrate the culinary heritage of the country that we had just visited, so I ordered *soufflé*, *escargots*, *boeuf bourguignon* and *crème brûlée*. The fact that I enjoyed munching on some snails more than my dessert confirmed that I am not a fan of crème brûlée! My stomach only felt slightly uncomfortable rather than as sickeningly full as it had been the previous night. Following another extravagant post-dinner theatre production, we headed back to our cabin. An early start, and a different country, awaited us in the morning.

BEYOND THE WALL

15: JEANS, VOLCANOES AND THE MAFIA
GENOA, POMPEII, SORRENTO AND MESSINA, ITALY
OCTOBER 2013

Upon docking in Genoa, it was clear that we should have been brave enough to have independently explored the city as originally planned. The historic centre appeared to be a mere fifteen-minute walk from the port. The persuasive sales pitch from the ship's excursion team, combined with a sudden bout of anxiety, had caused me to abandon any notion of independence. Consequently, we found ourselves being herded into another coach that would turn an easy profit for both the tour operator and cruise line.

The journey was just about long enough for our guide, Gabriella, to pepper the group with some quick-fire historical snippets: "Genoa is Italy's sixth largest city, but it was once a powerful republic. Most of you will have read about the Republic of Venice – well, our republic was also a wealthy and formidable maritime power from the eleventh to the eighteenth century. It was one of the commercial centres of the Mediterranean and Black Seas, expanding to incorporate Corsica, Monaco and Crimea. Genoa remains a valuable port, with lots of cargo ships and cruise liners like yours docking here throughout the year. Many ships are built and launched here."

"You seem proud of your city," an elderly man at the front of the coach commented.

"Yes, I love my home! I hope you all enjoy your visit."

Upon alighting, Mum and I put on our coats, as the gloomy skies indicated that rain was imminent. At least the cooler weather meant that I was not ruing my failure to pack any shorts. In fact, it was somewhat appropriate that I was wearing jeans because the origin of this famous item of clothing can be traced back to Genoa. The city was already famous for its corduroy when the Genoese Navy began equipping its sailors with durable, weather-resistant trousers that could be deemed an early form of jeans – indeed, Gênes is the French name for the city. It was not long before opportunistic merchants began exporting them around Europe. Other cities, including Nîmes in France, have also laid claim to the creation of jeans, although it is not a great surprise that mass production began in the 1870s with Levi Strauss & Co. in the United States of America.

I was only half-listening to Gabriella's instructions regarding our walking tour, instead opting to have a look at our surroundings and take as many photographs as possible. The pastel-coloured buildings by the port had given way to grander looking structures, suggesting that we were heading towards the historic centre. Many of the buildings had a slightly faded look, as if they had seen better days but were still undeniably important and respected.

"If you see the flag of St. George, it is because that is our city's flag – we are not displaying it to welcome English visitors!" Gabriella quipped.

Our initial walk through the city took us past numerous churches, theatres and the residences of various important historical figures, including an eighteenth-century reconstruction of the childhood home of Christopher Columbus. We soon arrived at Piazza de Ferrari, a popular and picturesque square with an impressive circular fountain occupying its centre. Water was shooting up from the multitude of spouts surrounding its base, with each one directed at its central basin. From there, water was being propelled into the air. The shape being created resembled a crème caramel – although I'd had enough of such desserts in recent days, it was a delightful fountain in a pleasant square.

"As I have already stated, Genoa has a strong history as an important financial centre, before and after it was incorporated into the unified Italy. Over the years, the square has been the home of important institutions such as the stock exchange and Teatro Carlo Felice, our famous opera house. Look in front of the theatre – there is a statue of Giuseppe Garibaldi, who is known for…"

"Biscuits!" a man from our group interjected. It was not exactly the most original comment, but it was enough to make most of our fellow tourists chuckle, which in turn resulted in a smug look on the man's face that clearly infuriated Gabriella.

"You British may think of biscuits, but to us he is a source of national pride. He was a general who was a key figure in the unification of Italy."

"They are nice biscuits, though..." the man muttered under his breath.

We were soon standing on the street that bears the Italian general's name. Via Garibaldi, together with numerous nearby streets and palaces, is a UNESCO World Heritage Site. Built in the sixteenth century, it was home to much of the Genoese aristocracy. Gabriella pointed out grand houses that belonged to the likes of the Spinola and Grimaldi families, with the city hall now located in the latter.

Cattedrale di San Lorenzo is probably Genoa's most famous building. The cathedral dedicated to Saint Lawrence was constructed between the twelfth and seventeenth centuries, incorporating Romanesque and Gothic architectural styles, with the façade's distinct black and white horizontal bands a symbol of nobility during the Middle Ages. I was unsure whether I found this look attractive, but there was no doubt that it created a striking image. A couple of lion statues, which almost looked as sad as the one I had seen earlier that year in Lucerne, were added on either side of the staircase in the latter part of the nineteenth century. Gabriella did not provide an explanation for their sombre expressions – maybe they were just bored out of their minds after standing guard for over a hundred years.

The group was shepherded through the cathedral in a brisk fashion that just about allowed me to make note of a couple of interesting additions. The chapels, frescoes and stained-glass windows were visually impressive, but they were not unusual in any way. The supposed presence of the relics of John the Baptist, however, was a little more intriguing. Various parts of his body are said to be preserved across the globe – the Nelson-Atkins Museum of Art in Kansas City claims to house the bone belonging to one of his fingers from his left hand, whilst numerous cities such as Damascus, Rome and Amiens have laid claim to various parts of his head. Without time for a proper inspection, I was left to imagine what obscure body part was stored in the cathedral's urn.

The authenticity of the relics may be debateable, but the unexploded bomb in the corner of the nave was more clear-cut. This was fired at the cathedral by the British battleship HMS *Malaya*, apparently in error, during the shelling of the city in 1941. The failure to detonate, and the cathedral's lucky escape, is commemorated by an inscription that translates to: 'This bomb, launched by the British Navy, though breaking through the walls of this great cathedral, fell here unexploded on 9 February 1941. In perpetual gratitude, Genoa, the City of Mary, desired to engrave in stone the memory of such grace.'

Our whistle-stop tour of the city was all but over; the only thing left to do was eat cheese and drink wine. What an onerous task! Most tours of this nature involve sitting down for a tedious sales pitch for something totally unwanted, such as a hat made from sheep genitalia or a jacket soaked in the blood of a penguin, but on this occasion we were invited to eat and drink some tasty produce and given the option to purchase some more. After being led into the basement of one of the city's grand buildings – possibly the city hall, most likely not – we were each presented with a generous portion of cheese from the Liguria region, including the sour-tasting soft cheese *prescinsêua* and *caprine da grattugia*, which is made from goats' milk. Liguria is known for its white wines, which is apparently due to the high limestone content found in the soil. Mum and I enjoyed our cheese and wine whilst pretending to be aware of their qualities and subtleties.

Although we had not visited the city's famous aquarium, which is one of the largest in Europe, or the peculiar Bigo Panoramic Lift, we had seen enough to gain some appreciation of this historic city. Tragically, the Ponte Morandi, a bridge constructed in the 1960s, collapsed five years after our visit. Forty-three people died and many more were injured when a 210-metre section gave way during a heavy rainstorm. After the remaining segments were demolished, it was replaced by the Viadotto Genova-San Giorgio in 2020. With safety a pressing concern, four robots have been designed to constantly inspect and clean the new viaduct.

Despite consuming an ample amount of cheese and wine, Mum and I soon found ourselves back in the buffet restaurant. With an unusual mixture of rice, pasta and burgers in our stomachs, we headed out to the top deck. The sky was a little gloomy and there was a slight chill in the air, so I kept my jeans and fleece on as we admired the view of the port and the landmarks of the city from our sun loungers. Despite the absence of the sun, it all looked rather picturesque from our vantage point.

My latest attempt to consume enough Italian food to cause internal organ failure was interspersed with our fellow diners' accounts of their day. Margaret and Geoffrey told us how wonderful their excursion to Portofino was, causing me to momentarily feel jealous. If we had opted to visit Portofino, however, we would have missed out on seeing any of Genoa. This is the nature of such brief visits: you have to quickly decide which location to spend your precious time in and which places to leave for another time. I was extremely fortunate that the prospect of returning to the region at some point in the future was a realistic one; therefore, there was no point in sulking like a spoilt brat because I had not visited Portofino. Another incredible theatre performance, a brief chat with Daniel and a couple of bottles of water rounded off our latest wild night on board this luxury cruise liner.

JEANS, VOLCANOES AND THE MAFIA

* * *

The ship was docking in Naples mid-morning, allowing us to have a post-breakfast walk on deck and take in the view of the surrounding area.

"Look over there – Mount Vesuvius," Peter urged, as he pointed towards the notorious volcano.

The highest of the two peaks was the typical conical shape, whilst the smaller one that partially encircled it is known as a caldera. The latter was originally taller but had collapsed.

"What will you be doing today?" I asked.

"We are going to Pompeii. I am looking forward to seeing it, although I hope the volcano does not decide to erupt again!"

"We are on an excursion to Pompeii and Sorrento. I'm a bit concerned we are cramming too much into our day, but I couldn't resist the opportunity to visit both. It's just a shame we won't see any of Naples other than when our coach drives through it."

The fear of missing out, or FOMO as the youth of today like to say, had caused me to choose the combined tour of Pompeii and Sorrento. Both places were far more deserving of the scant time we would be afforded to explore them, but this option proved to be more difficult to resist than a plate full of hash browns.

Our view of Naples was even more fleeting than expected, with our coach driver all too aware of the tight schedule that would involve him driving approximately a hundred kilometres in the space of a few hours. The gloomy weather of Genoa had been replaced by a bright-blue sky and the searing heat that is associated with southern Italy.

Upon arrival in Pompeii, our guide for the day, Adriana, addressed our tour group outside the entrance: "The ruins of Pompeii cover over forty square hectares. I would usually recommend spending a full day exploring the site, but I will show you as much as possible during our excursion. I hope you leave with a greater appreciation of this historic place."

"So, everything that we see today was once buried under ash from Vesuvius?" was the first question that emerged from somewhere in our huddle.

"Yes, Pompeii has a history going back to the eighth century BC, with the Oscans, the Etruscans and the Samnites building settlements here. The area became extremely prosperous during Roman rule, with its position by the Gulf of Naples making it an important strategic point and an attractive place for richer members of society. As I'm sure you know, the eruption of Mount Vesuvius in 79 AD saw the city buried in volcanic ash and pumice. This lasted a couple of days. We believe that many citizens managed to escape, but over one thousand bodies have been recovered. You will see the casts of some of those who perished, which I'm sure you will agree is very sad."

As we began walking through the site, the fact that this once thriving city had been wiped off the map due to the volcano in the distance was a sobering thought. Scores of people died in the place we were visiting as tourists. Although we had joked with Peter about the possibility of Vesuvius erupting once more, the somma-stratovolcano is indeed active. There have been numerous eruptions over the centuries, and because of the high population density in the surrounding area, it is considered one of the most dangerous volcanoes in the world. Some 600,000 people reside in the danger zone, with around three million living close enough to potentially be affected by an eruption.

Adriana led the group through some of the most popular sections of the ruins whilst explaining what we were looking at: "This used to be a bakery. You can see the oven over there."

It was fascinating, albeit in a rather sombre way, to be admiring excavated walls and columns that once belonged to buildings that were at the heart of a community. In addition to important structures such as the Forum, we were shown streets, homes and shops that were part of everyday life for the inhabitants of Pompeii.

"The Romans showed ingenuity to build sewer systems," Adriana enthused. "The Stabian Baths and the Amphitheatre may be impressive, but I think things like sewers and the pipes that helped control the water supply are far more interesting. The eruption of Vesuvius was tragic, but it preserved large sections of the city, providing an insight into what life was like back then. There are not many other places that have given us so much understanding of Roman civilisation."

The tragic nature of what occurred here is best demonstrated by the casts of the people who died in 79 AD. Large-scale excavations began in the eighteenth century, but it was Giuseppe Fiorelli in the 1860s who realised that the sporadic voids in the ash were spaces left by decomposed bodies. His technique of injecting plaster to recreate their form is still utilised today, although clear resin is now the preferred substance. We were shown numerous casts, positioned however they were when that person perished. Many were prostrate, but the most eye-catching was a cast of an individual crouched down with their hands clasped together as if they were praying for a miracle in their final moments. Whether or not this was something of an optical illusion, it helped conjure up an image of someone terrified of what was about to happen. I find that anything that allows visitors to form a human connection with historical sites or events is more striking and memorable than any passage from a book.

We spent an hour exploring the ruins before we sat down for the lunch included in our tour. The latest offering of Italian food, this time featuring Caprese salad and pasta coated in tomato-rich Neapolitan sauce, expanded my waistline even further.

"Did you enjoy Pompeii?" Adriana asked the group.

We all nodded in unison.

"Maybe you will come back in the future and explore it in more detail. I believe there are another twenty hectares not yet excavated. They continue to target small sections, so there will be more that has been discovered when you come back here. You can also visit Herculaneum, which was also buried following the eruption in 79 AD."

The coach journey to Sorrento took around an hour, during which time we were afforded picture-perfect views along the Gulf of Naples and the Sorrentine Peninsula. The Amalfi Coast, just over ten kilometres south of our route, may be more celebrated, but this was a stunning stretch of coastline. I took as many photographs as I could during our scheduled five-minute stop at a viewpoint overlooking the gulf, but I could not truly capture its beauty. The colourful buildings stacked up on the sweeping, curved bay complemented the late-afternoon sunshine shimmering on the water below. I had feared that the Italian coastlines, so often romanticised in popular culture, would disappoint when seen in person. I need not have worried.

Perched on a plateau overlooking the Gulf of Naples, Sorrento has been a popular holiday destination for the last couple of centuries. The seaside town is favoured by British tourists and those purchasing package holidays, with its proximity to Pompeii and the Amalfi Coast a considerable draw. There was certainly less road traffic than in Naples, and there was a more relaxed vibe. Adriana seemed aware that we were running behind schedule, so our walk through the centre of the town was fleeting.

We were led to a shop selling a variety of lemon-based products that the region is known for, where we were invited to sample a shot of *limoncello*. The liqueur, which typically contains lemon zest, sugar, water and over thirty per cent alcohol, may be hugely popular, but it made me instantly recoil due to its tart flavour. Judging by the look on Mum's face, she was not a fan either. People go crazy for this stuff though – bottles of limoncello are everywhere in this part of Italy. It is part of everyday life for locals, and tourists feel compelled to down a shot even if it makes them contort their face because of its sharpness.

"OK, you now have fifteen minutes of free time before we have to get back on the bus," Adriana instructed the group.

We had spent more time gagging on limoncello than being shown the town's attractions, so I was determined to photograph as much as possible. At least I would be able to prove to people that I had visited. I snapped away with my camera in Piazza Tasso, capturing images of the statues of the Renaissance poet Torquato Tasso and the town's patron, Saint Antonino. Judging by its pastel-yellow façade, even the sixteenth-century Baroque-style Santuario della Madonna del Carmine seemed to be a fan of limoncello. It was adjoined to a bar, so maybe the Church goes hand in hand with alcoholic beverages in this part of the world.

Some of the pretty, balcony-lined streets contained fruit and vegetable stalls – teeming with lemons, of course. We scurried around taking photographs whilst somehow resisting the urge to purchase the generic made-in-China souvenirs on offer. It seemed a nice town. The pastel-coloured buildings were pleasant on the eye and there appeared to be a laid-back pace of life that was most agreeable. It is just a shame that we only had a paltry fifteen minutes to take it all in.

The coach journey back to the ship seemed to take an eternity, partly due to the rush-hour traffic. I began to worry that we would be left behind, forced to make our own way to Sicily to re-join the cruise. When we finally arrived at the port, half an hour had passed since the scheduled time of departure. The sight of our humongous ship was a welcome relief – after being shepherded through various cities over the last few days, I really did not fancy the responsibility of organising our own route to Sicily.

We were fortunate that this was an excursion booked through the ship; otherwise we may well have been left behind. Still, our small group felt the need to run towards the ship in order to avoid further infuriating the passengers on deck waiting to set sail. Some had already started a sarcastic round of applause. We had missed our dinner slot, but I was not bothered. Sure, we were deprived of some fine cuisine, but after a long day of sightseeing, the thought of making small talk with our dining companions was not all that appetising. Besides, there was certainly enough food in the buffet restaurant to satisfy our hunger.

Mum and I had not seen any of Naples, but I returned to the city for a three-night stay in 2019. Along with my wife, Carol, I finally experienced its beautiful chaos. We walked the vibrant streets, enjoyed delicious pizza, indulged in some rum baba and took a day trip to the nearby island of Capri. As I mentioned earlier, you may not able to do everything you desire during a cruise stop, but at least you can form a good idea of whether you would like to return someday for a more in-depth exploration.

JEANS, VOLCANOES AND THE MAFIA

* * *

"Of all the places we have visited this week, the only one we will be exploring independently is in the heartland of the *Mafia*!" I informed Mum whilst letting out a nervous laugh.

"I'm not worried about the Mafia – we have the Triad in China!" Mum responded defiantly.

I imagine that many Sicilians are fed up with the island's links to organised crime, but the presence of the *Cosa Nostra* is hard to ignore. Active since the nineteenth century, the Mafia have not only exerted influence and created fear in Italy and around the world, but they have also been immortalised in popular culture. Hollywood films such as *Goodfellas*, *Casino* and *The Godfather* series have made the wider public aware of the 'family values' and 'honour' associated with these criminal organisations. There have frequently been complaints, however, that the extreme violence and terror inflicted by *mafiosi* have been glorified on screen.

Regardless, the Mafia have at times become entrenched in the fabric of Sicilian and Italian society. Protection rackets are the core activity of the Cosa Nostra – it has been estimated that up to seventy per cent of Sicilian businesses pay the Mafia for protection from thieves and other criminals. This, along with the fact that some politicians have relied on the support of such groups, has made it difficult to act against them. There have been periods where there have been concerted attempts to tackle the Mafia, with prominent figures put behind bars, but their presence still looms large over the island. Having said all that, it was doubtful that any *mafioso* would be interested in a couple of cruise passengers taking a stroll around Messina. Tourism is vital to the city's economy, which is unsurprising given its proximity to the mainland. A project that would have resulted in a 3.6-kilometre bridge spanning the Strait of Messina had been scrapped earlier that year, but the cruise industry continued to supply a steady flow of visitors.

Having spent much of the previous day in the shadow of Mount Vesuvius, we were once again within striking distance of one of Europe's largest active volcanoes. After all, Mount Etna is less than a hundred kilometres from Messina. I tried to reassure myself with the knowledge that the likelihood of running into volcano-related trouble was about as remote as being 'whacked' by a mafioso. My over-active imagination, however, meant that I now had to worry about both far-fetched scenarios!

It was another hot day, with a blue sky almost clear of any clouds. Sweltering in my jeans and clutching a basic map I had picked up from the cruise terminal, I took on the responsibility of guiding Mum around the city. We had already seen the thirty-five-metre-tall Madonnina del Porto when the ship docked. A golden statue of the city's patron saint holding the city's letter of protection stands on top of the monument, blessing all ships that enter the port.

Messina's most famous square, Piazza del Duomo, was the obvious starting point for our exploration of the city. As various tour groups were already gathering here, taking photographs of the *Fontana di Orione* without people obscuring the view of the ornate marble fountain proved to be a more difficult than expected task. The fountain depicts the mythical founder of the city, Orion, along with naiads, tritons, angels, and representations of the Tiber, Ebro, Nile and Camaro rivers. It was the work of Giovanni Angelo Montorsoli, who was a protégé of Michelangelo. Montorsoli was also responsible for some of the decorative work belonging to Messina's cathedral, which stands proudly behind the fountain.

Basilica Cattedrale Metropolitana di Santa Maria Assunta, which has a history dating back to the twelfth century, suffered catastrophic damage during the earthquake of 1908 and the aerial bombardment of the city during the Second World War. The reconstructed cathedral was not the most spectacular building I had ever seen but it was nonetheless pleasing on the eye. Due to the previous day's events heightening our fear of missing the ship's departure, we decided not to spend any time inside the cathedral. The sixty-metre-high bell tower, with its famed astronomical clock, was the most eye-catching feature of the building.

Although it was less extravagant than the one I had seen in Prague, the level of detail was impressive. Each day at noon, its figures are brought to life to recreate the history of Messina, including the legendary scene of the Madonna handing over the letter of protection. The presence of scaffolding on the bell tower, which seems to accompany me whenever I visit a city's most famous attractions, was not quite so pleasing. I am almost surprised that the entire Great Wall of China was not covered in scaffolding for the duration of my trek! The astronomical clock show would not commence for another couple of hours, so we moved away from the crowded square.

I had read that the best views of Messina were to be found at Temple Christ the King. This involved negotiating some beautiful staircases and a brief visit to another church, Santuario della Madonna di Montalto, followed by the final climb up the winding streets to Tempio Votivo di Cristo Re. Located on Viale Principe Umberto, the site of the former fortress, the octagonal-domed church was constructed at the turn of the twentieth century. The bell tower was also octagonal, with its rusty bell exposed to the elements due to the lack of an enclosure. The long walk and the intense heat had left us drained, but the splendid view overlooking the city and the Mediterranean Sea had been well worth our exertions. We still had over two hours to walk back to our ship before it departed, but I felt an unnecessary sense of urgency bordering on panic.

Just before we returned to the port, I spotted a shop selling clothing. It appeared to be an establishment of the budget variety – the absence of any signage was a clear indication of this – so I finally had the opportunity to buy some shorts that would be considerably cheaper than the sixty-euro garments on offer on board *MSC Preziosa*. After rummaging through the unmarked shelves, I found a suitable pair of shorts and some swim shorts for just five euros each. The bright blue and yellow swim shorts proved to be a sound purchase, as they accompanied me on several trips in the subsequent years, before finally succumbing to Father Time. Sicilian swim shorts are seemingly of good quality!

We left the largest island in the Mediterranean without visiting the Regional Museum, the Camposanto cemetery or the Galleria Vittorio Emanuele III. It was a shame that we did not sample any Sicilian food, but a relief that we did not run afoul of the Mafia or Mount Etna!

Most of our dining companions had taken an excursion to Taormina, which is one of Sicily's most popular and picturesque tourist destinations. Making enough small talk to avoid being deemed entirely unsociable was proving to be a gruelling task each evening. It was not that I disliked our fellow diners, I just struggle to engage in polite but meaningless conversations with people that I barely know. Rather than feeling more comfortable as the week wore on, I found it increasingly difficult to think of things to talk about. At least on the first night we all had the option of asking the obvious questions during the get-to-know-each-other stage. Nevertheless, I enjoyed the delicious food, wearing my smartest attire, watching wonderful theatre shows and wandering around on this extraordinary vessel. After spending most of the week visiting European destinations, we were setting sail for Africa.

BEYOND THE WALL

JEANS, VOLCANOES AND THE MAFIA

BEYOND THE WALL

16: LESSONS LEARNED
SIDI BOU SAID AND CARTHAGE, TUNISIA
OCTOBER 2013

Taking an organised excursion at our next port of call was more understandable, given that we were spending the day in another continent. The prospect of being left behind here was even more horrifying than it had been throughout the previous week. Having recently taken a day trip to Morocco from the Costa del Sol, I was about to add my second African country to my tally, despite only spending a matter of hours in each. Part of me felt guilty for the nature of my initial forays into North Africa, but I could not help but feel pleased that I had managed to squeeze these trips into broader, more generic Mediterranean holidays. Perhaps this was a sign that the socially awkward, somewhat cowardly version of myself had won the battle with my inner adventurer.

Our guide for the day, Youssef, provided the group with some information about Tunisia during the twenty-kilometre coach journey from the port of Tunis – the capital city that we did not get to explore – to Sidi Bou Said.

"Welcome to my country," he began enthusiastically. "We have the smallest land mass in North Africa but, in my opinion, we are thriving in a way that others are not. After we gained independence from France in 1956, there was a period of secularism."

He was referring to the policy that restricted religious influence, which led to ever-increasing tension between the government and the Islamic community.

"This officially remained in place until the Tunisian Revolution of

2011," he continued. "Part of the wider Arab Spring, these events saw a month of street demonstrations that led to the ousting of the secular dictator Zine El Abidine Ben Ali."

The protests were partly attributed to the self-immolation of Mohamed Bouazizi. The vendor set himself on fire not long after having his cart and produce confiscated. As I had discovered in Prague and China, this drastic act can be an effective way of highlighting a repressive regime or a seemingly hopeless situation. Tension had already been simmering, with leaked documents recently uncovering the corruption of the Ben Ali regime. People were fed up with living under a repressive dictator who had been in power since 1987. After initially trying to squash the protests, Ben Ali fled to Saudi Arabia. Over the following years, he was charged with various crimes involving theft, corruption and inciting violence. He died in 2019 whilst still in exile.

"We are now in the process of establishing a civil state that blends the policies of secularism and Islam," Youssef explained, referring to the principles that would soon be enshrined in the Tunisian Constitution of 2014. "Of all the countries that saw regime change during the Arab Spring, our nation is the one that has successfully established a democracy. It is still early days, of course, but we have made good progress."

Our guide concluded his welcome speech whilst clutching a hardback: "I will take this time to recommend that you purchase the book I am holding. It details a lot of the history of Carthage and Tunisia – it is very interesting."

This was met with collective silence.

We soon arrived at Sidi Bou Said. Known for its widespread blue and white colour scheme that was implemented in the 1920s, the village has become a tourist attraction. Once a popular haunt of European artists such as Klee, Macke – writing those names in succession makes me think of the British comedian Lee Mack – and Moillet, the market stalls selling souvenirs were an indication of how it has embraced the presence of coachloads of tourists. I put my camera to good use as Youssef led us through the narrow, cobbled streets. The whitewashed buildings, complete with ornate blue doors and *mashrabiyas* – a type of projecting oriel window enclosed with a wooden lattice – were certainly easy on the eye. I was pleased that the pretty village was not overcrowded; in fact, our group was probably the only thing disturbing the tranquillity! The clifftop setting of the village, overlooking an enticing beach and marina, added to the aesthetics. It was obvious why this was a place favoured by those seeking a temporary escape from the hectic city life in Tunis.

Looking back at my photographs, it is understandable why Carol mocked my fashion sense. The combination of black trainers, relatively long black socks and shorts was in complete contrast to the beauty of this charming white-and-blue village.

"I can't believe you wore long black socks and black trainers! I would not have walked next to you if I were there! I'm being serious!" was her damning verdict when flicking through my holiday snaps. These days my fashion faux pas are kept to a minimum by the watchful eye of my wife!

Youssef shepherded the group into a craft shop, seemingly owned by a friend of his, and then onto its rooftop terrace.

"This is a good spot for photographs," he suggested. "You can look out over the village. Some leather is being tanned on the other rooftops over there. We make lots of leather in Tunisia – it is important to our economy."

We all duly posed for photos against the backdrop of the whitewashed houses and perfect blue sky. As expected, the cost of being presented with this vantage point was listening to the sales pitch of the shop owner before exiting the premises. Thankfully, he did not go for the hard-sell, and we were able to leave without feeling pressured into buying any unnecessary trinkets. A few members of the group purchased a few items, so all parties seemed happy with the outcome of this arrangement.

Another short coach ride took us to the ancient ruins of Carthage. Youssef once again unsuccessfully encouraged us to purchase the book. Perhaps it contained some interesting information, but our guide's description of the site was enough to meet our needs.

"We will soon be arriving at Carthage," Youssef began. "This is one of the most historic sites in North Africa, and it was once one of the most affluent cities in the world. It was a Phoenician colony before becoming the capital of the Punic Empire. Legend states that Dido founded the city. Are you familiar with her?"

Hoping that someone would refer to the British singer who achieved global success in the early 2000s, I was left disappointed when an eager gentleman sat on the front row gave a more serious answer: "I believe she was an ancient queen who, after fleeing Tyre and founding Carthage, killed herself so that she didn't have to re-marry."

"One version of the legend says this, whilst another claims she eventually agreed to re-marry after being struck by Cupid's arrow. Unfortunately, Aeneas was then instructed to leave her to fulfil his destiny by founding Rome, prompting her to take her own life and pronounce a curse on the Trojans."

The accuracy of these events may be debated, but her enduring legacy in Tunisia, where she is regarded as a national symbol, is not in question.

"Carthage was destroyed by the Romans in the Third Punic War in

146 BC, before becoming an important city in the Roman Empire," Youssef informed us. "Many other forces seized Carthage over the years, with a period of Muslim rule followed by its capture by Christian Crusaders. As I mentioned earlier, it was a French colony until 1956. The constant fighting over this land is unsurprising, as its location on the Tunisian coastline makes it strategically important – ships must pass between here and Sicily when travelling through this part of the Mediterranean. If you want to learn more about Carthage, you should buy this book!"

His latest sales pitch went down as well as the others.

We could not fault his enthusiasm, however, as he diligently guided us through the ruins. We were shown towering columns, the remains of buildings and the different sections of this UNESCO World Heritage Site, including the Baths of Antoninus and the Archaeological Park. We were horrified to hear that first-born children were sacrificed at the Tophet. Youssef then informed us that we had twenty minutes to explore the site at our leisure. Mum and I took this opportunity to capture as many photographs as possible and admire the sight of the imposing columns against the backdrop of the Mediterranean Sea. Impressed by its magnificence, we could have spent longer than the tour allowed for – which is exactly what happened. Suddenly, we realised that we could no longer see any of our group. I checked the time and began to worry.

"It's been over twenty minutes. Where are we supposed to meet?" I asked Mum.

"I'm not sure. I was hoping you knew."

"Tour groups always wait for latecomers. We'll head back to the gate where we were dropped off. I'm sure it will be fine," I reassured Mum. I was probably trying to reassure myself more than her.

Hearts beating faster than they had at any time that week, we scarpered back to the gate. There was no sign of our coach or any of the group.

"They must be by the other entrance," I declared whilst attempting to mask the state of panic that was engulfing me.

We ran to the other gate, but our group was not there either.

"Unfortunately, your group has left," a Tunisian man sat on a stool informed us. "Don't worry, I will call the tour operator and see if another coach will pick you up."

The fact that he was not wearing any uniform or displaying any identification that indicated he was affiliated with the cruise company caused my panic-stricken mind to race away. I instantly assumed the worst: our coach had left without us, and now a stranger was organising our abduction! As he began speaking into a battered old Nokia phone, I

LESSONS LEARNED

had visions of being bundled into a stranger's car. We had always been amongst the first back on the coach for each of the week's excursions, and the tour guides had always waited ten or fifteen minutes for stragglers to return. Yet the first time that we were a few minutes late, we were being abandoned in a different continent! Would we have enough money to take a taxi back to the ship? Would the driver even accept euros?

"Where are you going?" the man asked as I paced along the car park trying to avoid having a full-blown meltdown and hoping that our coach would magically re-appear. "I have spoken to the tour operator – another coach will be here soon, and they will take you back to the ship."

Had this stranger come to our rescue or was he orchestrating our kidnap? In normal circumstances, I would like to think that I would have trusted him. There was no reason to believe that he was being anything other than genuine and kind, but my mind was a jumbled mess. I froze, unsure of whether to thank him or not. Despite my lack of acknowledgement, and the rudeness of my almost dismissive nature, he did not react with anger. Right on cue, a coach displaying the MSC logo pulled up beside us.

"Thank you!" I beamed whilst instinctively pulling out a few euros.

"I don't want your money – I just wanted to help," he calmly replied.

Not only had I dismissed his attempts to get us out of a tricky situation, but I had now insulted him by brandishing money in his direction. This taught me an important lesson: rather than making negative assumptions about people, one should view each person in a good light unless they have given you genuine reason not to do so. In a world where people perpetuate damaging stereotypes of those who find themselves homeless or have had to flee their home country to escape violence – to the point that they are dehumanised – I have learned to give everyone an opportunity to make a positive impression and avoid jumping to conclusions.

Our new coach companions were on the German-language version of the tour we had just taken. We ended up doing the same circuit of Carthage whilst pretending to understand what our guide was saying and ignoring the nudges and tuts of our fellow tourists. Any feeling of embarrassment was miniscule compared to the utter sense of relief that was flowing through me. When it was clear that the guide was telling us that we had some spare time to explore the site, we made a beeline for the coach, unwilling to risk even the remotest possibility of being left behind for a second time.

During that evening's dinner, Geoffrey and Margaret, who had been on the same tour as us, explained that the coach left without us because someone from our group had informed Youssef that we had prematurely returned to the ship because we were feeling ill. Perhaps they were disgusted by my long black socks and black trainers! I had assumed that Youssef had left us behind as punishment for not purchasing the book that he was constantly plugging.

Peter and Helen had taken an excursion to the Bardo Museum. Tragically, this was to be the site of a terror attack less than two years later. In March 2015, two gunmen opened fire as passengers of *MSC Splendida* and *Costa Fascinosa* alighted coaches outside the museum. The perpetrators followed those that fled inside, eventually taking them hostage. After a three-hour siege, the surviving hostages were rescued and the terrorists were killed. Twenty-two people, mostly European tourists, lost their lives as a result of the attack, with over fifty injured. Many of the victims were on the same MSC-organised excursion that Peter and Helen had taken. If Mum and I had booked the cruise a couple of years later and decided to visit the museum, we could easily have been caught up in the atrocity.

Later that year, another terror attack occurred in Tunisia. A gunman killed thirty-eight people at a popular tourist resort, thirty of whom were British citizens. Already reeling from the previous attack, this horrific event obliterated the tourism industry that is so vital to the country's economy. It took a few years for people to regain the confidence to visit Tunisia, which had shown signs of recovery until a global pandemic brought the world to a halt. Despite the terror attacks, Tunisia has seen the most successful democracy established out of all the countries involved in the Arab Spring. Women have more rights and freedoms than in many other countries in the region, and efforts have been taken to decriminalise homosexuality and abolish the death penalty.

Something even more distressing than being abandoned by our tour group occurred during dinner. "Mum, would you like some more water?" I asked.

"Mum? We were wondering what your relationship was. We had been debating this all week before concluding that you were a couple." Margaret interjected.

I had not needed to worry about Daniel mistaking us for lovers – our entire dining table had already done that! Feeling deeply embarrassed, and horrified that our fellow diners had been viewing us this way, I once again clarified that we were mother and son. Vowing to make the nature of our relationship clearer to everyone around me, from this point on I started including the word 'Mum' in every sentence whilst out in public!

LESSONS LEARNED

EPILOGUE

The final day of the cruise was spent at sea as we headed back to Barcelona. After visiting several cities over the past week, it was time to unwind. It took several circuits of the top deck, but we finally managed to snare a couple of sun loungers. Surrounded by nothing but the Mediterranean Sea, we relaxed in the sun. I even had some swim shorts to wear.

I used this downtime to look back over the previous twelve months. A year ago, I had been looking forward to trekking the Great Wall of China. The trip had felt like a life-changing experience, but it had not fundamentally changed my life. My desire to embark on more adventurous expeditions had soon given way to the reality of the life I had already chosen. With a nine-to-five job and a wonderful girlfriend, it had proven extremely difficult to pursue such lofty ambitions. Instead, I had compromised by taking several holidays and spending the occasional long weekend abroad. There may be limitations with this type of travel, but I was content with the knowledge that I was able to venture overseas without abandoning my professional and personal commitments. The fact that I am now married to Carol is testament to this.

Most stories of this nature would have had the China trek as its climax, with a series of shorter trips building up to the once-in-a-lifetime experience, but my journey followed the opposite path. This does not necessarily make it less worthy – it is just how my life unfolded. The desire for a deeper and truer form of travel still resides within my soul, but I have enjoyed all of my trips, no matter how short or limited, as they have allowed me to see more of the world than I would have if I had chosen to stay at home. After all, I have still managed to visit over sixty countries in six continents. Maybe I will one day go beyond the wall – metaphorically speaking – and undertake a series of daring escapades in remote locations. For now, though, I simply feel fortunate to have visited so many wonderful destinations and witnessed so much of the world's unmistakable beauty.

* * *

If you have enjoyed the book, the most effective way of showing your appreciation is by leaving a review or a rating on Amazon. This is of particular importance to an independent author like me.

You can also seek out my previous offerings:

The Adventures of an Introvert: Ten Countries, Four Continents; Minimal Eye Contact (2019)

Tales of an Unsociable Traveller: The Road from Wigan Pier to Tsukiji Fish Market (2020)

One can keep up to date with the latest news regarding future releases, read my blog and find links to my social media accounts (where I frequently post photographs from my trips) via my website:

https://theadventuresofanintrovert.com

Printed in Great Britain
by Amazon